REVELATION

AUTHENTIC POWER IN AN OVERWHELMING WORLD

KEVIN P. HOPKINS

ARCHWAY
PUBLISHING

This book is a work of non-fiction. Unless otherwise noted, the author
and the publisher make no explicit guarantees as to the accuracy of
the information contained in this book and in some cases, names of
people and places have been altered to protect their privacy.

Archway Publishing books may be ordered through booksellers or by contacting:

Archway Publishing
1663 Liberty Drive
Bloomington, IN 47403
www.archwaypublishing.com
1 (888) 242-5904

New International Version (NIV) Holy Bible, New International
Version®, NIV® Copyright ©1973, 1978, 1984, 2011 by Biblica,
Inc.® Used by permission. All rights reserved worldwide.

ISBN: 978-1-4808-8987-3 (sc)
ISBN: 978-1-4808-8985-9 (hc)
ISBN: 978-1-4808-8986-6 (e)

Library of Congress Control Number: 2020910837

Print information available on the last page.

Archway Publishing rev. date: 6/12/2020

For Ted,
I promised. Thanks for believing I could do this.

With love to my mom and dad,
The two people who've never given up on
me, no matter the trial. Thank you.

To my children – Kristen, Kendra,
Erin, and Braden
The ones who have called me "dad" and loved me
unconditionally your whole lives. Erin, thanks for
helping me get my thoughts edited and put down
when they were new and a bit random.

To John, Kenny, and Keith
My best friends, brothers, and ride-or-die partners

To Alvin and Keith
You helped me work through God's calling in my
life and taught me to keep my eyes on Jesus

I love you all.

CONTENTS

Prologue ix

Chapter 1: Structure, History, Context, Setting and Genre of The Revelation 1

SECTION I: "WHAT YOU HAVE SEEN"

Chapter 2: The Prologue 11

Chapter 3: The Greeting and Doxology............................. 19

Chapter 4: The Vision Begins 33

SECTION II: WHAT IS NOW

Chapter 5: The Letter to the Church at Ephesus................. 47

Chapter 6: The Letter to the Church in Smyrna.................. 59

Chapter 7: The Letter to the Church at Pergamum 71

Chapter 8: The Letter to the Church at Thyatira 87

Chapter 9: The Letter to the Church at Sardis 99

Chapter 10: The Letter to the Church at Philadelphia..........109

Chapter 11: The Message to the Church at Laodicea 125

SECTION III: WHAT MUST TAKE PLACE LATER

Chapter 12: John's Vision of Heaven 145

Chapter 13: The Lamb 155

Chapter 14: The Lamb Opens the First Four Seals..............165

Chapter 15: The Fifth and Sixth Seals Are Opened 177

Chapter 16: The Remnant..187

Chapter 17: The Redeemed..195

Chapter 18: The Seventh Seal and Four Trumpets of Wrath 205

Chapter 19: The Fifth Trumpet of Wrath 215

Chapter 20: The Sixth Trumpet of Wrath 225

Chapter 21: The Angel With the Tiny Scroll...................... 237

Chapter 22: The Temple and God's Two Witnesses.............249

Chapter 23: The Seventh Trumpet of Wrath 261

Chapter 24: The Woman, The Baby, and the Dragon 271

Chapter 25: The First Beast 285

Chapter 26: The Second Beast.. 297

Chapter 27: The Remnant Become Redeemed 311

Chapter 28: The Harvest of the Earth 325

Chapter 29: The Seven Bowls of God's Wrath.................... 333

Chapter 30: The End of the Great Prostitute 345

Chapter 31: The Lament and the Curse Over Babylon........355

Chapter 32: The Defeat of Satan and Judgment of the Dead .367

Chapter 33: The Great White Throne 379

Chapter 34: The New Heaven and the New Earth 391

Chapter 35: The Final Vision 401

Epilogue 409

Bibliography 413

About the Author..415

PROLOGUE

It is January 1, 2020, as I start this long-delayed project. In 1999, I was the pastor of the Sterling, Colorado Church of the Nazarene. In May of that year, for the third time in twelve years, I embarked on preaching my way through the Book of Revelation. I would, once again, attempt to share some new insight or idea with the group of people who called me "Pastor." Revelation has been something of a mystery for most folks. This has been true since the church first debated whether to include it in the Bible. When I was a graduate student, Dr. Roger Hahn had encouraged me to focus my personal studies, for the duration of my career, in one Old Testament book and one New Testament book. He pointed out that a church pastor becomes the local Biblical expert for his congregation and perhaps for the entire community. He taught a course in the Gospel of John, so I chose John in the New Testament. I later took another course in The Gospel of John from Dr. Hahn at Nazarene Theological Seminary. It was in that course that we discussed "Johannine" literature; that is, all the books of the Bible that bear John's name or attributed to the Apostle John. "The Revelation of John" was mentioned as an interesting anomaly. It is almost too old for the Apostle John to have likely written. Yet, it bears many connective themes from his Gospel and epistles (again, a fancy name for those letters we call First John, Second John, and Third John.) Revelation captured my imagination! The Revelation: what did it mean? Had people figured it out? Could I understand it? Did it matter today? I moved from the Gospel of John to The Revelation of John. I started spending time every week, diving into the mysteries and symbolisms of The Revelation. It has been a life-long pursuit that has led me to many discoveries that have helped me through the most challenging and darkest times of my journey.

On that beautiful spring morning in Colorado, when the service was over, a man named Ted Tomes (say, "Toms") approached me and said, "This is amazing stuff! You have got to write this down! You have got to write a BOOK!"

I laughed. It was just the first Sunday of preaching what I knew would be months of weekly sermons. This guy had no idea how boring this could get. He had no clue the sacred cows I intended to turn into hamburger and steaks. Still, each Sunday, Ted would come back and say things like, "Seriously Pastor, you have got to promise me you will write this book! Promise me!"

So, hoping to assure him, or just get him to stop, I promised that one day I would sit down and write the book. Every time I have studied in Revelation, every time I have preached a series or a single message through the years, my promise to Ted has come back to me. When Ted passed a few years ago, I felt a sense of loss and regret that I had not yet been able to send him a signed copy or at least a manuscript of the "book." Now it is time to remedy that regret. There are many things in my life that I cannot go back and replay or redo, but this is something I can do. If any reader finds my perspective useful, then God has truly blessed the effort. If not, that is fine, too. This effort is really for Ted and for the chance to keep my promise to him. If I do not write this book now, I have come to realize that it is something I will always regret, and I do not want ever to have to bear that kind of regret.

While my intent is certainly not to write a theological treatise, this book will undoubtedly contain many doctrinal elements and assertions. They come out of me, and so they are mine. If you disagree, I expect, respect, and understand that. I only ask that you consider what this ancient book has said to me across the years and measure it against the truth you find as you read and contemplate my perspective. This will not be a scholarly publication. There will not be excessive footnotes, endnotes, or cross-references. At the end of the book, I will include a bibliography for those of you who might be interested in the resources that I have found interesting across the years. Some are scholarly books that require a bit of knowledge in Biblical Greek language to benefit fully. Still, most are accessible by anyone who wants to learn something new.

Back when I was writing a doctoral dissertation, my advisor said, "Kevin, you can write your book another day. For now, write this dissertation." He thought that I tended to write in a more conversational tone, not in the appropriate tenor of the academic work in which I was then involved. Well, now it is time to write my book. It is meant for regular folks, whether churched or unchurched, highly educated, or simply educated to read and (hopefully) find some value. I intend to provide something through which preachers may take a pragmatic journey and find (again, hopefully) some thread of inspiration or affirmation. My sincere prayer is that any reader might walk with me through these pages and, at some point, think, "Wow! I never thought of that in that way. That helps me." If that happens even once, this effort will be what Ted thought it would be, and for which I have hoped.

A few years ago, while speaking at a men's retreat, I was approached by a small group of the guys attending the event. Because of my pointed and non-conventional presentation, they said, "Kevin, you really should come with a warning label!" I understood their point. I can tend to present things in a rather abrupt and confident manner. That can be a bit disconcerting to people not accustomed to my personality. In the interest of not taking you by total surprise, let me take a moment to issue a few warnings that might prove useful before we dive in:

1. I have never been a fan of the "traditional" or "typical" reading, teaching, or preaching of Scripture. Instead, I have always tended to push the envelope within somewhat responsible boundaries. I believe it is the essential task of the student to find the application, or truth that speaks to them on a personal level. I have always believed that my mission, as a preacher, lies in finding what moves my heart. If it moves me, I trust it will move others. I have always held the Word to be, as it says of itself, a force both "dynamic and active." I will try very hard not to depart from orthodoxy, but I will also strive to allow God's Word the freedom of its unique dynamic.

2. I do not hesitate to turn some sacred cows into hamburger! Those old cows never gave the milk folks needed from them anyway; so, please be patient as I carve up some steaks. I will try to be gentle and explain why I do not stick to the ideas previously penned, even people I have deeply respected. They were just doing what I am trying to do, share ideas about what God might like to do and say through His timeless Word. At

the same time, since I do not believe that God says anything to an individual today that He has not given to His entire Body, the Church, in His Word. I will try only to cut up the unorthodox cows and preserve the message that I believe God is speaking to His Church, past, present, and future.

3. These are *only* my insights and thoughts. They are only truth as the Holy Spirit might commend them to you. The Old Testament called any prophet to accountability with the people among whom he lived and spoke. I am your servant. I write these words in service to my brothers and sisters in the New Testament church in 2020. I remain accountable to you. If at any point, these words seem less than they should be, I pray your forgiveness. You are also certainly welcome to call me or e-mail me and discuss with me what you think I may have mistreated, or simply missed. I promise to have a discussion seasoned with grace. We are all still learning.

4. In the interest of consistency, I have made a conscious choice to speak of God in male personal pronouns. God is Spirit, and Spirit has no gender. Though I, and much of my anticipated audience, are deeply influenced by this perspective. Always, I pray it will not cause offense to women who read my thoughts. Because I'm a man, I tend to think of God as male. Because I'm Caucasian, I tend to perceive God as the same. I'm deeply aware that God is, in essence, neither. I'm grateful to belong to a church denomination that has ordained and empowered women and minority pastors and leaders from its very inception. I ask that you might extend grace in this area.

I shall try not to allow it to infringe on the real message, and I pray it will not create an annoyance or stumbling block to any reader. Apart from pronouns about God, or pronouns that are expressly male from the text, I will make every effort to use more inclusive gender pronouns whenever possible. The Book of Revelation is for Christ's Body, His Church. The Body of Christ in my day is a big tent. I will try to refer to us as "humanity," "humankind," or "Church," when each is fitting.

5. Throughout this book, scriptural references will be my translation, unless otherwise noted. I do not claim to be an expert in Greek and even less in Hebrew. There will be times in which I will purposely choose a direction from among the possible word meanings that may not be the most popular usage or choice. I will try to clearly explain each time I make such a decision and will make every effort to credit any copyrighted text that I directly quote appropriately.

Ready? Let us order some steaks and enjoy a feast together!

CHAPTER ONE

STRUCTURE, HISTORY, CONTEXT, SETTING AND GENRE OF THE REVELATION

(It is not as boring as you think — and it all matters!)

STRUCTURE OF THE BOOK OF REVELATION

Many theories and ideas exist concerning the structure of the Book of Revelation. Some see parallel storylines and complex plot schemes. In contrast, others see patterns in the symbolism and events portrayed in the book. Such things were not the craft of first-century writers and did not fit in apocalyptic (end of times) literature. Think about it: if the world is coming to an end, how many parallel storylines are there time to see to completion? Since our purpose here is to read this book from the perspective of the book itself, I would submit it seems wisest to allow the book to determine the outline we use. In the first chapter, John hears the one who looks like the Son of Man say,

> *"Write, then, what you see, the events that are happening now, and the events which will take place later." Rev 1:19*

There you have it. We will use that as our outline: "what you see, what is happening now, and what will take place later." Chapter one is what John sees at the moment in his vision. Chapters two through four are the messages to the churches to whom he writes. That is, the prophetic Word that is "now." After Chapter four, we find the vision that is yet to take place in John's world and ours. I understand that it is not at all a balanced outline. The third section is enormous in comparison to the first two. Still, this is the precise outline the text gives us, so I think it serves our purpose best to stick with that basic outline.

Now, a brief word about the nature of prophecy, as I believe it to be and function. I understand that many people think of prophecy as future-telling (not far removed from fortune-telling in some circles.) The truth is that prophecy is not future-telling. Examine, if you will, the books of the Old Testament that qualify as prophecy – Isaiah, Ezekiel, Jeremiah, Joel, etc. Each of those prophets was preaching. They were pronouncing God's Word from God to His people in a given moment. The utterance was pertinent. It was expressly for that moment. Would it be true in future moments? Of course! It is God's Word. It is true forever, like a laser beam that shines out from the moment it is spoken or

Prophecy Event Curve

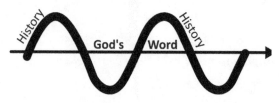

The intersection of history with God's Truth

written, through history. History will cycle back and forth, across and through it, but God's Word continually shines in a straight beam. At any point in which history intersects that truth, it will seem as though the prophecy applies to that very moment. But that is simply the nature of history running its curve and once again intersecting the beam of God's truth shining through it all. That is a very Johannine thought! Look at John in the first chapter of his Gospel:

> *"Life was in Him, and that life gave light to hu-manity. The light shines, and never stops shin-ing, through the darkness – and the darkness cannot infringe on it or understand it in any way." John 1:4*

What an awesome realization! Prophecy is God's Word – spo-ken or written through a person – and because it is God's Word, it will prove true forever no matter the circumstance or event. It may even have a different significance in hundreds of years, but it will still be the truth. You see, that is the fundamental difference between what is "truth" and what is "true." It may be true that it is sixty-five degrees Fahrenheit outside at this moment, but that will not continue to be the truth, even through the rest of this day. It will not continue to be the truth at this same time on any other day this week, let alone forever. Do you see how that shows us the awesomeness of God's truth? It will be true tomorrow, next week, at any time of day or night and for the rest of all time. Truth sets people free because truth has that kind of eternal power! The Book of Revelation is TRUTH! By that virtue, it may say several things to a variety of people throughout history. In the interest of our purpose in this book, let us try and keep to what it meant to those to whom John wrote, and what it says to us today.

THE HISTORICAL CONTEXT OF THE REVELATION

Here, again, scholars debate. That is what they do! After all, if they could not argue, what good would they be? Truth be known, they delight in it. I clearly remember from my intermittent stints at seminary that the coffee pot was always on in the cafeteria. No matter what time of day or night you stopped in, there was almost always a group having some sort of theological debate. We would even jokingly call each other's ideas "heresies" and label them with each other's names: the Smithian Heresy or the Palmerian Heresy. Of course, we were just giving each other a hard time. Still, I have many wonderful scholarly friends who will even argue something they do not believe, just for the sake of having a debate. I understand that such an exercise seems rather pointless to those who are not in academia. But I promise you; it is how most discoveries and thoughts come to light!

So, scholars debate continually about assigning a date to The Revelation. For our purposes, we are going to shoot right down the middle of the arguments, because I believe there, the truth most likely lies. Now, some clues tell us when this book was most likely written. There are references within the text that seem to indicate that certain events have, or have not, happened by the time the letter is finished. You can look up these theories if you like. Scholars generally agree that the right-down-the-middle time frame for the release of The Revelation is about 95 AD. That is ninety-five years after the birth of Christ. If, as we believe, Jesus lived to somewhere between thirty and thirty-six years of age, then Revelation is written around sixty years after his death. Close enough. But does that create any issues with the question of "Who wrote it?" Some scholars believe that 95 AD makes the book too old to have been authored by John.

I tend to believe that Jesus called men younger than himself to be his disciples. John and his brother James were fishermen apprenticed to their father. Right or wrong, I picture them somewhere around the ages of fifteen to seventeen. When He calls them, Jesus is around thirty years of age and will be their Rabbi for about three years. If that is close, then John was between eighteen and twenty when Jesus died, around 33 AD. The average life expectancy in Jesus' time was somewhere between thirty-five and forty years. That number can be a bit misleading when you realize how very high the infant mortality rate must have been. Still, if The Revelation appears in circulation around 95 AD, John would have to have lived to be over eighty years of age to have written The Revelation.

Now, that is not impossible. People certainly lived to that age in that day. If you want to believe that John wrote The Revelation, many scholars would agree with you, and the book itself attests to that very fact. Some believe that a student of John, an apprentice as it were, wrote or completed the book. That idea has a good deal of support among those debating scholars. But, since the text says its author is John, and the thematic material in the book is very consistent with the other Biblical writing attributed to the Apostle John, I am going to hold to that and believe John wrote it.

What was going on in John's world in 95 AD? Well, the Roman Emperor from 81 AD until 96 AD was Domitian, the younger brother of Titus and the son of Vespasian. Domitian was an extremely authoritarian ruler. He enjoyed the longest reign of any emperor since Tiberius, the second Roman Emperor, who had ruled from 14 AD to 37 AD. Domitian was a nationalist who sought to rebuild war-damaged Rome while strengthening military might along Rome's borders. He also wanted to expand the Roman Empire into the region of England and Scotland. Wildly popular among the people and military, the professional political class that comprised the Senate despised him. Domitian strengthened the Roman economy and saw it as his mission to restore the Roman Empire to the type of splendor it had known under Augustus.

Religiously, Domitian was committed to the traditional Roman religions, especially to worship of the Roman god Jupiter. He spent an immense amount of money, restoring the Temple of Jupiter. He also restored the practice of worshiping the imperial cult, going as far as proclaiming his brother Titus, his infant son, and a niece to be deities. Foreign religions, especially Judaism and Christianity, did not fare well under Domitian. Eusebius would report three hundred years later that Domitian was tough on Christians and Jews nearer the end of his reign. That timeframe would roughly correspond to the writing of The Revelation. Still, it appears that Domitian's mistreatments were limited to punitive taxes. They do not appear to approach anything as dramatic as throwing people to lions or having them serve as entertainment at the hands of gladiators. No trials or executions based on religious preference appear in any record set forth by historians contemporary with Domitian's rule.

Nonetheless, it is crucial to a proper understanding of the dynamic of The Revelation to bear in mind that the Christian movement in 95 AD was small, scattered, and unpopular with the ruling forces of the Roman Empire. Christians had already endured great persecution at the hands of the mentally imbalanced Caesar Nero. Roman religion was the focal point of spiritual life in the Empire. Foreign beliefs, like the veneration of ancient Egyptian gods such as Isis and Serapis, were tolerated, as they were something of a spiritual fad. Christianity was extremely unpopular. The New Testament Church in 95 AD was in its infancy, remote, disconnected, and virtually powerless against the heavy hand of Domitian and the Empire.

CONTEXT, SETTING, AND GENRE OF THE REVELATION

Emperor worship was on the rise. Traditional Roman religion, with its variety of pagan deities, was seeing a resurgence. The church believed that persecution, even more violent as had been seen under Nero, was inevitably coming their way. The most prominent living Apostle, John, had been exiled to the island of Patmos for his religious activism. The politically unpopular and scattered church often felt ineffective as the public chased after modern spiritual fads. Does this sound familiar? Does it not look, in many ways, like the place the twenty-first century Christian Church finds itself in the United States?

Into the stifling Roman Empire, John wrote to seven small and isolated congregations. Yet, he did not write just any letter in the standard form. Instead, he wrote to the churches using a unique literary genre, not seen for hundreds of years: apocalyptic. Apocalyptic literature was an ancient form that had been used by

Hebrew writers like the prophets Daniel and Zechariah. It is a highly symbolic style of writing in which mythical beasts or objects serve to represent known people or quantities in the reader's world. As we work our way through the text, you will become familiar with the pattern of symbolism in The Revelation.

But why, you might ask, would John write to the churches in such an ancient and often confusing form of literature? Why not merely send them letters that speak clearly of what he wants to say to them (or believes God wants to say to them)? Why risk mucking up the waters with symbolism and fanciful beasts? Remember our setting: An Empire that viewed religions outside of the Roman cults as suspicious. Rome tolerated other religions, as long as they were not a threat to the Empire, but Christianity is seditious at its core! The entire point of Christian faith is to proclaim Christ, the single Lord of all creation. If this letter to these seven churches were to be intercepted by an officer of the Roman Empire, there could be repercussions. But what if the message appeared in a form that none in Rome could understand? What if it traveled into Rome with the diaspora (the scattering of Jews from Jerusalem and Palestine 30 years before Revelation circulated) and was driven by the Christian message through almost-allegorical stories in those symbols? Then the letter would be seen by any interceptor as meaningless and pointless fancy. As such, it would more likely be discarded by the road than made out to be any issue by Romans. The Revelation is, in effect, a message in secret code, It speaks to a tiny audience who just happens to have former Jews and new Christians among them, who will be able to decode the symbols and meanings in the letter. They will understand its meaning and its message because it is a message that they, like us, desperately need.

SECTION ONE

"WHAT YOU HAVE SEEN"

CHAPTER TWO

THE PROLOGUE

Revelation 1:1-3

THE TEXT:

"Prologue: [1]This is the Revelation from Jesus Christ, which God gave Him to show His servants things that must soon take place. He made these things known by sending His angel to His servant John, [2]who now bears witness to all the visions he saw– that is, the message of God and the Word of Jesus Christ. [3]Blessed are both, he who reads out loud the words of this prophecy, and those who hear these prophetic words and obey them, for the time is near." Rev 1:1-3

WHAT IS THE TEXT SAYING TO US?

The Book of Revelation is, in essence, a letter. Theologians call this kind of letter an "epistle." That is a fancy way of saying "a letter from an Apostle." John wrote this letter to seven churches spread out across what is now Western Turkey, in an area about the size of the U.S. State of New Jersey. But if you compare it to all the other epistles in the New Testament, you will find one difference. It has a prologue! All of the other letters start with an introduction, which is typically just the name of the person writing the letter. Most of us grew up writing letters that began with, "Dear ____," and we would insert the person's name to whom we were writing the letter. New Testament epistles almost all start with the name of the person writing the letter introducing themselves and giving a bit of an idea as to why they have any credibility to be writing such a message. Not The Revelation! It begins with a prologue. John wants you to know the purpose of his letter right up front. He identifies himself as the one writing, but the words are not his. These words have come to John "...from Jesus Christ."

If you are reading these words from the perspective of a twenty-first century Christian, then you are very likely a Trinitarian. You are likely to believe that God, Jesus, and the Holy Spirit are all the same. Now, step back and bear in mind that John knew Jesus personally. John lived in a world in which the idea of a Trinity had yet to be defined. John knew Christ, and Christ said that everything He ever had to say was given to Him by the Father (John 12:49). So, John wants to show us that this "Revelation," this revealing of the heart and mind of God, comes to us by way of Christ who received it from the Father. Notice that John leaves himself out of this succession. He will introduce himself shortly, but at the outset, he wants the reader to know that this is God's message, given to Christ for God's people.

John also wants the reader to know that this is not some far-flung future vision. These are things which "must soon take place." Can you feel the urgency in that statement? These things *must* take place and *soon*! I grew up in Oklahoma. Throughout my childhood, late spring meant the approach of tornado season. It is no coincidence that the National Weather Service Severe Storm Warning Center sits in Norman, Oklahoma – right in the heart of "Tornado Alley." As I was growing up, I distinctly remember the beeping alert tone on the television that meant the weatherman was about to come on with a tornado alert or warning. A "watch" indicated that we needed to be aware that weather conditions were right to form tornados, but nothing was imminently threatening. A "warning" usually started with urgent words from the meteorologist like, "This is a tornado warning for Hughes County! A tornado has been spotted on the ground two miles southwest of Holdenville! If you live in Holdenville, go to your storm cellar NOW!" I spent many of my childhood hours in a storm cellar with family or friends, waiting out storms. Admittedly, there may not be quite that level of urgency in John's prologue, but it is close. The things and events about which John is writing are imminent. He believes they are to happen very soon.

Then, John shows us how this message got from God to him: an angel brought it. In Greek, the language in which The Revelation first appeared, the word translated "angel" means "messenger." God gave this message to Jesus, who sends it to John via a divine messenger, and John is going to send it to us in this letter. Exciting stuff! It makes us want to hear what is in the message! Imagine yourself, part of one of these small churches in 95 AD. Word circulates that a letter has come from John, who is in exile on the island of Patmos. All the families in your church come from around the city. They come to the meeting place and gather around the leader who will read the letter.

John already has everyone's attention, and we want to know

more! But, to our growing anticipation, John speaks a blessing over our little church group. The blessing is first on the leader reading, and then on all of us who are hearing the letter and take it to heart. Do you feel the calming effect that has on us as we listen to it? We are anticipating hearing this Word that comes directly from God. Still, it is essential to remember to be grateful that we hear it. We are, indeed, among the most fortunate people in the world. God wants to speak to us. God wants to include us in the plan. He will not leave us out.

Then comes a very intriguing statement. The blessing is not only for those who hear the message. It is also for those who hear and obey the words of the message. That's a pretty stout condition. Because, it infers that if you only hear, but do not obey, then the blessing is not for you. That seems somewhat staunch. Yet, it is in perfect keeping with the call to both hear and act in other places in scripture. James says,

> *"Do not be deceived into thinking it is enough only to hear the Word. Do what it says." Jas 1:22*

Matthew says,

> *"Everyone who hears my words and puts them into practice is like a wise man who built his home on bedrock." Mat 7:24*

The difference in The Book of Revelation is that the instructions which bear obeying occur, primarily, in the letters to the churches in chapters two and three. Most of the rest of the content of the book takes up the prophetic vision. Still, Christ wants the churches to know that the blessing of this letter comes, not only in listening but in following through.

I have recently had discussions with an influential person in my life and ministry. We have been discussing the fact that so many churches within our culture are "ingrown." By that, we mean that they have the kind of worship service that pleases themselves. They have activities for their church's kids. They have dinners and social gatherings for themselves. Often, in the majority of programming in these churches, the lost are entirely forgotten – or worse, intentionally excluded. I attended a service at a church only a couple of months ago, in which there was a big push for their upcoming sports leagues. They were going to have basketball, volleyball, and soccer leagues opening within the next few weeks. Sign-up for all leagues was to begin the following week. The number of openings was limited because so many had pre-registered at the end of the last season. Anyone interested in getting their child into one of the leagues was strongly encouraged to register that very day to guarantee a spot. One well-meaning mother asked out loud if they could invite friends or neighbors to join the league. She reported that their municipal leagues had become notorious for cheating and bullying play. The answer from the person making the announcement was, "Well, I suppose you might be able to invite outsiders, but let's make sure all of our kids who want a spot have one first."

I sat in stunned amazement. In part, I understood the sentiment of trying to keep our kids out of the cheating and violence for which the city leagues were becoming known. I am not so naïve as to think that churches never form alternative activities to shelter their kids. But it seemed rather exclusive to call the other kids "outsiders," or to suggest that the church intentionally save spots for "insiders." I heard a great deal in the worship service that day about reaching our world and being Jesus to others. Still, the announcement about making sure "outsiders" were not considered for a spot until all the "insiders" had one has haunted me since that day. John's final statement in the prologue makes such a thing even scarier! If the time of this apocalyptic wrath is near, perhaps I should be looking out even more carefully for those my church wants to reach?

HOW MIGHT WE SHARE THIS?

As a pastor or study leader, I have always treated the Prologue as a textual unit. I would let the text form an outline something like this:

I.   The prologue is God's Word, and it is from the heart of God.

II. These things are going to take place soon, to the churches to whom it was written and, perhaps, in our lives too!

III. The intention of Revelation is not terror or fear but blessing and gratitude. God is including you in His plans and wants you to be actively involved.

QUESTIONS FOR FURTHER STUDY OR REFLECTION:

1. Do you believe that God still speaks to individuals today?

2. How do you believe God reveals Himself to people today?

3. Do you believe God still speaks to people through "angels?"

4. What form do you believe angels take?

5. What does the term "Word of God" mean to you?

6. How do you believe God blesses those who read or hear this scripture?

7. What does it mean to you that "The time is near?"

CHAPTER THREE

THE GREETING AND DOXOLOGY

THE ASSURANCE THAT JOHN IS BRINGING GOOD NEWS

Revelation 1:4-8

THE TEXT:

"1:4From John, to the seven churches Asia: Grace and peace from the One who is, and who was, and who is coming and from the seven spirits which are always before His throne, 5and from Jesus Christ, the faithful witness, the first risen from the dead, and ruler of the kings of the Earth.

To Him who loves us and freed us from our sins by His blood, 6and made us a kingdom, and priests to serve His God and Father – to Him is the glory and power forever. Amen.

7Watch, He is coming with the clouds, and every eye will see Him, including those who crucified Him; and all the races of the world will weep for Him; so shall it be! Amen.

> [8] '*I am the Alpha and the Omega,*' *says the Lord God,* '*the one who is and who was and who is coming, the Almighty.*'" *Rev 1:4-8*

WHAT IS THE TEXT SAYING TO US?

A map showing the seven churches of Revelation

Having used the prologue to show the chain-of-authority by which this message comes to the reader, John issues his greeting and then a blessing. These are much like what we see in other epistles in the New Testament. He starts simply by giving his name in the introduction. Most New Testament epistles begin precisely this way. Here is the first affirmation that the writer is, indeed, John.

To whom is he writing? This message is for the seven churches in the Roman province of Asia – now Western Turkey: Pergamum, Thyatira, Smyrna, Sardis, Philadelphia, Ephesus, and Laodicea.

THE BLESSING

John begins his blessing on the churches with the words, "Grace and peace." This greeting is something akin to the angels' assurances surrounding the birth of Christ. In those accounts, the angels continuously repeat the words, "Do not be afraid." John's greeting seeks to serve the same purpose – assurance, and encouragement. John is, inasmuch, saying, "God has a message for you, and you should know that the heart of this message is not judgment but grace and peace."

Grace – the word means "unmerited favor." Remember the angel's words to Mary? "Greetings, you who are highly favored!" John's greeting serves to remind the churches to whom he is writing that, no matter how they have succeeded or failed, God comes to them by way of His grace. He is not coming to them to judge or condemn. He may have corrective things to say to them, but like any good father, He comes to love and to strengthen each of them. Grace is that powerful force in relationships that says, "No matter, what you have done, no matter what you have said, no matter where you have been, and no matter how you think you may have failed, you are welcome here. Come home."

Peace. It is such a strong word that it can stand alone as an entire sentence. Peace. We know very well what it means, even if we seldom experience it. The word in Hebrew is *shalom*. It is a greeting and a parting blessing. It translates, "peace on every side," or "the total lack of conflict or disturbance." We so often look at our world as those seven little congregations must have looked at theirs: as though peace is a fleeting dream. I am reminded of the words of Longfellow from the poem, "I Heard the Bells on Christmas Day" in which the poet cries out,

> *"Then, in despair, I hung my head. 'There is no peace on earth,' I said. For hate is strong, and mocks the song of peace on Earth, goodwill to men."*

If we pause to reflect on how little peace there is in this world, this is a natural sentiment to echo. We see constant fighting between governments and factions in the Middle East. We see turmoil in Eastern Europe, fires in the rainforest, and across most of Australia as I write this. Someone is always angry with the President of the United States. Our major political parties lay traps for each other and seldom ever speak to each other, except in angry tones. My neighbors take sharply divided stances on everything, from politics to sports. We even argue about whether or not Alice down the street should have her six dogs on leashes when she takes them out to walk around the block! Turmoil is everywhere in our world. Peace seems so inaccessible today. It was the same amongst the churches to whom John was writing. Their Empire did not like them. Rome had only conquered the people around them within the previous 150 or so years, and they lived in constant tension with the Empire. Rome itself was absorbed with trying to hold its borders in modern-day Germany and expand into what is now Great Britain,

Scotland, and Ireland. It was a world of unrest and distrust. Peace was often hard to find. Yet, John speaks to those small churches of "grace and peace." God wants to talk to you, and He wants to bring grace and peace in the process.

Then, John refers to God in an incredibly awkward manner in the Greek language in which the letter was originally written: "... from Him who was, and is, and is to come..." Greek is a precise language in many ways. The language has specific verb forms to show past, as differentiated from present, as differentiated again from the future. John has to engage in impressive linguistic gymnastics to say that God is all of these things at once. But that is his precise intention. He is trying to capture for his Greek-speaking audience a concept that his Jewish readers will already understand well – the idea of *YAHWEH*. Time and space cannot bind the God of Israel as they do the Roman deities. Unlike them, *YAHWEH* does not toy with His creation for His entertainment. He is not in danger of being taken over or having to quash a rebellion. He is sovereign, all-powerful, always-present, all-knowing, and all-loving. He sees all of history as though it were a single moment and directs it towards the purpose of being reunited with the creatures He created and loves. He influences kings and leaders. He leads armies and generals. He is at work in the scope and sweep of history and events around us. There is a plan, and God wants us to have an idea of where everything leads. Without taking time to teach Roman subjects all of the theology of *YAHWEH*, John tries to capture God's essence in this encompassing description.

"...and from the seven spirits which are always before His throne..." Rev 1:4

Remember those debating scholars? They get deep into the weeds on this one. Some suggest that John means the spirits of each of the seven churches which are always on God's heart and mind. That is not wrong thinking, but there is no support in The Revelation (or the rest of scripture) for that position. The "seven spirits before (or 'around') his throne," are much more likely the seven attributes of God himself. We see them in the very familiar verse from Isaiah 11 – a prophecy often quoted to describe the expected personal characteristics of the Messiah:

> *"The Spirit of the Lord shall be with Him, the Spirit of wisdom and insight, the Spirit of counsel and strength, the Spirit of knowledge and respect of the Lord, and He will delight in reverence of the Lord." Is 11:2-3*

Yes, it is a challenge to get seven out of that list. There are three pairs of attributes listed after the general attribution, "The Spirit of the Lord." Then there is this seventh trait of "delight in reverence of the Lord." But, is that a Spirit? Is the "Spirit of the Lord" a separate attribute from the other six? There may be eight, or five, or just six. Seven is a bit elusive. Is this even the right list? I believe it is the correct list. Numbers in the Bible are a tricky thing. Bear in mind that in either ancient Hebrew or ancient Greek letters may also represent numbers. Numbers and letters are, thereby, symbols. They may be good or bad. Three is a good number: Father, Son, and Holy Spirit, the Trinity. Twelve is a good number. It is the number of tribes in Israel or the count of Jesus' disciples. Seven is a good number. To the Hebrews, seven signified completion – a whole unit. Saying that something happened for seven days was to say that it happened until it was complete. Whatever event was next could now take place. Why say that God is seven sensible (those we could sense) spirits? It is John's way of saying that this message comes out of all the essence and power of God.

> *"...⁵and from Jesus Christ, the faithful witness, the first risen from the dead, and ruler of the kings of the earth." Rev 1:5*

The ultimate authority is listed last. This message from the all-encompassing and whole God comes to us through Jesus. Remember, John sees the relationship between Father, Son, and Holy Spirit as more linear than modern Trinitarians. By Jesus' own words, God sent Christ, and Christ sent the Holy Spirit. While John would not argue that they are not all the same, he accentuates their autonomy in this progression of the message reaching us. The ultimate judge is Christ. Jesus is, by His admission, the one who witnesses to the Father. (Compare with John 5:19) John then shows Jesus as "the firstborn from the dead, and the ruler of the kings of the earth." Here, John affirms that Jesus is the resurrected Lord. Christ, alone, is the one who defeated death and rose to life. He was not just the only one to do so, but the first – the promise that those who believed in Jesus would join Him in the resurrection from the dead.

It will be critical to remember this concept as we get deeper into The Revelation. Not only is He the Savior of those who believe and are part of His Church, but He is the ruler of those who believe themselves to be rulers on this Earth. It is not the Empire - any Empire - that rules God's people. They are subjects of the Kingdom of God. All other rulers, kings, emperors, prefects, governors, and authorities are *ruled*. They are illusions. They appear to be in power, but they are not. They are governed by Christ and only may act according to His purpose in this world. While it is wise to respect them, they are not to be feared. They are not the ultimate power – Christ is. Again, John is trying to convey a very familiar Hebrew thought to non-Hebrew readers: the concept of "I AM."

You see, if God is "I AM," then He is always present tense. He is not a has-been. He is not a will-be. He is neither washed up nor yet to come to power. At any moment in time, God *is*. In those moments in the past, God *is*. As though all of time happens in a single moment, God *is*. In the time that lies ahead, God already *is*. So incredible is His power that time cannot define Him. Space cannot confine Him. The "I AM" (a phrase considered too brash to be anything but rude in friendly Greek and Jewish culture) is the only one who can say those words. Everyone, everything else, is bound in time and space. That which was is dead and gone. That which is to come does not yet have life or form. All of us, and all of those who appear to rule us, are bound in the past, present, or future. The Empire is mighty, but it will one day fall. That means the Roman Empire, the British Empire, the Ottoman Empire, the Egyptian Empire, the Persian Empire, or the Empire under which you live right now. Empires fall. The Kingdom stands.

Pause here. Take this to heart. This is another one of the essential thoughts to bear in mind as you read the rest of The

Revelation. It may be one of the most crucial ideas to hold onto as you live your daily life. ***There are always these two forces at work in the world: Empire and Kingdom.*** They are almost always at odds. The world consists of Empires. The Empire determines your taxes, your liberties, and your rights. It governs your ability to do commerce and make a living. The Empire seeks control of all of its subjects and, perhaps, seeks to expand to control other people. The Empire is conquest, control, and constraint. In stark contrast is the Kingdom. The Kingdom supersedes all Empires. The Kingdom sets free the captives and breaks the bonds of the slaves. It brings healing to the sick, sight to the blind, strength to the weak, and life to even the dead! The Kingdom is about life, liberty, and love.

The two will always experience conflict, for the Empire will never accept the Kingdom. You must choose which rules your heart, your mind, even your life. In today's world, as in the world of the Roman Empire in John's day, people must choose Empire or Kingdom. We often confuse the two by treating national leaders as some kind of high order of priests. We attribute God's design to political movements, getting the structure backward. We try to choose the least offensive ruler for the Empire, based on our spiritual perspectives, all the while forgetting that the Empire is not the Kingdom. We end up behaving like subjects of the Empire more than heirs of the Kingdom. We seem to forget that we are only citizens of the Empire, but we are children of the King who rules the Kingdom. John is writing to people just like us, albeit in a very ancient time. In the trials and turmoil they face every day, those folks have lost sight of the Kingdom because they live in the shadow of the Empire. Because he writes in the authority of God,

John speaks just as loudly to us. Your King rules the Kingdom and the Empire. All other kings answer to him. You truly have nothing to fear.

THE BENEDICTION

John follows this incredible depiction of Jesus with the statement, "To Him who loves us..." It is a second benediction. Who is Christ? Who is this mighty ruler of kings and empires? Who is the One who will bring judgment on everyone and everything at the end of all time? He is the One who loves us. He is the one who paid the price for our freedom. We need not fear His wrath, nor His judgment for those are not for us to bear; for by His sacrifice, He elevated us to the offices of priests and rulers in His Kingdom!

> *"Watch, He is coming with the clouds, and every eye will see Him, including those who crucified Him; and all the races of the world will weep for Him; So shall it be! Amen." Rev 1:7*

Here we receive a command: Watch! Be alert. Keep an eye on the world around you, because He IS coming! The spirit of urgency and immediacy continues to be the theme. Why are these phrases in quotes in the text? While these are not quotes taken directly from scripture, they are ideas presented in both Old and New Testament scriptures. They are likely lines from contemporary worship songs or hymns in the church John knew. The references to Christ returning in the clouds comes from Matthew 24:30 and 26:64. Daniel also refers to "one like a Son of Man" coming in the clouds in Daniel 7. Yet, there, the "one like a Son of Man" is not coming to Earth, but going to the "Ancient of Days" (God).

The statement "every eye will see Him..." is a direct reference to Zechariah 12:10-14, which also expresses the concentric circles of those who will mourn his death. An important note here: bear in mind that this section is not a part of the prophetic utterance of John. This is still the introduction of The Revelation. John is not speaking prophetically here. He is speaking of what he believes to be inescapable *fact*. The return of Christ is not in any doubt – just watch. It is sure to come. Everyone who played any part in His crucifixion will see Him, and they will all realize that they tried to murder the King, and they will mourn for their sin. This is part of the benediction, a form that is supposed to bring comfort and assurance. Already, John is drawing a line of differentiation. Do you see it? The return of Christ is sure. It will bring assurance to those who belong to His Kingdom and not to the Empire. To those ruled by the Empire and who crucified the Christ, His return may well bring mourning and regret. From the seventh passage in the book, you must choose a side.

As heirs, we get to participate in the blessing rather than the curse. We experience pardon rather than judgment. Because He is gracious and merciful to us, we exalt Him and worship Him and confirm that He has power and glory for all time. Then John quotes God Himself, not from any previous scripture, but directly from the throne at this moment. God declares that He is the "Alpha and Omega," the beginning and the end. John finishes this quote with the descriptor of "who was, who is, and who is to come." There it is again that awkward language-defying Greek contortion that says, "I AM!" He'll repeat it in Revelation 22, at the very end of the Book.

HOW MIGHT WE SHARE THIS?

When I preach or teach the Greeting & Doxology, I break it into two sermons or lessons. I would recommend outlines that look something like this:

The Greeting

I. A message of grace and peace:
    Reminding us that God always comes to bring us peace, no matter what we might be enduring in any given moment

II. The reality of the spirits of God at work in our lives:
    What is it to experience the Spirit of the LORD? How might we know wisdom, understanding, counsel, strength, knowledge, holiness, and the fear of the Lord?

III. He who rules the Kings of the Earth is your brother:
    In any time, Christians need to center their minds in the fact that they serve a higher authority than the "empires" that contend for control over them

The Doxology

I. Living Free from Sin - How does this thought compare with the idea in Hebrews 12:1 about leaving sin behind like an old garment, or the doxology in Jude 1:24?

II. Heirs, not colleagues or friends

III. Living as Heirs Until Christ Returns

If we are heirs, and free from entangling sin, what should our lives look like in this world?

QUESTIONS FOR FURTHER STUDY OR REFLECTION

1. Are there still cities in the locations of the seven churches? What were they like?

2. Why is it significant that God was, is, and is to come?

3. What are the seven spirits before His throne? What do they mean to you?

4. How has the blood of Christ freed us from our sins?

5. Can you be called to be a "priest" if your vocation is to something other than ministry?

CHAPTER FOUR

THE VISION BEGINS
GOD IS WITH YOU AND HE HOLDS THE POWER
YOU HAVE BEEN LOOKING FOR

Revelation 1:9-20

THE TEXT:

"1:9I, John, your brother and companion in the suffering and kingdom and patient endurance in Jesus, was on the island of Patmos because of the Word of God and my witness to Jesus. 10On the Lord's Day, I was in the Spirit, and I heard behind me a loud voice like a trumpet, 11saying: 'Write on a scroll what you see and send it to the seven churches: to Ephesus, Smyrna, Pergamum, Thyatira, Sardis, Philadelphia, and Laodicea.'

12I turned around to see the voice that was speaking to me. And when I turned, I saw seven golden lampstands, 13and among the lampstands I saw one who appeared to be a human being, dressed in a robe that reached down to His feet, wearing a golden sash encircling His chest. 14The hair on His head was white like wool, as white as snow, and His eyes were like a blaze of fire. ¹⁵His feet were like molten bronze glowing in the furnace, and His voice was like the sound of cascading waters. ¹⁶In His right hand, He held seven stars, and projecting from His mouth was a sharp double-edged sword. His face was like the sun shining in all its brilliance.

¹⁷And when I saw Him, I fell at His feet like a dead man. Then He laid His right hand on me and said, 'Stop being afraid. I AM the First and the Last. ¹⁸I AM the Living One; I was dead, and now look, I AM alive forever and ever, and I hold the keys of death and Hades.

¹⁹Therefore, write down everything you will see, that is the events that are happening now and those which will take place later. ²⁰As for the mystery of the seven stars that you saw in my right hand and of the seven golden lampstands: The seven stars are the seven angels of the seven churches, and the seven lampstands are the seven churches.'" Rev 1:9-20

WHAT IS THE TEXT SAYING TO US?

With verse nine, John embarks on recounting his vision, his Revelation. He starts by affirming, once more, his identity. He also tells us where he is writing: the Island of Patmos. Patmos is a small island off the west coast of Turkey in the Aegean Sea region of the Mediterranean Sea. Just over thirteen square miles in landmass, it is a rocky island with beautiful beaches lined with palm trees. Tradition tells us that John was banished to Patmos after being placed in boiling oil by the Romans and emerging with no injuries at all. Tertullian reports, in *The Prescription of Heretics*, that this event took place in the Colosseum. This fact is not supported anywhere else in historical writings. Further, he relates that all who witnessed the miracle came to faith in Jesus Christ (also unsupported elsewhere in historical literature.)

There is nothing in The Revelation text to explain why John is on Patmos. He claims that he is in exile "because of the Word of God and testimony of Jesus." There is genuinely no reason to doubt the traditional interpretation that John is in exile for spreading Christian doctrine within the Roman Empire. To most Romans, Christianity was equivalent to magic. If Tertullian is accurate that some kind of miraculous event happened to John in public sight, it would be consistent with what we know of the reign of Domitian. It figures that Rome would have him removed to exile on a remote island where he will be, in effect, "out of sight and out of mind."

This is an account of a vision, yet the first thing John describes is hearing a voice that speaks from behind him. We will discuss a bit more on this kind of "bait-and-switch" literary device in a moment. Here, the vision recalls a sense of God speaking to Moses without letting Moses see Him. It reminds us of God talking to Elijah in a quiet whisper after He did not appear in the earthquake, wind, or fire. This, however, is not a hushed whisper.

It comes to John on the Lord's Day and is as loud to the Apostle as a sounding trumpet! The metaphor of the sounding trumpet is a way for John to say that what the voice said to him was both clear and unmistakable. The first instruction the voice gives is to write down what John is about to see and to send it to the seven churches in nearby Asia, which the voice names.

There is a short break in The Revelation, as John turns around to attempt to "see the voice which was speaking..." That would be a trick now, wouldn't it? How does one see a voice? As I warned you just above, here is another instance of the prophetic bait-and-switch. The construction serves to heighten the mystery and the reader's curiosity. The reader naturally wonders, "What does John see? Who is speaking these words to him?" Here is a literary mechanism that you should look for, and get used to, in The Revelation. Several times, John is going to write about something imminent, which sets a particular expectation in the mind of the reader, only to have the narrative play out differently than the set-up.

In verse twelve, we have every expectation that he will turn around and see someone. But, no, he turns to see...lampstands. Then he reveals to us that a man is standing among the lampstands. The man wears a floor-length robe and a golden sash around His chest. He is royalty. It is Jesus!

Remember that John said God gave this message to Christ, and Christ sent the message to John. Jesus does not look like He did the last time John saw Him. His hair is pure white like lamb's wool or snow. The color signifies that He is aged, royal, and must then possess the wisdom and wealth of both stations in life. His eyes are like blazing fire. Please note that John does not say Christ's eyes are fire. He says they were *like* blazing fire. The Greek word for fire here is *puros*. See anything familiar with this word? Fire can do any number of things, but primarily it either consumes and destroys, or it purifies! The process of sorting the precious metal from the impurities with which it naturally occurs involves immense heat. The precious metal melts, and the impurities burn off.

Have you ever sat by a fireplace or campfire and found yourself just staring into the flames? Fire is transfixing. It draws us in and captures our thoughts and focus. These thoughts are the essences of what John is likely trying to say here. The eyes of Christ are transfixing and attractive. They capture his attention. The fire, the zeal in them, is purifying and focused.

Bear in mind that those who have previously encountered God in visions in the Bible – Moses, Elijah, etc., were not allowed to look at His face. John is not only allowed to look at Jesus' face but is permitted, even encouraged, to stare straight into His eyes! That focus, purpose, purifying, and transfixing quality of Christ's gaze is the energy behind this entire vision. John gets to look into the all-seeing eyes of God in Christ. Though his human vision is limited and likely failing, in this vision, he will get to see the bright and cleansing perspective of Christ.

Where is Christ standing? He stands amid the lampstands. Each is within His reach. None is neglected or outside the care of Christ. The lampstands are His, and He can tend and protect them as He stands among them. This connection will be essential in a few verses when you find that the lampstands represent the seven churches to whom the letter speaks.

Then, John makes a curious observation. Christ's feet are like "bronze yet in the fire." They are not molten, they have form, yet they are white-hot. The Greek word used here to describe Jesus' feet is not used anywhere else in scripture. It looks to be a hybrid word from a Hebrew word that means "white," and the Greek word for "brass." It may be a term used by tradesmen. But what does it mean? There is a verse in the Old Testament that says,

> *"What a beautiful sight upon the mountains are*
> *the feet of the messenger who brings good news!"*
> Is 52:7

The Israelites lived in a country surrounded by mountains. Warring enemies typically came right down the valley in the middle of the country to attack them. If help were to appear, it would have to be provided by allies over the mountains. (compare with Ps 121:1-2) If a friendly force were to arrive and sweep in to save Israel, they would send a forward scout to come running down from the mountains to let Israel know that help was coming. Feet deliver messages – both good and terrifying. White-hot feet symbolize that there is a critical message coming. It is hot off the press, or from God's mouth, as it were. Whatever message Christ is about to utter to His churches is of white-hot importance!

Having described Christ's appearance amongst the lampstands, John mentions that His voice was "like the sound of rushing waters." I spent a good part of my formative childhood years in the forests of the Pacific Northwest. Coursing through those woods were rivers that often terminated in waterfalls. I remember following trails and clearings toward the ever-present sound of water to discover a rushing river or a beautiful waterfall.

One of my favorite waterfalls to this day is Snoqualmie Falls in Washington State. In the Spring, during the snowmelt, this twenty-seven-story-high waterfall generates so much mist that, from the observation platform, it seems like it is consistently raining. The sound is a deep roar that defies any description. If you concentrate just slightly, you can feel the vibration in the ground under your feet. The thundering in your ears is all-encompassing. It is hard to know if you feel it or hear it more. The sound comes from every direction and fills every sensory capability you have. Again, John is trying to express how transfixing and encompassing the person of Christ is to his senses. The voice is felt as much as heard. It surrounds and fills the mind, body, and senses. There is no missing it, no mistaking what it says.

In His right hand, Christ holds seven stars. In John's century, that would look something like holding seven pinholes of light. In my century, I envision holding seven, twenty-seven-million-degree fusion reactions that produce enough heat and light to drive entire planetary systems. I do not know that astronomers in John's day could grasp that our sun is a star – or the immense power possessed by some of those stars they could glimpse in the night sky. Perhaps it does not matter, but I love the thought that Christ can hold these immense engines of the universe in His hand. John explains that these stars are the symbols of "the angels" of the seven churches. These are their spiritual engines. They are the heart of God at work in each church. Each church has a light at its core. Each church is driven, as it were, by a quantum reaction. The kind of power available to each of these tiny congregations is unfathomable and, just as with us, likely to be largely untapped. Christ is affirming, through His Revelation, that no matter how challenged your church (or your life) may seem, the power available to you is truly incredible. So, it is fitting that the final descriptor John uses of Christ's face should be that it shines like the sun in all its brilliance. While he is allowed to look into Christ's eyes, His face shines so bright that it might be painfully uncomfortable to gaze into His face.

Do you pick up a theme here? Lampstands, eyes of fire, feet like bronze in the fire, stars, the brilliance of the sun in his face?

Light.

Remember, it is John writing here. The same guy who starts his Gospel with the words, "In Him was life, and that life was the *light* of humanity." (John 1:4) In any of John's writings, it is helpful to watch for the theme of "light." God is light. God brings light. He lights the way for us. He shines among us by His presence like a light from inside a tent. John 1 says,

> *"The Word became flesh and pitched His tent among us, and we have seen His glory, the glory of the only Son, whoever came from the Father, full of grace and truth." John 1:14*

You likely understand how it might be to camp in a tent when the light is on the inside. Everyone outside can see everything you do by the silhouettes cast on the walls of the tent! For John, that is how it is to live with God in our midst. Because the light is inside with God, everything He does, every move He makes, is evidenced to us directly. We, among whom God lives (amongst whose lampstands He stands, right?) get to see His glory and every move He makes amongst us.

From his mouth comes a double-edged sword – a direct reference to Hebrews 4:

"For the Word of God is alive and dynamic. Sharper than a double-edged sword, piercing so surgically that it can divide soul from spirit, joint from marrow, and can lay bare the thoughts and intentions of the heart." Heb 4:12

The power of the words He is about to speak in the vision lies in their truth. This is something of a cloaked mission statement for The Book of Revelation. By its nature as apocalyptic literature, it will lay bare the truth of what we can expect in the end times. This vision will define what is coming from the Holy Spirit and how your soul might respond. The truth of The Revelation will reveal the thoughts and intentions of all actors – God, Jesus, the revealer, the enemies of God, and people - whether they follow God or deny Him.

John is so overwhelmed when he senses Christ's encompassing and powerful presence that he says he passed out or lost the ability to stand on his feet! Yet John remains aware of what is going on in the encounter. The old man says, "Do not be afraid." It is the greeting that almost always comes to humans from God. He is not here to judge just yet. He has a message to share, and John needs to hear and convey that message.

Who is he? He is the "first and the last." It is likely a bit redundant for you now. But this is how we know that this is Jesus. He is the living one who was dead but came back. In all of history, only Jesus and Lazarus returned from death. Having been resurrected,

He now lives forever. He holds the keys to death and Hades. The one who holds the keys controls access. Death is no longer a locked door beyond which no one can travel or return. Then, John uses a name that his Greek readers will quickly recognize – Hades.

Wait, Hades is not originally from the Bible. It is the name of the Greek god of the underworld. He lives under the earth in a place of immense material mineral wealth. His realm is also called Hades, and he rules it with his wife, Persephone. To Greeks, it is the place souls go after they die. It is something of a blend of Heaven, Hell, and Purgatory. For ancient Greeks, it was the grave. It was inescapable. Once you were in Hades, you stayed there forever. But John says Christ has the keys! We could spend multiple volumes of books trying to survey all of the afterlife myths, beliefs, and theories that people have held throughout history. Indeed, entire books exist simply to examine the Greek concept of Hades. John does not want us to get hung up here. He wants us to understand that, no matter what your idea of an afterlife, Christ holds the keys. Death holds no threat over those who are in Christ. Hades cannot keep them. Hell cannot imprison them. Those who belong to Christ will be with Him in His presence, no matter what grave might try to separate them. If He has to come to retrieve them, He can. He has the keys.

The implication to the author is evident. John need not be fearful of the things he is writing. Christ tells John to write down what he sees – what MUST happen. Again, here is that sense of urgency. Then, as if to show that He is not interested in making the symbolisms too hard for ordinary folks to understand, Christ explains the first two. The lampstands are the churches. They give light for seeing, for worship, for reading, and learning. Each seems but a candle flame – flickering and delicate – but behind each is a star. The power behind each church is an infinite nuclear reaction generating more power than a person can comprehend – endless light and guidance, immense gravity and warmth, eternal energy, and strength.

HOW MIGHT WE SHARE THIS?

When I have preached or taught this section, I have treated it as a single section. I would use an outline similar to this:

I.   Am I open to hearing God's voice in my life?

II. Am I committed to being obedient to whatever God might ask of me?

III. Am I willing to walk in God's Spirit and accomplish His priorities in my life?

QUESTIONS FOR FURTHER STUDY OR REFLECTION

1. What does John mean by "the suffering, kingdom, and patient endurance that are ours?"

2. What does John mean when he says he was "…in the Spirit?"

3. From where does the term "like a Son of Man" come? What does it mean?

SECTION TWO

WHAT IS NOW

THE LETTERS TO THE CHURCHES

CHAPTER FIVE

THE LETTER TO THE CHURCH AT EPHESUS
RETURN TO YOUR FIRST LOVE

Revelation 2:1-7

THE TEXT:

"2:1To the angel at the church in Ephesus write: These are the words of the One who holds the seven stars in his right hand and walks amidst the seven golden lampstands. 2I know your deeds, namely your hard work and persistence. I know that you cannot stand wicked people, and so have tested those who call themselves 'apostles,' but are not, for you found them to be liars. 3You have persevered and have patiently endured hardships for the sake of my name and have not grown weary.

4But I hold this against you: You have forsaken your first love. 5Consider how far you have fallen! Repent and return to the things you did before. If you do not repent, I will come to you and remove your lampstand from its place. 6But you have

this in your favor: You hate the practices of the
Nicolaitans, which I also hate.

⁷Let the person with ears hear what the Spirit
proclaims to the churches. I will allow the one
who prevails to eat from the Tree of Life, which
is found in the paradise of God." Rev 2:1-7

THE CITY AND CHURCH AT EPHESUS

The first church to receive a message from Christ is the church at Ephesus. Before we dive into the text, let us take a quick look at what Ephesus, and the church at Ephesus, was like at the time this letter arrived. Ephesus was a busy port city on the estuary of the Kaystros River, just inland of where it drained into the Aegean Sea. A few hundred years earlier, it was the home of one of the Seven Wonders of the Ancient World – The Temple of Artemis. In its glory, the Temple is estimated to have been nearly four times as large as the Parthenon in Rome. When John wrote to the church at Ephesus, the Temple of Artemis stood complete and was famous throughout the civilized world. Because it was readily accessible by sea, it is highly likely that tourists and pilgrims flocked to Ephesus to worship at or visit the Temple. The Temple stood until sometime in the 400's AD when Christians closed it, as the Roman Empire converted to Christianity. There is ample evidence that Ephesus was second only to Rome as a center of commerce and trade. It enjoyed two factors that contributed to its fame. First, it was an ancient and famous port. Then,

A map showing the location of Ephesus

it was the water terminus of the main section of the Royal Road, built by the Persians to carry goods from Susa (in present-day Iran) to the Aegean. Even as empires rose and fell, the Royal Road continued to be a primary conduit of travel, goods, and communication. Because of its prominence as a center of trade and commerce, and because it had a sizable Jewish synagogue, Ephesus made an excellent candidate for missionary work by the Apostle Paul. Tradition holds that the Apostle John moved from Jerusalem to Ephesus and spent his entire ministry there; and that it was from Ephesus that Domitian exiled him to Patmos. There is a tradition that says John brought Mary, the mother of Jesus, with him to Ephesus and cared for her until her death. Though we do not know these things for sure, the traditions are ancient and supported by time and veneration. It would make perfect sense that John would have been somewhere in that area to find himself exiled to Patmos, just off the coast near Ephesus.

The church in Ephesus was started by the Apostle Paul and led by Apollos, Aquila, and Priscilla. (Acts 18) Paul spoke only to members of the Jewish Synagogue in his first hurried visit in Acts 18. In Acts 19, Paul returns to Ephesus to strengthen the new group of believers there. This time, Acts tells us that Paul spent his first three months in Ephesus speaking in the synagogue until they expelled him. Scripture then tells us that when Paul was barred from the synagogue, he went to the "lecture hall of Tyrannus" (Acts19:9). There he stayed for the next two years; the most extended time Paul spent in any one place in his ministry besides Rome. Not only did Paul plant a vital church in Ephesus, the Book of Acts tells us that because of Paul's stay in Ephesus, "…all the Jews and Greeks who lived in the province of Asia heard the Word of the Lord." (Acts 19:10) This may explain why Christ, through John, sends His first message to the church at Ephesus. It seems to be the focal point from which all Christians in Asia received their first witness and exposure to Christ.

WHAT IS THE TEXT SAYING TO US?

The section begins with the direction of Christ that John writes, "To the angel at Ephesus…" This serves to remind the Ephesians that God has an angel assigned to watch over their church. Not only that, but they are under the care of the "one who walks among the lampstands," Christ, Himself. The message that Christ shares with the Ephesians is interestingly similar in tone to the epistle to the Ephesians from Paul. It is, primarily, encouraging. Christ compliments the church for its hard work, perseverance, and careful vetting of those who claim to speak for God yet turn out to be false prophets. Christ further credits the members for their perseverance, endurance, and tirelessness in faith and ministry. Theirs is not a problem church. It is one of the most faithful and loyal churches in all of Christendom. Ephesus is a model church. Yet, Christ has a corrective to speak to them.

A word of caution to the twenty-first century reader: you and I live in an incredibly divisive and combative world. Social media is filled with hateful responses to even the most innocuous of assertions. There are days that I believe I could post to social media something like, "The sky is blue," and reasonably expect a variety of posts in disagreement. Some would even include hateful personal attacks! It might be easy for us to project our own cultural approach to criticism or correction onto the words of The Revelation. All but two of these churches are going to be the recipients of some kind of corrective from Christ. Whenever possible, it appears that He offers praise first, followed by corrective. I would ask that you try to picture in your mind a small church in the year 95 AD. They likely meet in someone's home, where they share a meal and then turn their collective thoughts to Christ. They have no Bible, no printed study materials, no videos. They enjoy none of the things that we have come to believe are so integral to the ability to study God's Word. They have what they know of Christ from the Apostles, and they have each other for accountability. They likely discuss current events and how they might best respond to them in a Christ-like manner. They probably talk about the Roman Empire, the law, their businesses and how successful they are, their children, and the issues around raising Christian children in a blatantly pagan city. They have no twenty-four-hour news channels, no newspapers, no magazines, no radio on which they can hear someone's opinion of the news for that hour. There are no media outlets to shape the information delivered to them in any given news cycle. Jealous yet? They have each other.

Perhaps this is something missing in our culture, even in our church. When they speak to each other in corrective terms, it is in love and out of concern for their collective witness and influence in their community. Each must be encouraged to walk as uprightly as possible for the good of the ministry of the group. Anyone who is out-of-step with the example of Christ would genuinely take to heart any correction lovingly offered by their friends. After all, they could not run off to the next church down the street. There was no other Christian church in town. They did not get mad and go off to start their own – no one would come. I am asking you to read these correctives to these churches as though you are reading them to yourselves. Do these issues exist in my life or yours? Do we need to introspectively consider each of these words of correction to live in a more Christlike manner? I think it is very likely that we each need some word of correction from this ancient book. One of the Twelve Steps of Alcoholics Anonymous reads, "We took a fearless and searching moral inventory..." I invite you to consider each of the correctives to these fledgling churches in that spirit. Each serves as a fearless and searching inventory of our own hearts and attitudes. Such an approach is indeed essential if we believe that "the time is at hand."

"But I hold this against you:" Wow! That will get your attention if it is coming from Jesus. "You have forsaken your first love." The imagery here is from marriage. We all remember how intense our first love felt. Older now, we understand that it was naïve and blind. But there was something so fierce and earnest about it, wasn't there? Unjaded and undamaged by the years that would follow, we could lose our entire heart in a moment. Many of us who may no longer believe in love at first sight, did then; and fell into it with reckless abandon. Oh, to have that trust and faith again! I believe we all long to be able to love like that, at least in some respects, into our old age. It is the same in our faith-walk.

I remember as a thirteen-year-old just having come to faith in Christ, how I longed to see my classmates come to faith. I testified to them at school about what had happened in my heart. I dragged some of them to church and then dragged them to the altar to invite Christ into their hearts. I wanted everyone to have the same joy I had found! But, over time, I became more realistic and complacent. I understood that other kids went to different churches where this "personal relationship with Jesus" stuff was not taught. Others enjoyed their life apart from Christ too much to hear about giving it all up for Jesus. In high school, and then college, Jesus became someone that we all talked about, but few wanted to know. My Bible went on the shelf with my dictionary and thesaurus. It became merely another reference book in my set. The raging fire of my first days in the faith settled into a barely glowing ember. Christ moves almost immediately to give the Ephesians credit for hating the practices of the Nicolaitans.

They were a sect that believed in living life through excesses of food, drink, and sex. But I am not sure his encouragement here relieves the burden of the corrective.

By the time I went to college, I had become a social Christian whose heart had drastically cooled. My friends and I would often return from a night of bar hopping and gather in one dorm room or another to discuss religion. We were unreasonably hard on those whose sin was different from ours. We did not even consider that, to some, we were a living irony. We would talk about God and Jesus – how they loved us just as we were and how we were not nearly as bad as those who were stealing money, or property, or having illicit sex, or cheating on their spouses. Those were horrific people; we were just young and careless.

While I'm not saying that drinking is a sin, the Bible is clear that excess can be. We were living in excess. My flame had grown low. My heart had become complacent. I resorted to criticizing what I perceived to be the worse failures of others to make myself feel like I was, perhaps, not so "lost." Throughout my career, I have seen thousands of Christians literally in the same place. Having lost the enthusiasm and fire of their first love for Christ, they had settled into a cooled spiritual existence. They kept the religious hours dutifully. They would not only show up for church most Sundays, but they would attend the educational hour before church and, perhaps, even a Sunday evening homegroup. But their conversations often drifted into comparisons of us-and-them.

It was as if the church was a fortress, with the good people inside and the bad people outside. As long as they could find someone whose failure could be deemed to be worse than their own, they could maintain their comfortably cool compromised

Christian complacency. Now, I am not judging, only observing my personal experience and its commonality with others. For, you see, I believe this is the truth of relationships of every kind. Our relationship with Christ, our marriages, our friendships, our work relationships are subject to the loss of our first love. We are, by nature, fickle. We get excited about what is new. Once the shine wears off, we become more lackadaisical, in every aspect of our lives.

Hating the practices of the Nicolaitans is a good thing. But where is your first love? If you were consumed by that zeal and faith that you had the day you first knew Christ, the Nicolaitans would not even matter. You would look for people who were open to hearing and having what you have to share. You would be consumed again by the need to meet the needs of others, rather than criticize those whom you simply deem to be "worse." Find renewal. Seek revival. Go back! Return to that first day of that first love and love like that again, before it is too late. Then Christ offers a warning. "If you do not, I will remove your lampstand from its place." Where is its place? Close to Christ. The warning is that, as our hearts grow more distant from God, our church will be moved away from His presence – separated from Him. This is the punishment of the Devil and those who fell with him. They were separated from the presence of God. This is the punishment of Adam and Eve after their sin. They were separated from God. Sin brings separation and distance in a relationship that was designed to be close. It is a dire warning.

In closing this section, we are introduced to this literary device, which will become familiar by the time of the seventh utterance: "Whoever has ears, let them hear what the Spirit says to the churches." That is us. We have ears. God knows this because He created us with them. He is not just talking about physical ears but also about "spiritual ears." Of course, He means the ability to hear with wisdom and discern what this Word says to us. Just hearing someone read those words makes each of us want to be among those who can hear! It is an ingenious literary device that *makes* us all the more willing to apply the truth of what we just heard to our own lives and circumstances. Included in the device, is typically a final promise: "To the one who is victorious (who prevails), I will give the right to eat from the Tree of Life, which is in the paradise of God." Ah! See what He is saying there? The warning was that the one who did not repent and go back to their revival faith might lose their standing in the presence of God, right? The promise is that the one who repents and finds victory over the corrosive forces of time and complacency will eat from the Tree of Life. That is in the Garden of Eden! That is where Adam and Eve lived – in paradise, where they enjoyed God's immediate presence every moment.

Think about this, though: Adam & Eve were in the Garden of Eden with God. In the Garden, there were two important trees: The "Tree of the Knowledge of Good and Evil" and the "Tree of Life." The Bible defines Adam and Eve's sin as disobeying God and eating fruit from the Tree of the Knowledge of Good and Evil. As a child, I wondered why someone would be removed from the Garden for merely eating from a tree! My uncle had an orchard, and we went out and sneaked peaches off the trees sometimes. Would we get kicked out of the family for such sin? The answer was a bit more theological. If in their disobedient state, Adam and Eve had gone on to eat the fruit of the Tree of Life, they would have been destined to live (theologically) in permanent sin. God had to remove them from the Garden of His immediate presence so that they could be redeemed from sin before facing the prospect of living in it forever. The promise here is the opposite of the curse. Sin will be removed from the equation of our lives by redemption in Christ. The promise to the one who sees victory over sin is an intimate, fulfilling relationship with Christ and each other.

HOW MIGHT WE SHARE THIS?

I have always preached or taught each of the messages to the churches as a singular unit or message. That is likely obvious from the quantity of the content above. I think each message stands on its own merit for today. There are many ways in which to approach this section, and I haven't always used the same approach. Still, with the thought of allowing the text to speak for itself, I might suggest an outline like this:

I.   What are the great things about your church?

II. In what ways might you say your church has "lost its first love?" In what ways could you say that you have lost your first love?

III. If your ears were sharp, what would you hear in this message today?

QUESTIONS FOR FURTHER STUDY OR REFLECTION

1. What were the deeds and perseverance of the church at Ephesus? What can we learn about the things that the church faced?

2. What did your faith look like at first? How has it changed? Is it warmer or cooler?

3. What steps might you take to see revival and renewal of our first love – spiritually, relationally, personally?

CHAPTER SIX

THE LETTER TO THE CHURCH IN SMYRNA
HOLD ONTO YOUR FAITH

Revelation 2:8-11

THE TEXT:

"2:8And to the angel of the church in Smyrna write: These are the words of the First and Last, who died and came to life again. 9I know your struggles and your poverty – you are the rich ones! I know about the slander of those who call themselves 'Jews,' but are not; they are a synagogue of Satan. 10Do not be afraid of anything you may be about to suffer. I warn you, soon, the Devil will throw some of you into prison to test you, and you will suffer persecution for ten days. Be faithful, even to the point of death, and I will give you life as a victor's crown.

11Let the one with an ear, hear what the Spirit says to the churches. The one who prevails will, in no way, suffer harm from the second death."
Rev 2:8-11

THE CITY AND CHURCH AT SMYRNA

A map showing the location of Smyrna

Smyrna sits only about thirty miles north of Ephesus. While not mentioned in the Bible outside of The Revelation, it shared with Ephesus and Pergamum the distinction of being one of the three most beautiful cities in the Roman Province of Asia. Built on a bay of the Aegean that reached nearly 30 miles inland, it was, even more than Ephesus, a port of sea trade and a terminus of goods coming to the sea from inland. Smyrna was a center of learning, with one of the most ancient medical schools in Turkey. The city was the center of a great deal of Jewish emigration. Many signs point to the fact that Jews had already begun relocating to Smyrna before the fall of Jerusalem in 70 AD. The resulting "diaspora" scattered Jews throughout the Roman Empire. It appears that there was more than one Jewish synagogue in Smyrna at the time John's message to the fledgling church at Smyrna clearly delineates them from the synagogue. His terse assessment of the synagogue will play out many years later. Those very Jews will turn against John's disciple – Polycarp – and martyr him by burning him at the stake in Smyrna.

Little is known about the church in Smyrna, outside of what we find in The Revelation. Historically, we see that the church at Smyrna was significant. Tradition holds that it was started by the Apostle Paul during his third missionary journey, but that it traced its apostolic heritage through John. In the fourth century BC, Tertullian would mention the credibility of Smyrna tracing its Christian roots from Polycarp back through John and other apostles that Polycarp may have heard at some point as a result of his association with John. At the time Christ addresses the church through John and The Revelation, it appears that they have undergone persecution. This persecution likely arose from Domitian's obsession with the Imperial Cult, which deified past Emperors and worshiped them as gods. There is some historical evidence that Domitian tied the ability of a merchant to do business with particular buyers to the vendors' willingness to proclaim allegiance to the Imperial Cult. This was particularly true of those who desired to do business with the Roman Government. If this is the case, the church at Smyrna (and later, at Laodicea) may face financial persecution and the scorn of local Jewish merchants, for having the courage to disavow the deity of dead emperors. At Smyrna, John hints that they may have more trouble on the horizon.

WHAT IS THE TEXT SAYING TO US?

The address to Smyrna is unique because it is one of only two churches addressed by Christ in The Revelation to which there is no corrective, but only encouragement and assurance. After the formal greeting, "These are the words of Him who is the First and Last, who died and came to life again," you will notice there is none of the formulation, "I have seen your deeds." Instead, there is a more compassionate address: "I know your struggles and your poverty, but you are the rich ones!" God is a merciful God. Isaiah 42 prophesied of Him,

> *"He will not break a bruised reed, and a faintly burning wick he will not extinguish;" Is 42:3*

Is the church at Smyrna perfect? Not likely. Yet, in His wisdom, God knows when to challenge a church with correction, and when to encourage it with compassion. I love the immediate peek behind the curtain, as it were: I know you are persecuted and feel impoverished against the wealth of those who are hitting you – but you are actually the rich ones! It is a quick and poignant reminder to that church, and to ours, that they are the ones whose Father owns the cattle on a thousand hills. They are the ones who serve the God who created the entire universe, who created light with a word, who rules the kings and leaders of the Earth. (Note: Part of the genius of a circulated letter to multiple churches is that everyone gets to read and benefit from the messages to the other churches besides their own.)

Now, a quick warning. I do not believe that Christians are good, and Jews are bad in God's sight. The accusation here is that the tormentors are not even real Jews. Rather than the more typical statement, "I have seen your deeds," there is this assurance that, "I have seen their slander." They are not real Jews, because Jews have laws against bearing false witness and slandering others. Jews have laws from God about treating even the stranger in their land with fairness and kindness. Their actions give them away. They do not belong to God; they belong to Satan.

There is an undertone here that meshes with John 8:19-47. There, Jesus had a sharp debate with Pharisees over what must have been one of the most whispered-about highlights of His life. He was born of a virgin. You get it, yes? You and I, who have attended Christmas services our entire lives, have heard the Christmas story recited by kids, adults, and even Linus from Peanuts. It has become something we read over and about which we do not think twice. Of course, Jesus was born of the Virgin Mary. But what if it was your daughter, or your sister, who turned up pregnant and when her dad asked her who the baby's father was, she responded, "Well, I know this is kind of hard to believe... but it is GOD!" I know what I would say if it were one of my daughters!

I am certain it was no more believable then. Why would God come to Earth in such a way? I have honestly asked myself that very question hundreds of times, and I can only come up with one real answer. Given the sovereign power to choose whatever way He desired to come to be with us, He chose that way. The Word became flesh born to a virgin girl in a forgotten town, in a nasty place, with no family or friends around, so that no child would ever feel like Jesus was born too high to be able to relate to them. He came in such a way that people could always whisper and gossip and say horrible things about Him, so no person who was just as trashed by the cool kids would ever feel like Jesus might not understand. In John 8:19, we get to witness firsthand what John saw, as Jesus claims to do what He hears from His Father. Then those wicked snakes strike out at him with the most evil thing they have, "Oh, your father, eh Jesus? Yes...please...tell us again...*who is your father?*" Jesus does not flinch. Instead, he doubles down and proclaims that they do not know God, or they would bear fruit to God. Instead, He says, they bear fruit to their father, the Devil!

These are the moments when I am convinced that it is the Apostle John who wrote The Revelation. He was there, at Jesus' side, in that entire crazy John 8 experience: Jesus protecting the woman caught in the act of adultery and the face-off with the Jews. As a result, you can almost feel him relating the two events as God says, "Those are not really Jews. Those are a synagogue of Satan!" He goes on, "Do not be afraid of anything that is about to happen to you. Satan is going to come and throw some of you into prison." Is Satan himself going to do this? No. His followers will, those folks in Satan's synagogue. What are they going to do? They will persecute you for ten days.

Now we come to another of those number riddles in The Revelation: Ten. We had seven stars and seven lampstands. We understood the angels and power behind each of the earthly lights that shine in the world for Jesus is His churches. In Jewish numerology, the number seven represents completeness or wholeness. Three is one of those numbers of completion; so is twelve. But ten? Ten is kind of between the stability of seven and the wholeness of twelve. Ten is akin to whole-and-then-some. It would be enough to be persecuted for seven days, but you are going to have to endure ten days. It is long enough to die without water, to languish without food. The trial that is coming your way is not going to be a weekend campout without any Internet. It is going to be, for some of you, a severe test. We do not like to think in these terms in the twenty-first century church. We like to sing about victory and hear about blessing. We seldom preach about enduring trials or tribulations. Christians in our day have a hard time believing that God would allow extended punishment, let alone torture, for His people. But in Smyrna, God gives them the heads-up that exactly that kind of persecution is coming. What would you do if God clearly told you, "I am sorry, but you are going to unjustly suffer for an extended time because you have been faithful to me?"

That sounds like the story of Job! Why did Job get tested? Because the Devil wanted to hit the man who was most trusting of God. I do not like that message. I do not preach it unless God makes me. I avoid that thought like it was poison. But it is the truth. Sometimes the faithful feel beaten and impoverished, and, just when it seems like it could not get any worse, the persecution comes. Have you ever felt like that? I think most of us probably have at different times. Those times cause us to question just how tough God believes us to be. His promise was not that we would never suffer. His promise was that He would not leave us or forsake us to suffer alone. Remember that verse from Isaiah? The promise was not to fix the bruised reed, simply not to crush it. The promise was not to add flame to the faintly burning candle, simply not to snuff it out. He is telling the people at Smyrna that it is going to get worse before it gets better. Now you can probably see why there is no corrective or scolding here. There is no reason to scold a church who must be told that the Devil is about to have his way with them.

Then the charge: "Be faithful." Even if it means to the point of dying, be faithful. Now, I would really like to write some great platitude about the virtue of being faithful in the face of torture and death; but I cannot. I am sorry. I do not want to suffer torture. I am not afraid to die, but I am in no hurry. Everything in me wants to shout, "No!" Take that vision away. Take that prophecy off of us. We do not deserve that. We have been good. We have not forsaken our first love like those sorry louts down in Ephesus. We have been faithful and true. We do not have their wealth. We do not get to live their carefree life of luxury. We are outcasts here. We get constant grief from that synagogue of meanies. Do not make us go through life-threatening trials, too. Please? God?

I do not like reading this message to Smyrna because it is a message to me as well. You have experienced it, just as I have. Sometimes this world is so unfair that the one who is already beat down gets hit some more – and then some more. Faith is not just serving God when the sun is shining, the birds are singing, and everything is peachy. The Revelation is a book about where the real power lies. It is about where believers find the authentic resource to face life, Empire, and Satan. Faith connects us to that power.

Then the promise. Endure in faith, and you will be the victor. Oh, there it is...my twenty-first century worship song! I will win, at least eventually. But what my worship leader forgot to include was that it might well be after deep testing. The crown Christ mentions here is that ring of laurel leaves that the Emperor, or his general, wore when returning from a significant victory in the battle for the Empire. All the citizens would line the street and proclaim their adoration for their hero. Rome knew no greater honor than to wear the Emperor's sign of victory. But the Kingdom has a higher honor. Victory for the Kingdom does not mean expanding the borders or vanquishing the foe. Victory in the Kingdom means the Empire, the world, has been totally defeated. The power of any other force or Empire, whether of people or of Satan, has been totally routed. It has no influence over the victor anymore, forever. That is the kind of victory God wins. Remember His words to Moses and the Israelites, as they were being chased out of Egypt by Pharaoh's army? Pinned between the army and the Red Sea, they start to whine at Moses that it would have been better to have died in Egypt as slaves than to be cut into pieces in the desert. Then Moses says,

> *"Stand still. Watch God act. For the enemy you see today, you will never see again, forever." Ex 14:13*

Have you forgotten Whom you serve? Have you forgotten He created all that is and that nothing has come into being except by His Word? Have you confused the source of all power in the universe with that puny Empire or that silly little bunch of gossipy devils down the street? Stand still. Stop pacing around and worrying yourself sick. Stop losing sleep and tossing and turning all night. Having connected yourself to the mighty power of God that enables you to stand in the face of anything...just stand still. Let the one whose ears are ready for this assurance hear clearly what God is trying to say to him or her today. You are not merely victorious over the Empire. You serve the one true God, with power over death and Hades themselves. You will not merely walk down the street past the Satan lovers in victory. You are going to walk right past the grave and into Heaven in victory!

HOW MIGHT WE USE THIS?

When I have preached this message to Smyrna, I have used an outline something like this:

I.   God sees when the church is struggling

II. God knows what the church is about to face

III. God brings perseverance and ultimate victory

QUESTIONS FOR FURTHER STUDY OR REFLECTION

1. Can you find out what kind of things the church at Smyrna had endured?

2. Why would this church be impoverished in the wealthiest city in Roman Asia?

3. Is there any historical evidence that Christians in Smyrna were persecuted until the martyrdom of Polycarp?

4. What is meant by the term "second death?" (Hint: the answer is in Revelation 21:8)

CHAPTER SEVEN

THE LETTER TO THE CHURCH AT PERGAMUM
LIVING IN THE MOST EVIL PLACE ON EARTH

Revelation 2:12-17

THE TEXT:

"*2:12Next, write to the angel of the church at Pergamum: 'This is what the one with the sharp two-edged sword says: 13I know where you live, where the throne of Satan is located. You bear my name, and did not renounce your faith in me, even in the days of Antipas, my faithful witness who was publicly executed, where Satan lives.*

14But I hold against you the fact that you have in your midst those who hold to the teaching of Balaam, who taught Balak to put a stumbling block before the sons of Israel, to eat sacrificial meat and to commit fornication. 15In the same way, you also include those who hold to the teachings of the Nicolaitans as well. 16So, you must repent. If you will not, I will come to you quickly, and I will fight them with the sword of my mouth.

[17]Let the person with an ear, hear what the Spirit proclaims to the churches. To the one who prevails, I will give a share of the hidden manna, and I will give them a white stone, and upon the stone, a new name is carved which no one but the recipient can know.'" Rev 2:12-17

THE CITY AND CHURCH AT PERGAMUM

Ephesus, Smyrna, Pergamum – they form the triad of the most prosperous and beautiful cities in Roman Asia (now Turkey). Pergamum is the furthest north of all seven churches, and just about straight north from Ephesus and Smyrna. Pergamum was an ancient city, founded under Greek rule. Peaceful and compliant, it transitioned smoothly to Roman control. Unlike Ephesus or Smyrna, it was not a seaport. Pergamum sits about sixteen miles inland from the Aegean. It sits on and around a high flat-topped mountain, which featured Pergamum's acropolis. Rather than a center of trade, like Ephesus or Smyrna, Pergamum was a center of culture, learning, medicine, and worship. On its acropolis was the second largest library in the civilized world. Only Alexandria boasted a more extensive library. Also, on the acropolis were immense temples to Zeus, Dionysus, Athena, and other Greek deities as well as a massive altar for sacrifice.

A map showing the location of Pergamum

The Great Altar of Pergamum (now housed in the Pergamum Museum in Berlin) sat prominently atop the plateau. At the base of the mountain was a temple to the Roman Imperial Cult. Many historians point to Pergamum as the first site of such a temple. It served as the epicenter of Emperor Worship in the Roman Empire. As a seat of government for hundreds of years and through three dynasties, Pergamum was the seat of influence and wealth in the region.

The church at Pergamum was, according to tradition, founded by Antipas, a disciple of the Apostle John. History tells us that

Antipas was martyred in Pergamum during the reign of Nero, perhaps 20-25 years before The Book of Revelation was written. Legend relates that Antipas was roasted over a fire in a large metal bowl shaped like a bull. He was martyred for casting out demonic spirits that the local population worshiped and loved. It is sufficient to say that history portrays Pergamum as one of the most idolatrous cities in the Roman Empire. It was a place of extremely diverse pagan worship, and a place very unfriendly to Christianity.

WHAT IS THE TEXT SAYING TO US?

The opening of this letter to the church at Pergamum is the only one to come from "the one with the sharp two-edged sword." This is an allusion to the truth, the Word that comes from the mouth of Christ. Again, look at Hebrews 4:

> *"For the Word of God is alive and dynamic. It is sharper than any double-edged sword. It cuts so deeply it can divide even soul from spirit and joints from marrow; it justly lays bare the thoughts and attitudes of the heart." Heb 4:12*

God creates with His Word. God battles by His Word. Nothing in creation exists apart from God's Word, and nothing can stand against it. Ultimately, it is one of two weapons that will defeat Satan (Rev 12:11). That is the kind of power that brings this message to the church at Pergamum. If I were preaching this message, I would read the next statement in my best *Sopranos* impersonation: "I know where you live!" But it is not really like that, is it? It is truly a word of assurance. Again, the statement is not, "I know your deeds," but more along the line of the compassionate tone of, "I know what you have to endure."

Then, look at what Christ says here, "You live where Satan has his throne." Everything in me says, "Whoa!" Not where Satan is powerful, or where Satan likes to visit often, but they live where Satan has his *throne*. I guess, as a kid, I always thought that Satan's throne would be…in Hell? But it makes sense that Satan could not cause much trouble from there. The more scholarly part of me wants to believe that this must simply be a way for Christ, through John, to say that Pergamum is a horrific place. If I rely solely on The Revelation to define its own symbols, things are simplified. I am forced to deal with the fact that Christ very intentionally says that Pergamum is home to the *throne* of Satan. This language means that, when Satan is thrown out of Heaven in Revelation 12, He takes up residency in Pergamum.

If you grew up similarly to me, you have likely grown up in a church culture that gives the Devil an awful lot of credit for an awful lot of things. I was in line once at a Christian bookstore. One of my favorite pastors/authors had just released a new book, and I ran right out to get a copy. There I stood in line at the Christian bookstore with my single little book. The lady in front of me had seven or eight books in her arms. As she laid them on the checkout counter, I took notice of the titles. They were all books about spiritual warfare. Most were specifically about Satan or the power of the Devil. She turned and caught me reading her book titles and took the opportunity to strike up a conversation. "I am really getting into spiritual warfare!" she exclaimed.

"Yes, I see that," I answered. "It looks like all of your books today are about the Devil?"

"Yes, they are," she responded. "I think we need to know everything we can about the enemy to do effective spiritual warfare with him, don't you?"

Why do people ask me these questions? Can they not read my warning label? I tried my best to deflect her question and said something rather lame like, "Yes, I suppose it is useful to know our enemy."

Well, that just struck her wrong.

"You suppose? Don't you understand that the Devil could kill you where you stand if you are not covered in the full armor of God? Don't you understand how important it is to know everything about him that we can, so we can foil his plots in our lives, our churches, and our world?" I could tell she was irritated with me now.

I said, "Ma'am, I have obviously offended you, and I am sorry. That is never my place or my right. I am simply of the opinion that, until I know absolutely everything there is to know about Christ, I dare not read or study about the power of the Devil. I am afraid of the dark. I would scare myself silly reading about the pure essence of evil!"

My new friend looked at me in some odd mix of disbelief and pity. She picked up her books and left. I reflected on that encounter for days. We teachers, preachers, authors, even musicians – in the church of Jesus Christ have done Christians a horrible disservice. We have presented the Devil as though "he" were a person. We have so personified him that we have reduced him to what would fit in flesh and bone. Now, please, do not get me wrong. The Bible clearly teaches that the Devil is a defeated foe since the cross of Christ on Calvary. The Bible clearly says his roar is merely an appearance of ultimate power, an illusion, not a reality of power. But come on! We are talking about the single personal embodiment of all evil in creation – all of it. Satan is not just a person, but the personification of all of the evil that ever exists at any moment. He is not all the evil that ever was or ever will be, because he does not transcend time as God does. But in any given moment, Satan is the embodiment of every ounce of evil that lives in the world. People talk flippantly about facing down the Devil, speaking directly to the Devil, or commanding Satan to do their will.

I understand what they are saying. I even believe that we have the right to tell the Devil to flee, and he must. But my dear friend, take a moment to think what it would be like to legitimately be in the very presence of all the evil in the entire universe right now. I get scared at horror movies. I react emotionally to suspenseful TV programs. I am not sure that any of us has any context to understand what it would honestly be like to be in the actual presence of Satan. Yet, Christ says to the church at Pergamum, "You live in the town where Satan has his throne!" That should get our attention.

"You bear my name…" the imagery at work here is the picture of the bride who takes and bears her husband's name. We, the bride of Christ, carry His name, known as Christians. The term literally means "Little Christs." Then, this beautiful testimony of them: "…and you did not forsake me even when they martyred my faithful friend and witness Antipas *right where Satan lives*." Oh, that we could be this faithful. I pray that one day God can say of us that we carried His name, and we did not forsake Him, even in the face of the martyrdom of others who were faithful.

I remember once hearing Chuck Colson speak. Colson had been one of the insiders in President Nixon's administration and was convicted of crimes related to the Watergate scandal and sent to prison. He shared the one fact that persuaded him of the truth of the claims about Jesus. He was convinced because all of Jesus' disciples were martyred or exiled for their faith, yet not one recanted their testimony. Colson told of how loyal all of Nixon's inner circle, known as "The President's Men," were to him. Yet, when faced with some prison time, all but one of them instantly turned on the President to save their own necks. Colson testified that, when he heard that Jesus' disciples were all willing to die for their testimony of Christ, he knew that Christ had to be real. People do not die for a lie. Antipas was John's friend and disciple. His death surely affected John deeply. If the tradition is genuine, Antipas was killed for casting out demons; demons the Pergamids liked!

The crime against Heaven is so heinous that, here, Christ repeats Himself. Anytime you are reading along in scripture and find something repeated – pay attention – it is crucial. Christ says that they murdered Antipas at the very spot where Satan lives. These folks have kept their faith in the most evil place on Earth. They have stood in the face of the wickedest presence in creation. Knowing they could also die for their witness, they continued to identify themselves as Christians.

The next phrase is so particular that you could honestly read it with specific words like: "But I have this one little thing against you…" Well, it is not really a little thing, is it? Christ says, in effect, that the church at Pergamum has held onto His name. Still, they have allowed the evil around them to corrupt them in some very significant ways. What are those ways? They have this spiritual problem in their midst. They have people who participate in a kind of sin reminiscent of an Old Testament character named Balaam. You can read the story of Balaam in Numbers 22. I'll give you the *Reader's Digest* condensed version.

Balaam was a pagan seer. Balaam sees that Israel has already crushed two kingdoms on their way to the Promised Land. They are about to encounter the kind of kings who give Balaam a great deal of money to prophesy on their behalf. Balaam sees an opportunity to swindle some kings out of great money! But God gets ahold of Balaam and warns him not to speak against Israel. King Balak of Moab calls on Balaam to prophesy against Israel. Still, God tells Balaam not to go, so at first, Balaam refuses. But his beneficiary, Balak, insists and so Balaam goes. Angered that Balaam is going, God puts an armed angel in his path, but only Balaam's donkey can see the armed angel. The donkey refuses to advance on the armed angel. Balaam beats his donkey mercilessly until God allows the donkey to speak! Then Balaam's eyes are opened to the presence of the angel in the path.

Interestingly, God then tells Balaam that he can go with Balak but must only say what God tells him. The two of them visit three different high places, building seven altars in each one. In each location, Balak begs Balaam to prophesy against Israel, but he will not. The final site is called Peor, and though Balaam continues to speak positively about Israel, even when threatened by Balak, he seems to soften his prophecy against Israel's enemies with an utterance about "fate," rather than a clear word from God. Because of this, Balaam comes to notoriety as a wicked person in Hebrew history. Numbers 25 accuses Israel of taking part in the "heresy of Peor." Numbers 31 places the blame on evil advice given by Balaam, and he becomes a person killed in retaliation against Midian, also recorded in Numbers 31, Deuteronomy, and Joshua. Here, in The Revelation, we are shown a bit more of the story. Christ says that Balaam's sin was teaching Balak how to put a "stumbling block" in the Israelites path. He did this by encouraging them to eat meat sacrificed to idols and to partake in sex with pagan priestesses – temple prostitution. Now, realize that history does not bear all of this out against Balaam and Balak. But in Jewish tradition, their names became connected with the sin and deception of taking part in pagan worship activities and rituals. Paul addresses this same issue of compromising faith by partaking in meat sacrificed to pagan idols with the New Testament church at Corinth.

It would be easy to justify eating the meat that was a by-product of pagan sacrifice. History tells us that the priests and priestesses would sacrifice the animals in the pagan temples, bleed them out, offering the blood as a tribute to their gods. What was leftover was a perfectly good carcass, the meat from which could feed a family for days. That meat was valuable. So, the temples had meat vendors out in the market who would sell the flesh. The temple priests and priestesses got the proceeds. If you understand that those gods they worship do not actually exist, why not buy the bargain meat and eat it? Paul says, "Sure...as long as in doing so, you do not provide a *stumbling block* that might hurt the faith of a non-believer." (1 Cor 8 or Rom 14) There is that term – it is Balaam's stumbling block. Somewhere along the path of history, the Jews equated temple prostitution as a "stumbling block," a sin against God. In the pagan temples, a priestess-prostitute typically led worship. She would announce the oracle of the day from the false deity, then accept offerings of sacrifice and money. For a particular offering of greater worth, she would have sex with the one who brought the donation.

An aside: This is most likely why Paul says, in 1 Timothy 2:12, "I never let a woman speak or teach in the church." It is not because they are not capable or worthy. It is not because God could not call a woman. It was because almost all of the people coming to those fledgling churches that Paul started were coming from the world of temple prostitution. If a woman got up and delivered a Word from God, there was an immense risk that men new to the church would misunderstand and approach her for sex. Paul was not putting women down but trying to protect them!

But Jewish tradition called these sins by the names of Balaam and Balak. Christ is saying to the church at Pergamum, "You are participating in this ancient deception by eating sacrificial meat and participating in sex with temple prostitutes. You are using your knowledge that the gods they serve are not real to take advantage of their system and to benefit personally. You are living in compromise." That is bad, right? But then, it gets worse.

Christ then speaks to the fact that they have members in their church who hold to the ways of the Nicolaitans. Remember them? We met them in the message to the church at Ephesus. The Ephesians hated them, but there are folks in Pergamum who join in their excesses in food, drink, and sex. There are people in the church who claim to belong to Christ but live just like the pagans around them. These people partaking of these excesses may even be claiming that they are, in some way, a blessing from God! Aren't you glad there is no one in the twenty-first century church living like that? Aren't you glad that Jesus is scolding those wicked people in Pergamum who would dare to live like that, and that none of us would ever do such a thing? Can you even imagine that people would claim to be Christians and eat to gluttony? The nerve! Or that folks would sit in church claiming to know Jesus as their "personal Lord and Savior" and go out on Friday night and get blind-stumblin'-porcelain-worshipin' drunk? Surely not! Or that there might be people who would call themselves Christians and post all kinds of holier-than-the-average-bear platitudes, scriptural quotes, and Jesus memes on their social media platforms, but be on four different adult dating pick-up sites looking for their next sexual partner? Not in our church...I mean...we would never do such a thing...right? Not us. I am feeling a little sick at this point.

It is us. It is a significant part of the twenty-first century church. The church around us, among us, within us...lives in compromise with the world. A few weeks ago, I attended a church as a guest. The pastor said, clearly, members of one of the political parties were not allowed to become members in his church unless they repented of their political party affiliation. He said they were not required to join the other party, but they had to repent of and quit their current party, or they could not join the church. I sat in stunned disbelief. Now, I have to confess to you, and you may stop reading right here because of my confession, but please hear me out. Then, if you think I am a heretic, I understand.

As I write this, Donald Trump is President of the United States. To be honest and transparent, I did not vote for him. I did not vote for his opponent, either. One was a non-convicted criminal in my mind. The other was a serial womanizer and verbal abuser. I had watched the latter through the primaries. He made up petty derogatory nicknames for his political opponents. He brushed off his former womanizing ways. He even dismissed an awful recording, in which he said incredibly demeaning things towards women. It bears mentioning that the tape was from fifteen years previous, and he was unaware that he was recorded at the time. But, he did nothing to express remorse for the words. He never apologized. He doubled down, saying that he did not ever like to apologize. I just could not vote for him with a Christian conscience. So, I did not vote for either of them. For the only time in my life, I left the race for President unmarked.

I have seen the man change while he has been in office. Whether he is sincere or not is not for me to judge, but I have seen him change. As a Christian, I pray for the transformation of anyone who accepts the claims of Christ in their lives. As such, I give the President every benefit of every doubt every time. He has done a much better job than I was afraid he might do, and he appears to have walked into a better place than he once was. I pray for him daily and hope God is at work within him.

But I must never forget that he leads the Empire, not the Kingdom.

He is not a high priest. He leads the Empire. Our form of government will never allow him to be king or emperor, but he leads the Empire just the same. I am deeply convicted that I must be discerning of what is taking precedence in any decision made by my President, or my Congress, or friends and countrymen. Are we putting the Empire first, or the Kingdom? (I told you it would matter.) I love my country. I love my President. But my love for the things of the Empire must never compromise my love for Christ. Oh, my friends, this is a point at which I can so easily fail. Take off your halo and sit on it, please?

This is just as hard a test for most of you too! The temptation is strong to compromise our faith with excess, food, drink, or sexual pleasures. We tend to believe that we are cagey enough to make exceptions to what we know is God's will. Our tendency to think that we are smarter than the rest of the pagan world is a powerful influence. Throughout my career in the church, I have seen businessmen and women, civic leaders, government authorities, even law enforcement officials compromise their core beliefs. They have chosen shortcuts that they reckoned at the moment were beneficial to the good. They thought the short-cut was preferable to the proper way of doing things because it would result in the same outcome with less hassle or process. Compromises that looked like practical shortcuts at the beginning turned out to have tragic consequences before the end. See? God's "one little thing" is not such a little thing. It is the sin of compromise, and it affects every one of us at multiple points in our lives.

Interestingly, the threat here is not of taking away the lampstand. Christ does not threaten to distance the offenders from Himself. The threat is much more urgent. He threatens to come and fight them with his double-edged sword of truth. He is promising to expose them! He will reveal the truth about them and their compromising sins. When we involve ourselves in compromise, that is the fear that hangs over our heads like a huge dark cloud, isn't it? The fear of exposure is smothering when we are committing compromise. Christ makes it clear. He will come and fight. That is not a fight any of us can win. That is not a fight any of us want even to see coming. Let the person with an ear turn it to the truth now, before it is too late. Repent. Turn and go the other way. End the compromise and return to living as you know you should, even if it looks like the longer, harder way. Then, you will know the freedom that comes from living in the truth on that path.

The reward? Christ promises to give the one who endures to the end "the manna." There existed for many years after his martyrdom, a tradition said that the relics of St. Antipas would sometimes exude oil that came to be known as the "manna of the Saints?" Oil was frequently used for medicinal purposes and believed to have healing properties. Manna was the bread that God provided the Israelites to eat in the desert as they escaped from Egypt in The Book of Exodus. The tradition connected with Antipas artifacts must have already been known in John's time. He alludes to it here. I will give to the one who prevails that mysterious and healing sustenance – and one more thing. I will give him a stone with a name on it, which only he and I will know. That is the mark of a changed life! Jacob becomes Israel, Abram becomes Abraham. Sarai becomes Sarah. The aspect of the name of God is added to, or replaces, their former identity when they stop compromising (each of them was) and live the life to which God calls them! The promise of being given a new name is the promise of redemption. A new name means a new reality – the past forgiven – a new future ahead as we walk with God. The final reminder is that God has such power that He can, literally, rewrite your life and future!

HOW MIGHT WE SHARE THIS?

Whenever I have preached or taught this section, I have used an outline something like this:

I.   When you live next door to Satan, life can be challenging

II. Do not let Satan rub off on you

III. The promise of a life redeemed

QUESTIONS FOR FURTHER STUDY OR REFLECTION

1.   What temples existed in ancient Pergamum?

2.   What sites in Pergamum might have constituted the "Throne of Satan?"

3.   What can you learn about the life and martyrdom of Antipas?

CHAPTER EIGHT

THE LETTER TO THE CHURCH AT THYATIRA
YOU ARE DOING BETTER – DO NOT LET
FALSE LEADERS TAKE YOU DOWN

Revelation 2:18-28

THE TEXT:

"2:18Then write to the angel of the church in Thyatira: 'These are the words of the Son of God; whose eyes are like tongues of fire and His feet as molten bronze. 19I know your works, namely, your love and faithfulness and service and your endurance. Your recent behavior is better than your earlier behavior.

20But I hold against you that you have tolerated that woman, "Jezebel," who calls herself a prophetess and who teaches and deceives my servants, to commit ritual fornication and to eat meat sacrificed to idols. 21Now, I have given her time to repent, but she did not want to repent of her fornication. 22Behold, I will cast her into a sickbed, and I will cause those who commit fornication with her great tribulation. *If they will not reject her behavior,* ²³*then I will kill her children with the plague. Then all the churches will know that I am the one who searches mind and heart, and I will give to each of you in accordance with your deeds.*

²⁴*Now I say to the rest of you in Thyatira, you who do not hold to this teaching, who have not learned what people call "the secrets of Satan," I will not put any other burden upon you.* ²⁵*Only hold on to what you have until I come.*

²⁶*And to the one who prevails and who keeps my works until the end, I will give authority over the nations,* ²⁷*and he will rule them with an iron scepter and crush them like shards of pottery.* ²⁸*Just as I received it from my father, I will give the morning star to him.* ²⁹*Let the person with an ear hear what the Spirit proclaims to the churches."' Rev 2:18-28*

THE CITY AND THE CHURCH OF THYATIRA

Unlike Ephesus, Smyrna, or Pergamum, Thyatira was never a large metropolis. Still, though small, it was a center of regional commerce. Though it did not offer the variety of goods that one might have found in its larger neighbors in Roman Asia, historians tell us that Thyatira had trade in which it specialized, offering

A map showing the location of Thyatira

some of the most sought-after commodities of its time. So specialized was trade in Thyatira, that it was home to several influential guilds of artisans. Archeologists have discovered evidence of
guilds of coppersmiths and of those who dyed cloth - particularly
a specific color of deep red, or purple, that was famous throughout
Roman Asia. In fact, this trade is mentioned in the Bible. In Acts
16:14, Paul encounters a woman named Lydia in Philippi. The
Bible records that she was a dealer in purple cloth, and a wor-
shiper of God. For a small town, Thyatira had a broad influence
in Roman Asia. Yet, aside from its mention in Revelation 2, and

the mention in Acts 16 that Lydia was from Thyatira, it does not appear anywhere else in the New Testament. There is a tradition that attributes the founding of the church there to Paul. Still, no Biblical or historical reference bears this fact out. All we know, we hear from John in The Revelation.

WHAT IS THE TEXT SAYING TO US?

The message to the church in Thyatira bears some deeply rooted Jewish symbolism. The introduction to the letter starts by affirming the person of Christ using imagery from the first chapter. Then, an intense affirmation for the church's "love, faithfulness, service, and endurance." Christ even credits the church with improvement in its behavior. They are doing better than they had been previously but then comes the corrective, and it is more personal and direct than any yet issued to the other churches. What Christ holds most against the church at Thyatira is not so much an attitude or a spirit as it is a person. They tolerate "Jezebel" in their church. Now, the person's name is probably not actually Jezebel. That is a Palestinian name, and not likely the name of a person in a Greek-Persian-Roman city or church. The name Jezebel is representative and taken from a real person in Jewish history. Who was she, and what was wrong with her?

You will find Jezebel in 1 Kings 16 and following. She was the princess of the Kingdom of Phoenicia, the daughter of the King of Tyre and Sidon. Phoenicia sat along the eastern shore of the Mediterranean Sea. Her name is, literally, Jeze-Baal. Her father was King Eth-Baal. Their names reveal that they are worshipers of the false fertility god, Baal. Jezebel, in what was likely an arranged marriage meant to bring peace between neighboring kingdoms, married Ahab prince and heir to the throne in Israel. She persuaded Ahab to blend the worship of Yahweh with the worship of her fertility god, Baal, leading Israel into the worst kind of idolatry and polytheism (the worship of more than one God, expressly forbidden by the Law of Moses). Because Baal was a fertility god, the worship ceremony dedicated to him often included sexual acts and elements. Jezebel systematically murdered the prophets of God and replaced them with priests and priestesses of Baal. She prostituted Israel. It took generations for the divided heart she brought to Israel to be mended, and then only by exile. Her name came to represent the epitome of wickedness, especially in women, and it is in that vein that it appears in The Revelation. This woman in Thyatira apparently belongs to the church of Jesus Christ but seems to have continued to teach elements of the pagan religion from which she came. Further, she appears to have been a leader in the pagan temple. She refers to herself as a prophetess and teaches the specific pagan elements of ritual prostitution and the consumption of sacrificial meat.

Pause a moment. I need to draw a clear line of definition between the use of the name Jezebel here in The Revelation, and the ways in which it is sometimes used in the twenty-first century church. Because of the wickedness of the original Queen Jezebel, and because of the use of the name to indicate a wicked woman in The Revelation, there has been a movement for decades among some evangelical churches in America to use the name to shame any woman whose behavior that her church, or their leadership, want to paint as "wicked," or "immoral." As a result, many of God's daughters have been shamed out of congregations or churches, accused of lying, infidelity, or some form of general wickedness. In many cases, our sisters, thus accused, were not truly guilty of anything. They only disagreed with sinful conduct among the male leaders of their own households, or their church, or both. In some cases, these ladies had possibly fallen or been betrayed into some real sin. But none of them deserved to be shamed and called by the name of the Biblical epitome of evil. They may have failed. They may have sinned. But it is unlikely they tried to drag an entire congregation into pagan rituals or compromise. People fail.

Might I encourage you, if you are part of a congregation that has ostracized anyone, especially a woman caught in a public sin, consider the example of Christ? Before you cast out a soul who needs the church more in their time of shame than they ever did in any time of joy, consider the damage you could do. At some point, we must realize that the corporate move to judge and condemn a lost soul among us, may be every bit as evil and pervasive as the sin of the Biblical "Jezebels" – and even worse than that for which we might judge or shun another.

In Thyatira, there is no doubt of the depth of wrongdoing that Christ is pointing out in the person the church is tolerating. She is, indeed, leading the church astray with elements of her former pagan spirituality. She is dividing their hearts between God and false gods in the same way that the original Jezebel seduced Israel. Christ says she was given time to repent and turn away from her evil, but she did not. So, in only the message to Thyatira, Christ proclaims judgment on an individual. She will be cast onto a sickbed, and those who have participated with her in sin will be stricken with great troubles. Now, I know that many preachers have had a hey-day with this passage and speculation that Christ is referencing some sexually transmitted disease in this passage. While that might be possible, it is not the direct intention of this text. Christ is simply saying that, for her refusal to repent, she will become very sick. Those who have joined in her sin, if they do not repent, will suffer equally agonizing consequences. Finally, if her children do not repent and break the generational cycle of sin that she represents, they will die. One way or another, Christ will end the cycle of sin in their church and in their lives.

Because this corrective is aimed at a single person, and specific transgressions, it may seem easy to dismiss by those of us who are not fornicating or eating sacrificial meat. In fact, Christ goes on to say to those in Thyatira who have not participated in the named sins, that He is not going to put any further burden on them. Her judgment will stand as a reminder to the rest of the churches in Asia. Each person determines their judgment by their deeds. Wait, are we not saved by grace? Are not our deeds meaningless in the light of grace? Here, Christ connects us to one of the most worrisome scriptures in the New Testament: Matthew 25:31-46.

In Matthew 25, Jesus offers us His version of the final judgment. He gathers all people from all time and separates them, the obedient to his right, the guilty to his left. Then, he judges them on a simple set of criteria:

> *"I was hungry, and you gave me food. I was thirsty, and you gave me something to drink. I was a stranger, and you took me in." Mat 25:35*

Or they did not. Both groups recite the exact same clueless response,

> *"Lord, when did we see you like this, ever, and do (or not do) these things for you?"*

Jesus responds precisely the same way to each group:

> *"As you did (or did not) do these things for the 'least' of my brothers, you did (or did not) do these things to me." Mat 25:40*

The Bible is straightforward that you and I are justified (saved) by the grace of Christ. If God did not choose to see us as washed of sin by the blood of Christ, we would have no hope. It is only by grace that we are saved. But Christ is clear that we are individually responsible for what we do with that grace. Jesus' account of the judgment indicates that we will be judged on nothing but works or, at least, the attitude that we hold in our hearts that drives us to minister, or not. Christ says as much to the church at Thyatira: "I will reward each of you in accordance with your deeds."

Finally, this exciting promise: the victorious one is the one who keeps Christ's *works*, not just His Word, to the end. We expect to see Him calling us to keep His Word. Yet, here, He promises a great reward to the one who keeps His works! This is another of those key Johannine thoughts. Look at the epistle of 1 John 2:

> *"Whoever claims to be a part of Christ must walk as Jesus did." 1 John 2:6*

A few years ago, I was standing in line at a sandwich store, awaiting my turn to step up and place my order. In front of me was the most densely tattooed person I have ever seen. The back of his neck, his arms, the backs of his hands, his legs, every square inch of his skin that I could see was covered in ink! His hair was cut short. Into the hair on the back of his head was cut the letters "WAJD." My holy pastoral mind immediately started to judge this walking comic strip. What manner of blasphemy must this "WAJD" cut into his hair be? At that moment, he turned and smiled at me. He had piercings in his ears, at the side of one eye, in his nose and lips. Good heavens! What kind of heathen had I happened upon in the sandwich shop? He spoke, "Good afternoon, my friend!"

Taken back a bit by his friendliness, I responded, "Good afternoon to you, too. May I ask, what do the letters 'WAJD' represent that you have cut into your hair?" He turned to face me and said, "The one who claims to know Jesus must not simply ask 'What Would Jesus Do?' but must commit himself to 'Walk as Jesus Did,' First John 2:6!"

He smiled broadly. I said, "Amen," but my smile hid my deep shame and disappointment in myself. I had assumed that I had a right to judge him because of his appearance. He carried more ink than the Sunday paper, but his heart was better than mine. He looked like a train-wreck but was walking right. I looked like a white-washed tomb and was about as stinky inside. I remember sitting in my car with my sandwich and asking God to change my heart.

The promise to Thyatira, and to all others who would read this charge, was to keep the works of Christ and be made a ruler over the nations with the same force an iron hammer would have over clay pottery. And finally, the promise of the morning star. What does this mean? It is one of those themes that continually rings through the writings of John. Think of the Gospel of John, chapter one. The Word was from the beginning, and it was the Word's right to bring everything else into being that exists. Contained within that Word was life and that life was the light of the world.

Light. The Jews have several words for particular times of the day. There is a word for that time in the morning, before the sun comes up, when there is only the faintest glow on the horizon, and the stars can still be seen. There is that one heavenly body that shines brighter than all the rest – the morning star. It is the promise that the new day is beginning, even though the sun is far from rising. In John's Gospel, Judas leaves the "last supper," to go out and betray Christ, and John says, "…and it was *night*." (John 13:30). The word means, literally, "the dead of night," or "pitch black." Judas betrays Christ, and there is no light in the sky. Later, John portrays the betrayal of Christ by Peter in John 18:27. Peter betrays Christ not once, not twice, but three times. Three times worse than Judas.

But look at what John says: as soon as Peter utters his third betrayal, John says, "…and at that very moment, a rooster crowed." Now, Jesus had predicted this would happen. But why the rooster? When does a rooster crow? In the morning, in the very early morning before the sun even peeks above the horizon, while it is still so dark that you can see…the morning star! Judas betrays Christ in the hopeless dark and goes and hangs himself in hopelessness. Peter betrays Jesus three times worse, but at the moment when there is a hint of the new day in the sky. The morning star shines brightly in the dusky sky. The light is coming. For John, this statement communicates hope. To the one who is victorious over the sin that can creep into our Christian walk, Jesus promises the morning star – the hope of redemption. If you have an ear today, perhaps you needed to hear that there was that kind of hope for you.

HOW MIGHT WE SHARE THIS?

In preaching or teaching the message to the church at Thyatira, I have used an outline something similar to:

I.   The good that lives in us all – and gets better some days

II. The evil we all tolerate - that gets worse as we live with it

III. Our responsibility to fight our own battles until we overcome

QUESTIONS FOR FURTHER STUDY OR REFLECTION

1. What can you find about Thyatira in historical references?

2. What happened with Lydia from Thyatira in the Book of Acts?

3. Who were the prophets who had face-offs with the original Queen Jezebel?

4. How did those confrontations turn out?

5. What kind of compromise in today's church would be similar to the sins of Jezebel listed in this account?

CHAPTER NINE

THE LETTER TO THE CHURCH AT SARDIS
WAKE UP!

Revelation 3:1-6

THE TEXT:

"³:¹To the angel of the church in Sardis write: 'These are the words of Him who holds the seven spirits of God and the seven stars. I know your deeds; you have a reputation of being alive, but you are dead. ² Wake up! Strengthen what remains and is about to die, for I have found your deeds unfinished in the sight of my God. ³ Remember, therefore, what you have received and heard; hold it fast, and repent. Because if you do not wake up, I will come like a thief, and you will not know at what time I will come to you.

⁴ Yet you have a few people in Sardis who have not soiled their clothes. They will walk with me, dressed in white, for they are worthy. ⁵ The one who prevails to the end will, like them, be dressed in white. I will never blot out the name of that

person from the Book of Life but will acknowl-
edge their name before my Father and His angels.
⁶Let the one with an ear hear what the Spirit says
to the churches." Rev 3:1-6

THE CITY AND CHURCH OF SARDIS

A map showing the location of Sardis

Unlike Ephesus, which is mentioned several times in the New
Testament, Sardis is only mentioned in The Book of Revelation.

All that we know about the congregation is what we read from John in Chapter 3 of The Revelation. The city of Sardis was significant for several reasons. It had been the capital of the Kingdom of Lydia. As such, it ruled what is now Western Turkey from the 1200s BC to the mid-500s BC. Sardis was the center of commerce and rule for the Kingdom of Lydia until the Persians conquered it in 546 BC. It featured a tremendous market and specialized in dying woolen fabrics and producing beautifully colored rugs. A stream that flowed through Sardis, right through the market, was renowned for containing gold flakes, which were melted into nuggets for trade.

The Sardinians were the first known culture to mint coins. Their first coins came from the early 500s BC and were a combination of silver and gold called "electrum." Within a short time, the Sardinians discovered the process for separating the precious metals. They established the first circulated coinage using both metals. Sardis was known for its beauty throughout the civilized world. Its beauty is a significant factor as we address the message from Christ to the church at Sardis.

WHAT IS THE TEXT SAYING TO US?

Christ's message to the church at Sardis centers around appearances versus reality. It is a fitting message for a church in a city of splendor and wealth. The introduction is much like that to Ephesus. "These are the words of him who holds the seven spirits of God and the seven stars." It is an affirmation that it is still Christ who is speaking in the vision, and Christ who has a message for the church at Sardis. Unlike the message to the church at Ephesus, there is no affirmation in the letter to Sardis. The corrective comes right away, and it is firm: "I know your deeds; you have a reputation of being alive, but you are dead." Christ does not mince words, does He? They live in a city that is all about appearances: beautiful rugs and brightly colored clothes and decorations. Their culture has rubbed off on their practice of faith. Their faith has atrophied behind a façade of vitality. Christ says, "Wake up!" It is not too late, but they must take action soon before the remainder of their faith simply dies out behind the false front. If I sat through the warning to Ephesus and felt like I was in the clear and was still honoring my first love, Christ might just come back and get me here for hypocrisy! How many churches do I know that are all about program and staff and beautiful facilities and busy ministries, yet lack real intimacy with the Holy Spirit? How many people do I know who talk the faith, act the part, sing well, can do the spiritual jumping jacks, can speak in tongues or prophecy, and yet have no intimate depth with God?

In the middle years of my ministry, the megachurch movement arose. Out of that grew the entire "seeker-sensitive" emphasis, in which churches made tremendous attempts to be more non-confrontational and accessible by newcomers. I attended seminars and workshops, went to educational events, earned continuing education credits, and even got certified in two different areas of consulting for church growth! We modeled worship for each other in the new style with the latest lighting effects and platform setup. We tossed out the pews and got beautifully upholstered chairs so that everyone had their own "space." We dimmed the lights until you could not find a place to sit if you came after the music started. We even went as far as to create fake smoke! Wait; what? It is true. I was a rock concert kid. When we went to rock concerts, there was always smoke in the air from cigarettes (or other smoking materials.) That light show was only impressive because there was smoke in the air through which you could see the beams of light. So, in my lifetime, churches (that is right, churches) created smoke so that their light show was more impressive than those without smoke. My conservative denomination condemned smoking but manufactured fake smoke, so the light show looked cool. I came away from worship at a mega-church with friends a few years ago. The first question they asked was, "What did you think of worship this morning?"

I tried to waffle my way out of answering the question, but they pressed until I responded. "Well, I have a couple of questions," I began. "If God is light, why is it so dark in church? And, if the church is already on fire, why must we make fake smoke?"

I am afraid I must confess to you that it was not just gentle sarcasm on my part. Something was missing. I later referred to the typical church service in that large American city as "a rock concert and a do-betta speech." We have perfected the "hip" and the "cool." We have mastered the appearance of holiness, but where is the power? Much of what passes for worship today is simply a façade. It looks and feels highly programmed and focused on making everyone feel like they can hide in the dark. The music is so loud that if you do not know the songs, it is no problem. No one will know if you are singing along or not. But where is the substance?

I should update you at this point. Those same friends changed churches in that big city about a year ago. They recently invited me to attend their new church, and I was happy to go. The worship team took the platform and immediately invited the congregation into a more intimate, less showy, worship. The leader explained the purpose of their worship service. He called them to seek the presence of God, not simply to make each other feel good nor to appeal to the emotional side of those gathered. He said their worship was offered to God, not designed for people. No flashing, sweeping lights. No trendy costumes, or ear-shattering volume. The songs were not about victory or overcoming or winning; they were about adoration, drawing near, collapsing in God's presence. The pastor came to the platform to speak and said something like, "We know we are different. If you are new here, we do not mean to shock you, that is the very last thing we want. We are here to draw intimately close with God at every opportunity. We believe that only by knowing Him in intimacy, will you find the kind of strength and assurance. Those attributes allow you to show His grace and love to the folks you are going to be among the rest of the week."

My heart nearly screamed in my chest. "This! This is what I need!" His message was not showy nor bombastic. It was simple and focused. It had only one point. Even I could understand and remember a one-point sermon. The service and sermon had none of the trappings of a seeker-sensitive, mega-church. The church was unashamed that they might make you a bit uncomfortable with their attempts to pull us all closer to God. It was so foreign to me, so strange, to be part of a church service that was all substance and no appearance. It was antithetical to almost everything I had been taught to pursue in the past 30 years of ministry. But it was real. Jesus will not have to write a warning to that church for being exceptional in appearances, but lacking substance. When we got into the car again, my friends asked, "What did you think of church today?" Did you catch the difference? They did not ask me about worship; they asked me about *church*.

Because my thoughts had been immersed in this writing, I said, "Well, it is certainly not Sardis!" Of course, I then had to explain what I meant, but you understand. As I write this, I am constantly bombarded on social media and in church leadership meetings with questions about why the world is leaving the church. We ask ourselves continually about what is going on or what has happened to the world that they no longer value church. That is precisely the opposite of the question we should be asking. The more pertinent question is, "What happened to the church that made us so useless to the world?" By trying to be more relevant, did we become irrelevant? By seeking to become more seeker-sensitive, did we become insensitive to the need of the human heart for deeper intimacy with God? Did we unintentionally become Sardis? In many cases, yes, we did. But there is hope.

We are not dead. There is still a piece of the living and breathing Body of Christ yet alive in us…in all of us! Lord Jesus, please do not come in the night and take what remains. Give us time and wisdom to reclaim what we have and what we know to be right. In a world of brightly-colored garments, help us to be the ones who walk in the purity of unstained garments – and similarly untainted motives. Let us be the ones whose names are not blotted out of the Book of Life. (See what John does there? He hasn't even mentioned the Book of Life yet. He is giving us a bit of a preview!)

Then this final promise that is so very powerful: "I will not blot his name from the Book of Life but will acknowledge that name before my Father and His angels." John remembers that Jesus had spoken of those who would come to Him at the final judgment and say, "Lord, our friend, whom we knew so well! Did you see everything we did in your name – casting out demons, healing the sick, and preaching your *Word?*" Jesus said,

> *"Then I shall have to say to them, 'I am sorry, I*
> *do not know you. Go away." Mat 7:22-23*

It is possible to have put on the act of knowing Christ. We may have said the right words, done amazing things, and even given God credit; yet, done all of those things merely for the appearance of holiness. The promise of Christ in Revelation 3:5 is to the one who serves in intimacy and honesty: Christ will acknowledge his name, "Kevin! My friend! Welcome home!" in front of God, the Father, and all the host of Heaven. He knows me. The Christ of Heaven, the King of Kings, and Lord of Lords...knows me! Do you sense what this repeated device is starting to do? Don't you feel it pulling at your heart to want to be one of those who can hear?

HOW MIGHT WE SHARE THIS?

I have likely played my entire hand as to how I would preach or teach this exhortation to the Sardinians. Still, my outline would look something like this:

I. Sometimes there is nothing positive to be said about my walk with God

II. Sometimes I have to admit I am great at appearances, but lack relationship

III. It is never too late to grasp what is left and do with it as Christ desires

QUESTIONS FOR FURTHER STUDY OR REFLECTION

1. What were the major trades in Sardis that made them appear so wealthy?

2. What would it be like to live in the place where the first precious metals were formed into coins? What would it be like to be the first to have money?

3. What kinds of things does your church do that really only promote appearance, rather than encouraging intimacy?

4. What practices in your own spiritual journey have become mere appearances, but may not really fostering intimacy with Christ in your life?

5. What part of real faith is left in your heart right now? How can you focus on living in that truth in order to be more intimate with Christ and allow Him to bring back revival and intimacy between yourself and Him?

6. What is the first step you can take, right now, to start to rebuild your authentic relationship with Christ?

CHAPTER TEN

THE LETTER TO THE CHURCH AT PHILADELPHIA
GOD LOVES YOU MORE THAN YOU CAN IMAGINE

Revelation 3:7-13

THE TEXT:

"3:7And to the angel of the Church in Philadelphia write: 'These are the words of the Holy One, the True One, the One who has the Key of David, who opens the door that no one can shut, and shuts the door so that no one can open it. 8I know your deeds. Look! I have placed before you an open door, which no one has the power to shut because I know you have little strength. Still, you have obeyed my command and did not deny my name. 9Watch! I will cause those who belong to the synagogue of Satan, who call themselves Jews (but are not, they are liars) – watch, I will force some of them to come and grovel at your feet so that they will know I have loved you. 10Because you have obeyed my command to endure, I will preserve you from the hour of trial, which will come upon the entire Earth to test the inhabitants of the Earth.

> *[11]I am coming soon. Keep what you have so that no one takes away your crown. [12]As for the one who prevails to the end, I will make him a pillar in the Temple of my God, and he will never leave it. I will write on him the name of my God and the name of the city of my God, the new Jerusalem, which descends from Heaven from my God, and I will write on him my new name. [13]Let the one with an ear hear what the Spirit says to the churches.'" Rev 3:7-13*

THE CITY AND CHURCH OF PHILADELPHIA

The second-to-last message is to the church in Philadelphia (this one is in Turkey, not Pennsylvania). As you are likely aware, the name comes from two Greek words – *philos* – which means "love;" and *adelphos* – which means "brother." The city of "loving brothers" or "brotherly love." This is likely a reference to the ruler who founded the city in tribute to his brother; not necessarily a statement of how people there treated each other.

Philadelphia sits on a fault line. The city has been hit throughout history by many earthquakes, a few of which nearly leveled it. If you research historical writings and references to Philadelphia, you will likely find some comment of mild surprise that the city was not abandoned at some point. But it has not been. There is still a Turkish city of about 10,000 people there, about one-fourth of whom are of Greek descent. There is still a sizeable Christian population in the city. They will happily show you the foundations of what they believe was the first church in the city – and the place where the recipients of The Revelation met to worship. There are also mosques and synagogues active in Philadelphia to this day.

A map showing the location of Philadelphia

Because it was continually in need of rebuilding, Philadelphia was never a "wealthy" city. A center of trade and inland commerce, it was always able to generate substantial income. The side of the city up against the mountains was famous for its wine grapes and wines. Yet, rehabilitating after earthquakes kept the taxes high and the residents under continual financial strain. Even today, the city is noticeably dirty and less resplendent than the other cities in the region. We know of the church only what is mentioned in The Revelation, so, we will dive in.

WHAT IS THE TEXT SAYING TO US?

Philadelphia is one of only two churches mentioned in the addresses in Revelation chapters two and three to whom no corrective is addressed. The other is Smyrna, discussed earlier in Chapter Six of this book. These final two churches provide a bright contrast. In Philadelphia, Christ finds no fault; and in Laodicea, He finds no good. This message to Philadelphia is unique. In every church greeting before this, there has been a reference to Christ previously seen in the introduction. We have heard things like, "These are the words of Him who holds the seven stars and walks among the golden lampstands." Or we have heard, "These are the words of the Son of God whose eyes are like blazing fire and feet like white-hot bronze." But here we get something a bit quizzical because it is not mentioned before this greeting:

> *"These are the words of the Holy One, the True One, the One who has the Key of David, who opens the door that no one can shut, and shuts the door so that no one can open it." Rev 3:7*

It is pretty easy to understand what Christ means by "the Holy One" and "the True One." Those are simple attributes that are easily ascribed to Jesus, but what in the world is this "Key of David?" Well, this mystery is not too hard to solve. Just do a search in your Bible software for the "key of David." You will likely get a hit on Isaiah 22:

> *"I will place on his shoulder the key to the house of David; what he opens no one can shut, and what he shuts no one can open." Is 22:22 NIV*

That was easy, and it fits perfectly. But what is it saying? Isaiah 22 is a prophecy written to foretell the punishment and anguish the Israelites would suffer at the hands of the Babylonians in about 597 BC. You can read the chapter. The prophecy is accurate; the men of Jerusalem did not face the Babylonians in some honorable battle. The Babylonians cut off the city from all trade and besieged it. The fighting men starved to death or snuck away in the middle of the night and ran! The Jews have always believed that the Babylonian exile was punishment for generations of compromise. For years, they worshiped one set of idols or another, and could never settle themselves to worship only Yahweh. In Isaiah 22, the prophet is proclaiming their judgment, besiegement, and being carried away into Babylonian exile. Shebna, the keeper of the Temple, had failed. He had resigned himself to surrender to the invaders. In Isaiah 22, he is, in fact, digging his own grave in a final act of total surrender. The prophet is not having any of that. Shebna will lose his position. The old will give way to the new. Eliakim, the son of Hilkiah, will take Shebna's place, if only for a short time. He will get Shebna's robe and sash – and he will get Shebna's keys to the

Temple. God says he will drive Eliakim into the stone like an anchor peg who will hold his ground to the very end. But, if you read to the end of the chapter, you see that even that sturdy anchor will be sheared off in the coming judgment, and Jerusalem and her Temple will fall.

But the key is not lost. Christ still holds the key to God's house! The Temple in Jerusalem was rebuilt after the Babylonian exile, then rebuilt again by King Herod into something even more splendid than it was during the reign of King Solomon. Then, about thirty years before John writes The Revelation, it was ransacked, burned, and razed to the ground – never to exist since. But Christ still holds the key to God's House. The anchor still exists in Christ. The Kingdom will not fall because the anchor pin will not break off. Jesus has the key to the Kingdom. He promises that He will open the door into the Kingdom, and no person or force or influence or ruler will ever be able to close it. And whomever He shuts out, will never be able to gain entrance.

Christ says to the Philadelphians, "I know you and your efforts. Look! I have placed before you an open door which no one can close because I know how exhausted you are, so I'll hold it open for you!" Even though they are not rich, but spent and impoverished and feel weak, Christ affirms that they have obeyed Him and not forsaken His calling. Then He repeats the command to "watch" or "look." He promises a victory to them that He has not guaranteed to any of the other churches – it is a personal victory that they will see come to pass. He promises that He will drag at least some of the Jews (again, he refers to them as a "synagogue of Satan") over to their door to fall prostrate at their feet. Compare this thought with Isaiah 60:

*"And all who held you in contempt shall come
and bow down at your feet." Is 60:14*

Or compare it to Isaiah 49:

*"They shall bow down before you and lick the
dust off your feet." Is 49:23*

Who is God talking about, through Isaiah, in those scriptures? He is talking about the Gentiles coming to grovel at the feet of the Jews...the Children of Israel! In this ironic twist, Christ promises this little church that He will cause the Jews who have abused them to fall prostrate at their feet and to see that God loves these Christians more than those who call themselves His chosen people. Once again, what is Christ going to show? His love. How will He show it? In preservation.

We save those we love. We give our lives for those dearest to us. In fact, all of our earthly priorities and our capacity of love can be measured by answering one honest question: If the world were coming to an end and you could rescue ten people, who would they be? God says He would save you because He loves you. Do you feel the power in that statement? No matter what the Empire of your country's government does, no matter what the Empire of men and women do, no matter what the Empire of spiritual forces that would crush you might do – Christ will save you because He loves you! You have absolutely nothing to fear. You might appear needy, exhausted, weakened, and alone. You are not. Christ will save you because He loves you that much.

When retained to consult with church boards about strategic

planning, I have often asked, "What would you do if money were no issue, and *you weren't afraid?*" You see, it is fear that so often paralyzes us as people and as churches. Why do we fear? Because we do not understand from whence our power comes! Do you realize what Christ, through John, is doing here? He is preparing you for everything that is about to come in the pages of The Revelation! He is giving you the last piece of valuable insight before you launch off into the dark jungle of symbols and apocalyptic events. He wants you to remember that He has the key. He opens and closes the doors. No one else in the universe has that power, only Him. He is going to open and close the doors to your benefit. He is going to save you through everything you are going to hear about because He loves you! If you did not just set this book down and run around your house shouting for glory, you are not getting this yet! Christ has just handed you the most critical key to understanding everything else you are going to hear or read in The Revelation. God wants to anchor you into the wall of the Kingdom like an unbreakable peg until the very end of life – or the very end of the world. You are going to come through whatever lies ahead because the One who holds the key is with you and loves you and will preserve you no matter what. You have the power on your side!

When will this happen? Soon. Will you go through it alone? No, Christ says He is coming soon. Hold on. The one who overcomes will be made by Christ to be a pillar in His Temple! Not only will you be kept, but you will be honored. Sound familiar?

> *"Peter, I am trying to tell you that you are*
> *Petros – the rock! And on that rock, I am going*

to build my church, and not even the gates of Hell will be able to keep it out!" Mat 16:18

It is the same promise, but Christ writes this one to the Church at Philadelphia, and you and me. That is how much Christ believes in us. Are we worth it? Just as much as Peter was. What did Peter do? He denied Christ three times...but he came back. The love of Christ – catch this now – the love of a brother drew Peter back to stay. After Peter denies Jesus, Jesus is crucified and then resurrected, and Jesus is appearing to disciples everywhere. Only John records that Peter, afraid to face Jesus, flees way up north to Galilee, where Jesus first found him fishing and goes back to his former life of fishing. That disciple thing did not work out too well. He had promised to love Jesus until death! But he had failed. He had promised that ultimate *agape* love that says, "Even if they kill me, I will love you!" But he did not. He denied Christ all through the night – three times in all. Until the rooster crowed, just like Jesus had said it would. He was as bad as Judas or worse. He had failed. What could Jesus possibly do but strike him dead on sight now? It was better just to go back from where he had come. He was a dumb, rock-headed fisherman anyway. Jesus probably had not called him Peter (*Petros*), the rock, out of confidence. He was probably just making fun of him. Fishing was better. It is what he knew best. It was much safer.

In John 21, his brothers come to find Peter, and he invites them to quit with him and just go fishing. They join their friend and they fish all night – and catch nothing.

(If I were preaching this, I would pause right here and smile a wry smile. For this one, you have to go back to Luke 5, where

Jesus first calls Peter and Andrew. They were in their fishing boat. They had fished all night and caught nothing. Jesus comes to the shore and calls out to them, asking if they had caught anything. They reply, no, they have been skunked. Then Jesus says, "Cast the net out on the other side of the boat!" Bothersome people. They are always offering advice when they do not know what they are doing. Yet, when they cast out the net on the other side of the boat, the Bible says they caught so many fish that they could not haul the net into the boat!

In John 21, this guy appears on the shore, and he calls out, asking if they have caught anything. They say, "Nope! Been skunked all night!" And the guy says...ready for this? The guy says, "Why not try casting your net out on the other side of the boat?"

Now, you and I are not as stupid as Peter. We would have caught on right there, right? But not Peter. He has been up all night. The great and expert fisherman is about to go hungry on his first day back. He cannot even catch fish well! So, he and his friends throw the net out on the other side. As soon as they pull at the cords that close the loop of the net and trap fish inside, they cannot even lift it. It is so full of fish; it reminds them of...

Peter's heart bursts inside his chest. He cries out, "It is the *Lord!*" His friend has come to get him! The words were true! The promises were true! He is here! Jesus is here! Peter leaves his friends to worry about the huge catch. He puts on his clothes (to go swimming?). It is a symbol of his shame. He dares not meet Jesus naked. (Remember how Adam and Eve were ashamed because, in their sin, they knew they were naked?) He dives in the water – clothed - and swims to the shore and runs up the beach to see...

Jesus. It is Jesus. The friend he let down. The guy he failed. The guy who has every right to hate him or stone him, or at least beat him up. Peter's shame and failure are lost for a moment in the realization that Jesus has cooked them breakfast: he has already got fish that have never swum in the water – and bread that never grew in a field. Loaves…fish. Remember all those leftovers from the feeding of the 5,000? (John 6) That was a lesson to the disciples about the fact that Jesus always has enough to provide for everyone. It was a big lesson for them. Still, Jesus asks Peter to bring some of the fish he has just caught. Get it? Now Peter is the little boy with the lunch of loaves and fish – bringing his bit to the Master to feed everyone! See?

They sit down and eat. Jesus comes over to Peter and calls him by his proper name, not his friend- name.

> *"Simon, son of John, do you love me – do you AGAPOS me? Do you love me so much that you would die for me?"*

Peter's answer is almost feeble. But, for the first time in his life, Peter is honest about his own heart.

> *"Lord, you know I philos you. You know I love you like a brother."*

Jesus accepts Peter's answer and calls him to tend His little lambs. Weird response. Feed His lambs? I am a fisherman, not a shepherd. But, OK. Feed His lambs. See, the old Peter would have complained at that task. The old Peter would have thought that lamb tending was for the little girls and boys. This Peter does not grouse. He takes this calling to heart. Maybe Jesus is taking him back?

A second time, Jesus asks Peter,

> *"Simon, son of John, don't you AGAPOS me?*
> *Don't you love me with all your heart? Would*
> *you not die for me?"*

Surely this time, Peter must have had to bite his tongue. You know he WANTS to say, "YES!" but again, he answers out of the honest capacity of his broken heart:

> *"Lord, I do love you! You KNOW I love you! I*
> *philos you! I love you like the dearest of brothers!*

Jesus responds, but this time He calls Peter to feed His sheep – the big ones. Well, it is a better chore than lamb tending. Peter offers no complaint.

Then, John recounts that Jesus asks Peter a third time, but in English, you cannot see that the words Jesus uses change slightly:

> *"Simon, son of John, do you…philos me? Do you*
> *truly love me like the dearest of brothers?"*

Now some translations here say that the third time Jesus asked, Peter was hurt. But the Greek word is a funny kind of word that can indicate that this is the kind of hurt that makes a person take stock of themselves. Jesus changes His word for "love" here – to

Peter's honest account of himself. He meets Peter, where Peter is at the moment. Do you see what is happening? He is calling Peter back, but more than that, He is keeping him. He is not going to let Peter run away. He is not going to let Peter fail. He is preserving him...because He LOVES HIM!

I imagine Peter; his heart filled to the brim with the joyful realization of what Jesus is doing – calling him again. Weeping, grabbing Jesus in a huge bear hug, he cries out:

> *"Yes! Lord! Yes! I philos you! I love you as my*
> *dearest brother, and I always will!*

He is back. Jesus is back. Peter is back. He has been saved and preserved.

I did not forget where we were, I promise. I wanted you to see the glory that must be filling John's heart at this moment when he hears Jesus saying to the Philadelphians how much He loves them and will preserve them. John knows it is the absolute truth because he witnessed how Christ did precisely that for Peter. He loves them so much that He is going to write His name, the name of His New Kingdom, and their new name in that Kingdom on them. He is going to wash away all the things that they have been called before and absolutely redefine who they are. They will get a new relationship with God, a new walk with Christ, a new Kingdom in which to live, and a new untarnished name by which to be known. Come on. You have got ears. You have got a heart. You have been hurt before, even shattered perhaps. You have wished that you could wash all the bad away and stand blameless before God and everybody.

Those are words we have all longed to hear all of our lives. Lord, give us ears to hear that!

Now it is about to get real tense, real fast.

HOW MIGHT WE SHARE THIS?

When I have preached this message, whether in a study of Revelation or by itself, I have used an outline something like this:

I.   God has the power – He can open or close any door at any time

II. My place in God's plan is obedience. Will I step or stop, depending on what He does?

III. Do I understand how much God truly loves me? He is going to save me.

QUESTIONS FOR FURTHER STUDY OR REFLECTION

1.   What doors would you like to see opened in your life right now?

2.   What doors do you feel have recently closed to you?

3.   Can you begin to understand a direction that the open doors and the closed doors might be making clearer to you?

4.   What would you do right now if you weren't afraid of anything?

5. If you stop and listen to God, can you discern where He is calling you to be right now? Could you pray about it the next couple of weeks and be open to wherever He might call?

6. Do you understand how very much Christ loves you? How would you express it in words or writing or a song?

CHAPTER ELEVEN

THE MESSAGE TO THE CHURCH AT LAODICEA
I CANNOT FIND ANYTHING GOOD IN YOU

Revelation 3:14-22

THE TEXT:

"3:14And to the angel of the church in Laodicea, write: 'These are the words of the Amen, the faithful and true Witness, the Origin of the creation of God. 15I know your deeds, that you are neither cold nor hot. I wish you were either cold or hot! 16But, because you are lukewarm and neither cold nor hot, I will vomit you from my mouth. 17You say, "I am wealthy, and l have become rich and lack for nothing," yet you do not see that you are wretched, miserable, poor and blind and naked, 18I advise you to buy from me gold purified by fire that you might be rich, and white garments that you might be clothed so that the shame of your nakedness might not be exposed, and then medication to apply to your eyes that you might regain your sight.

[19]Those whom I love I correct and discipline; therefore, be diligent and repent. [20]Look! I stand at the door and knock. If anyone hears me calling and opens the door, I will come in to visit him, and I will share a meal with him and he with me.

[21]The one who prevails to the end will be allowed to sit with me on my throne, just as I also prevailed and sat down with my Father on His throne. [22]Let the one who has an ear hear what the Spirit says to the churches." Rev 3:14-22

THE CITY AND CHURCH AT LAODICEA

With Laodicea, we come full circle to the last church whom The Revelation addresses. Laodicea is the furthest church inland, and the furthest to the south of all the churches addressed in Revelation 2-3. Laodicea lies on intersecting trade routes with Ephesus to the west and Smyrna and Sardis to the north-northwest. In the time that John writes The Revelation, Laodicea is a very wealthy city of commerce. They specialized in textiles (they produced black wool that was renowned throughout the Roman Empire), medicine, and banking. The Jewish synagogue there was filled with powerful and influential tradespeople and merchants. As we mentioned before, under Domitian, the Imperial Cult movement was strong. Historians believe that one of the significant Greek temples in Laodicea was converted under Domitian to serve as the temple of the Imperial Cult. So strong was the Emperor's desire to

A map showing the location of Laodicea

push people toward worshiping former Emperors (and, one day, himself), that there is evidence that those who refused to worship the Imperial deities were disallowed from doing business with the government. Influential buyers were discouraged from doing business with them.

It is interesting to note that Jews were typically recognized throughout Rome as being monotheists, that is, worshipers of only one God. Throughout most of Roman history, Jews were allowed an exemption from the edicts of Imperial worship. As long as they were part of the Jewish synagogue, and most early

Christians were, Christians enjoyed the same immunity as their Jewish friends. The problem arose when they were kicked out by, or separated themselves from, the Jews. As a separate group, they were no longer recognized monotheists. They could fall under penalties and restrictions for not participating in worshiping in the Imperial cult – sanctions that often appear to have included a prohibition from doing business within the city. These sanctions likely contributed to the poverty of the church in Smyrna. They may be behind the compromise we find in Laodicea.

Despite the pressures of the political setting in Laodicea, there is ample evidence the church went on to thrive. Archeologists have uncovered what they believe to be the sites of at least twenty Christian churches there, and we know that Laodicea became the seat of a Christian bishop (a bishopric). Still, among the seven churches in Revelation, they certainly receive the harshest message.

WHAT IS THE TEXT SAYING TO US?

Just as there are two churches among the seven who receive no corrective guidance in the group, there are two who receive no real encouragement – Sardis, and Laodicea. While Sardis received praise for the faithful among them, there is not even a hint of affirmation for Laodicea.

Here, again, Christ introduces Himself using terms that are not included in the initial vision in The Revelation. In fact, the three titles that He uses for Himself here are unique and remarkable. First, He says that these are, "…the words of the Amen…" It is an engaging construction with only one precedent in scripture: Isaiah 65:16, in which the instruction is that both blessings and oaths are to be given or taken only in the name of "Amen." The Hebrew word *"amen"* simply means "so be it." It is an affirmation of whatever words or actions have come before. To this day, we end prayers with "amen." We are saying, "let it be so." Here, He is affirming His place as the one who ratifies all blessings and oaths. As the "faithful and true witness," Christ is the one who truly represents the Father. As "the Origin of the Creation of God," John is hearkening back to The Gospel of John 1:

> *"By His hand, He created all things, and with-*
> *out Him, nothing that has been created was ever*
> *created." John 1:3*

Ultimate power over anything in the world belongs to the one who created that thing. Christ created everything we see, so Christ has absolute authority over all of it. The one who is bringing the message to the church is the one who has the power to do whatever is needed to make things right.

Then Christ says he knows their deeds, that they are neither red hot nor ice cold. Of course, these terms are metaphors for their spiritual condition. Still, they likely have roots in the reality of living in Laodicea. At the archeological site, researchers have uncovered several lengths of an aqueduct that brought water to the city from a hot spring several miles to the south in Hierapolis. The water would have left the site of the spring at scorching temperatures. However, as it descended to the city, it cooled and arrived in a lukewarm state. We also know the spring water around Laodicea is very hard with minerals. It tastes horrible to most people. While it could serve as drinking water, many historical records contain complaints about its taste. There could be no more explicit metaphor for uselessness.

This is also an allusion to the medicinal use of mineral water. The hot springs above Laodicea attracted folk in need of their therapeutic qualities. People have long sought out hot springs for help with arthritis and joint deterioration. Some believed in drinking the steaming water for healing; others simply wanted to soak in it. To the north of Laodicea lay Colossae. There, icy springs bubbled up from the ground with great-tasting and refreshing ice-cold water. Water that cold can reduce swelling and decrease pain in certain circumstances. When Christ says, "I wish you were one or the other!" He is expressing that He wishes they were healing in one way or another, but they are not, and because they are not – they are worthless for any kind of healing. They are just a bad taste in His mouth. His promise is, then, to vomit them out of His mouth. That is a pretty clear metaphor. Not only are they lukewarm, Christ next addresses their arrogance.

"You say, 'I am wealthy! I have become rich and lack for nothing!'" The problem at Laodicea was not insufficiency, nor laziness. They had plenty, and they were industrious. They had simply become so busy being busy that they had forgotten God. Christ speaks to them out of precisely what has made them so proud. Remember? They had banking, the coveted black wool textiles, and medicine. They had likely compromised their faith and accepted Imperial worship, to not be banned from the attractive income available in commerce. Their lack of convictions, however, had made them wealthy and arrogant. Christ hits them right where they live:

"You say, 'I am wealthy! I have become rich and lack for nothing!' Yet you do not see that you are miserable, wretched, poor, blind, and naked!"

In a city known for its medicines and salves, particularly remedies for the eyes, Christ tells them that they cannot see. What are they missing? They do not comprehend the poverty within themselves. This message stands in stark contrast to the message to the church in Smyrna, who thought they were poor, but whom Christ called rich. In Laodicea, it is the opposite – they think they are rich. Nonetheless, Christ just lays into them with this litany of descriptors: "…wretched, miserable, poor, blind, and naked!"

Wretched. The word means "unhappy, needy, or of low quality." Who could be happier? They were wealthy. They thought their life was of very high quality. Christ says they are mistaken. Miserable? A word that means "wretchedly uncomfortable or dissatisfied." They thought they lived in comfort and satisfaction. Christ indicts them. "Poor, blind, and naked." In rapid succession, Christ hits them at the very points of which they were most proud! Remember? Their fame was banking (gold), medicine (especially eye remedies), and their famous black textiles. Christ discounts the things that have kept the Laodiceans so busy making money. It is as if, to Christ, those wealth-producing trades do not even exist, and the people have been left impoverished, blinded, and naked. As is true for most of us – their most impressive strengths were also their most glaring weaknesses. The things that made them proud, also made them arrogant. Christ calls them to repentance.

Repentance, from the Old Testament Hebrew word *shuv* or

shub (but the b makes a v sound), literally means "turn and go the other way." Christ advises they buy gold from Him – the pure value of a heart refined by His Word and by living out their convictions. He calls them to get from Him white garments. White is the color of purity. Black is the color of evil. Their black wool was famous, not inherently evil. But Christ is speaking in metaphors here. Their nakedness was figurative. It was spiritual. In being busy, they had sacrificed their purity of purpose and heart. To their shame, they had exposed themselves to the world as lukewarm and compromising Christians, who stood for nothing substantive. Finally, Christ calls them to get a salve for their eyes so that they might regain their vision. As I get older, I do not know that there is anything I value about my health more than my eyesight.

A couple of years ago, one of my coworkers suddenly experienced extreme blurriness in one eye. By day's end, the blurriness was affecting both eyes, rendering him able only to discern shadows and outlines, but no details. It was scary. His doctors determined that he had an infection. The doctors prescribed antibiotics, and over the next few days, his eyesight cleared to normal again. I remember how scared he was in that moment at lunch when his vision in one eye suddenly blurred. He was near panic. I also remember visiting him that evening when both eyes were affected and hearing the anxiety in his voice. Would this continue to get worse? Would he ultimately lose all sight? Our eyesight is invaluable to us. Life would be, well, wretched without it. Christ calls the church at Laodicea back to seeing clearly in a spiritual sense. He is talking about getting their priorities straight, regaining their passion for the things of God, and doing again the things that truly matter.

Christ says one almost-good and encouraging thing to Laodicea: If I did not love you, I would not chastise you. It is tough love, isn't it? Any of us who have ever parented understand precisely this sentiment. When my dad would punish me as a lad, he would often say, "This hurts me more than it does you." I always wanted to say, "I'll bet not!" But, even as a lad, I was wiser than that. Now, as a father, I understand what he meant. It is very important that we not coddle Laodicea. It is just as vital that we see that Christ's stiff admonishment to them comes from love. The historical perspective that the church there went on to survive for centuries and to do meaningful ministry is a reasonable assurance that they heard the message and took it to heart.

The message to the church of today is pointed and clear. All around us are reports that the twenty-first century church in America is losing ground. Membership and attendance are down. Offerings are drying up as the generations who emphasized tithing are dying. A younger generation is taking over, who are suspicious of giving their money to organizations that lack a clear missional directive with which they can get on board. As I write this, one of the largest denominations in history is discussing how it might break into two factions over social issues. But the truth is, they do not have the financial backing to support two administrative and organizational structures. I believe that, should they not resolve their differences, both factions will struggle, or die, due to their inability to survive financially without each other. The church across our nation is in trouble.

Then I look at the church all around me. Is it red-hot with revival? No. Is it healing and refreshing in the way it touches and brings renewal to others? No, it is not that either. It is just...

church. Sunday morning Sunday school hour has nearly disappeared. Sunday night services are no more. Wednesday night church activities have given way to sports practices, school activities, and busy-ness. Families are left grasping for any moments that they can find to spend together.

I remember, twenty years ago, coaching my daughter's soccer team and standing up to those who drew up the schedule. I asked them not to schedule the team I coached for Wednesday practices, scrimmages, or Sunday matches. In that day, they accommodated us. Today, they would look at me like I was crazy. The sacred things of our culture are passing away. Yet, the church walks on, neither red-hot with revival nor refreshing with healing. It is like I live in Laodicea. I often wonder how much longer God can put up with churches who have fellowship dinners for themselves, sports leagues for their own kids, Halloween alternatives for their own families, and any number of ingrown activities that serve themselves while ignoring the world. We are great at being seeker-sensitive – but no one is seeking us. The descriptive term I hear most often used of churches in my culture is, "They have got great music!" Yet, I cannot find any call to have great music in the Bible. We have gotten so busy being busy and taken such care not to offend anyone in our society, that we have become lukewarm and worthless. To the church at Laodicea, and to us, Christ has one more very quizzical thing to say.

By now, you have likely noticed a particular rhythm to the messages to the churches. There is an introduction that, but for these last two churches, references some attribute of Christ from the initial vision. There is that piece about "I know your deeds," followed by a detail of what is right or what is wrong with their deeds. There is typically some sort of statement of corrective or encouragement; then, there is the call to repentance and the bit about "he who has an ear to hear." But to Laodicea, Christ says one extra and unique thing. While His message to them has been tough – He says He is just on the other side of the door.

To the church at Philadelphia, Christ promised that He had the key to the door that He would open and hold open for them. Remember, He referenced back to the Jewish Temple of David and the guy who had the keys and could control which doors he opened, and which he locked. He promised the church at Philadelphia that *He* would open the door that could never close and close the door so that it would never open. To those without any power, He gave an assuring message that He held the ultimate power. However, now, to Laodicea, He takes a very different position. There is a closed and locked door. Christ says, "Look, I stand at the door and knock (and continue to knock)." The Greek verb is of the tense that starts at a point in time but goes on and on forever. The word picture here is not that Christ is banging on the door. He is just gently knocking, almost just tapping quietly, continually. Why would He do that? I am kind of thick-headed. It is noisy in my house. If God wants my attention, He'd better bang on that door! But that is not God's way.

Do you remember the story of Elijah from 1 Kings? Elijah is this fire-brand prophet that takes on Queen Jezebel and her god, Baal. Jezebel and her people believe that Baal controls the rain. Elijah marches into her palace and declares that it will not rain again until he says so. Then he leaves. Lots of things happen, but no rain falls. They search for Elijah, but he has vanished. Finally, he has a massive showdown with the priests of Baal in which they cannot get fire to fall from the sky to burn up their sacrifice because Baal is false and cannot hear them. Elijah taunts them, even asking if their god is on the toilet and unable to hear! (Yes, the Bible says this.) Then Elijah steps up and calls God to bring fire from Heaven on his sacrifice, and God does. God sends fire so intense that it even vaporizes the rocks of the altar on which they are sacrificing.

In victory, Elijah gets proud. While he has only done as God has instructed to this point in the story, he now does his own thing. The king is in his chariot, fleeing back to Jezreel. Elijah decides to use the power of God to show off, and outruns the king's horses, on foot. The queen promises to kill him. He gets scared and runs out into the desert, finally lying down to die. God comes to Elijah and tells him to get up and get ready because God Himself is going to visit Elijah. There is a mighty wind that even breaks rocks – but God is not in the wind. There is an earthquake that shakes the world to its foundation – but God is not in the earthquake. There is a fire so intense that it melts the rocks (these are all things that Baal was supposed to control) – but God is not in the fire. Then, in 1 Kings 19:12, the Bible says that after the fire, there came a gentle whisper. And God was in the gentle whisper.

Back to the door. Christ does not rage and batter His way into our lives. He quietly whispers. He gently knocks. He is hoping you will hear. If you hear and open the door, He will come in and fellowship with you. He will stay and share and laugh and live with you if you will only open the door. You see, the weak need a door held open for them, but the busy can easily miss a gentleperson's knocking. To the powerless, Christ will bring power. To those who think they have power, He will wait until they open the door. Whether you are weak or strong today, Jesus is at the door.

What will you do? Leave Him out there? Open the door? Walk through it with Him, or stay comfortably right where you are? The promise is that He will come in and make himself at home with you. More than that, He will allow you to occupy the throne of Heaven with Him, just like God welcomed Him to occupy the throne together. This is vitally important. Do you see what Jesus is doing here? He is inviting you into His family. More than that, He is inviting you to participate in the Holy Trinity.

I know, right? How can that be? Well, bear with me one more moment, and I will show you what I mean. Take a look at the prayer that Jesus prays for His disciples in John 17:

> *"21 I pray that they will all be one, in the exact same way you and I are one—as you are the same as me, Father, and I am the same as you. May they also be in us so that the world will know you sent me." John 17:21*

Bear in mind: this is Jesus praying. I just believe that if anyone's prayers were ever heard and answered by God that it might be Jesus' prayers. Look at what he prays for here. He prays for this unity among believers – that we would all be one. How unified? Just like He and God are unified. Wow! But wait, think about this – they are…the Trinity. Father, Son, Holy Spirit – totally unique but exactly the same – three-in-one. When Jesus is praying this prayer, the Holy Spirit has not yet been released into the world. There are just Christ and God the Father. Yet, Jesus prays that we would be one exactly like He and God are one. He says, "I in you…you in me…may they also be in us." I could be wrong.

I am only a guy and not that smart and not that highly educated, but it looks to me like Christ is praying for you and me to join in the Holy Trinity! Throw rocks at me if I am wrong, but that is what it looks like to me. Why? What is the purpose of this kind of unity with each other and with Christ and the Father? "So that the world may know that you sent me."

Several years ago, I was invited to co-officiate a wedding for friends. The groom had been raised in my denomination, and the bride had grown up Greek Orthodox. At the rehearsal, I met her priest, Father Saros. He was bedecked in some fancy garb, but was always smiling, very kind, and had a great sense of Godly humor! We got along well and made it through the wedding with no glitches. After the wedding, there was a dance. The first two hours of the dance were traditional Greek dancing, then the old people would go home, and the young people would dance to more modern music. There was amazing food and all kinds of wine and a traditional Greek band for the first two hours. They played a song that reminded me of the Jewish *Hava Naguila*. The people formed a large circle, hands on each other's shoulders, and began to dance a very simple step, and the circle rotated. Father Saros asked me, "Do you know this dance?"

I said, "No, I have never seen it or learned it."

He asked, "Would you like to learn? Come, dance!"

I agreed. The folks opened up two spots, and Father Saros and I stepped in. With just a couple of minutes of observation and helpful ribbing from the people around me, I picked up the order of the steps and around we went! After twenty or thirty minutes, the Father and I ducked out. The circle closed, and the dance continued. Back at our table, Father Saros asked me, "Do you know what the dance signifies?"

I answered with a question, "Community?"

"Yes," he said, "but more than that. Our dance represents our part in the Holy Trinity." Now he had my attention.

He continued, "You see, you cannot make a circle to dance with two. That is why with only two, they call it a square dance!" His eyes twinkled behind his broad smile. "But, you can make a circle with three!" He continued, looking ecstatic to be teaching me something new. "God is Father, Son, and Holy Spirit, yes?" he asked, but continued without my answer. "God is happy to dance as three, but the dance is more fun with more. God created humankind to have fellowship with Him. Christ prayed in John's Gospel for us to be one with Him, to join in the dance. When we agree to be part of God, He opens up a space in the Holy Trinity, and makes room for us! We can dance as long as we want. We can take breaks. We can even quit. If we come back, God will always open up a place for us as if we had never left. Millions of us dance, from all denominations. God has room for everyone who comes to the circle of the Holy Trinity by faith!"

I remember sitting there in stunned amazement. For my entire academic and ministerial career, I had struggled to explain the profound mystery of the Holy Trinity. Now, this big happy guy with the epic beard had just explained it to me in the simplest of terms – and it made sense! Every time I hear the prayer of Jesus in John 17:21, I smile in memory of Father Saros, and in recognition that Jesus is, once again, inviting us to join the dance.

Now go back to Revelation 3:21. Is the promise not the same? Christ says that the one who overcomes will be invited to sit with Him on His throne, just like He overcame and was invited to sit on God's throne with God. He is inviting us to join him and the

Father right where they are. Remember, we are talking about a spiritual place without the limitations of time and space. No one is too fat so that there is not room on Christ's throne for him. No one is too big to fit. No one is too slow or does not know the steps well enough to be included. Christ wants His overcomers to join Him on His throne, the same one He shares with the Father. He wants us to be a part of Him. That is the kind of unity to which Christ calls us. It is the unity He promises to those who overcome this world. Maybe I am crazy, but that sounds like music to my ears.

HOW MIGHT WE SHARE THIS?

Because of the density of precious things here, I have often broken this section up into two messages or lessons. I have used outlines something like this:

Living in Laodicea
I.   Why is it a bad thing to be lukewarm?

II. How do people or churches become lukewarm?

III. How do we reclaim passion or return to being a healing influence?

Jesus is At the Door
I.   Why does Jesus even want to come into this mess?
     a.   God in the chaos of Genesis 1
     b.   God in the chaos of the manger of Luke 2

    c.   God in the chaos of our hearts today

II. How do I open the door and let Him in?

III. What happens after I let Jesus in?

QUESTIONS FOR FURTHER STUDY OR REFLECTION

1. Describe what you believe a "lukewarm" Christian looks like.

2. Which of those traits do you find in yourself right now?

3. In your life, how would it look to be on fire, or cooling and soothing to others?

4. What steps would you prescribe to Christians who wanted to seek revival?
   (i.e., prayer, fasting, Bible study, worship, fellowship, service to others, etc.)

5. Which of those steps is lacking in your life right now?

6. When might you have a chance to begin to remedy that?

7. How can we influence our church, if it appears to have cooled to lukewarm?

8. Why do you believe Jesus would want to be part of our lives?

9. If you believe He does, do you believe there is ever a time he gives up wanting that?

10. What is the deepest separation from God you have ever seen someone redeemed from?

11. What does Jesus mean here when He says He'll come in and have a meal with us?

SECTION THREE

WHAT MUST TAKE PLACE LATER

CHAPTER TWELVE

JOHN'S VISION OF HEAVEN
THE HEAVENLY THRONE ROOM

Revelation 4:1-11

THE TEXT:

"4:1After this I looked, and amazingly, a door was opened in Heaven, and the first voice which I heard like a trumpet spoke to me: "Come up here, and I will reveal to you what must happen after this." 2Immediately I was in the Spirit, and I saw a throne standing in Heaven, and someone was seated upon the throne. 3The One seated there was like jasper and carnelian, in appearance, and an emerald rainbow surrounded the throne. 4Twenty-four thrones encircled that throne, and on the thrones sat twenty-four elders dressed in white robes with gold crowns on their heads. 5From the throne came lightning and rumbling and thunder, and seven blazing torches (which are the seven spirits of God) were burning before the throne.

⁶There was also before the throne something, like a glassy crystal sea.

All around the throne room flew four cherubim, covered with eyes on the front and the back. ⁷And the first cherub was like a lion, and the second cherub was like an ox, and the third cherub had a face like a human, and the four cherubim, each of whom had six wings, were covered with eyes on the outside and on the inside, and day and night they never stopped chanting,

> "Holy, holy, holy, Lord God
> Almighty, Who was and Who is
> and is the One who comes."

⁹And when the cherubim give glory and honor and thanksgiving to the One seated upon the throne who lives forever and ever, ¹⁰the twenty-four elders lie with their faces to the floor before the One sitting on the throne, and they worship the One who lives forever and ever, and they threw their crowns before the throne, chanting,

> ¹¹'Worthy are You, our Lord and
> God, To receive glory and honor and
> power, Because You created, all things
> And by Your will, they existed, yes
> were created.'" Revelation 4:1-11

WHAT IS THE TEXT SAYING TO US?

With Chapter 4 of The Revelation, we begin the third major section suggested back in Revelation 1:19, "…what must take place later." A word of warning: some of the things from Chapter 4 on are things that have already happened. Some of the things prophesied in the remaining portion of the book can be seen as either having happened or being yet-to-happen. Still, other things are pretty clearly yet to come at the time of John's writing The Book of Revelation. Some scholars believe that everything in the Book of Revelation has already happened. We will discuss the options as we encounter them. You can draw your own conclusions and applications. Throughout the discussion, bear in mind our initial conversation about the constancy of God's Word about the cyclical nature of history. God's Word may have intersected history in John's day, intersected again at some point in between, crossed through history in our day, and will affect history in the future. Truth remains truth in any historical frame of reference.

After all the references to doors being opened or closed, or Christ standing at a door, the text says that John sees a door opened in Heaven, and a voice calling him to come in. Do not miss the play on words here. For Philadelphia, Christ promised to hold open a door that no one could close. To Laodicea, He said He was the one who stood at the door and continually knocked so that someone might open the door for Him to come in. Immediately as John's vision turns heavenward, Christ opens His own door – the door to Heaven – and invites John to "come." Did you hear that?

"Come." John had heard those words as a very young man.

"Come, follow me." Jesus had said to him and his brother that day when they had been fishing. It was the call of a Master to a disciple – of a Rabbi to his protégé. Now, it is the call to come and see the things which "must happen after this." Notice the surety. These are the things that must happen. These are not options. These are not things that may happen. These must happen – and will.

John does not say he responded and went Rather, that he was immediately "in the Spirit." These are the exact words he used to describe the spiritual state he was in when his vision began in 1:10. This is most likely John's way of letting you know that he continues in this prophetic trance-like vision. The call to "Come up here," would then serve to indicate that John is going deeper – stepping in closer to God Himself. There is a mystical aspect here you are supposed to sense. The real truth about any moment in time – past, present, or future – lies with God, who is not anchored or limited by time. Does that not raise your sense of expectancy? What will John see? What does God so want us to know that He would call one of us into His very presence? Let's find out!

Again, here is that device you need to get used to watching for in The Revelation: John is called to see the things that must take place but, the first thing he sees is the person on the throne. Then, he cannot make that person out! I want you to see the similarities here with John's first encounter in the Spirit with Christ in 1:10 (and in the following verses), and this more profound encounter in the Heavenly throne room. In 1:10, you will remember he said that he turned to see the voice that was speaking to him and, instead, saw the One standing among the lampstands. Remember also that the voice in 1:10 was a sound, "like a trumpet," a theme, once again, repeated here in chapter four. He answers the call, follows the voice through the door, and sees...someone on a throne.

The one sitting on the throne is not described in human form, but in comparison to precious or semi-precious gemstones. The word "jasper" is prevalent in scripture. It is going to serve to describe the light that comes from the walls and foundation of the New Jerusalem in Revelation 21. Jasper? I grew up in a science teacher's home. One of my dad's favorite hobbies was geology and minerals. Jasper is most commonly blood-red. Now, there could be some real symbolism here, if Jasper were only red, but it also comes in greens and browns and creams.

Additionally, Jasper is opaque. It does not shine, reflect, or refract light! Ezekiel 28 says that Satan's garments were covered in "precious stones like Jasper." But Jasper has never been a rare stone or gem. Many scholars believe that the ancient word for Jasper connects, not to our modern opaque stone, but to another precious stone that appears nowhere else in the Bible, the diamond.

Carnelian, on the other hand, is a stone that has been known from antiquity. Carnelian is a translucent, blood-red gemstone that has been prized for centuries. It is also mentioned as part of Satan's bedazzled garment in Ezekiel 28:13. More importantly, it is the first gemstone that represents the tribes of Israel in the description of the High Priest's breastplate in Exodus 28:17.

Care to guess what the twelfth stone is? That is right; it is Jasper. The mention of these stones in relation may simply represent the extreme wealth of the Kingdom. Yet, they may also stand for the Alpha and Omega, the First and Last, and the entirety of God's people from all tribes.

The rainbow that encircles the throne is no mystery. It is the sign and seal of God's covenant with Noah that he would never again flood the Earth with water. Then, there is this curious comparison that the rainbow was, somehow, "like an emerald?" Well, emeralds are green. Rainbows contain a hint of green, but they are not mostly green. This construction in the Greek likely serves simply to say that the glorious splendor of this rainbow encircling the throne of God is so amazing that it just defies simple description!

Twenty-four elders – are they configured in a circle, in two concentric circles, twelve in an arc on the left and twelve in an arc on the right? The suggestions through history have been myriad. Let us suffice it to say that the concept comes from 1 Chronicles 24, where, during the reign of King David, Israel is reestablishing the practice of proper worship within the Temple. The descendants of Levi – one of the twelve sons of Jacob/Israel were assigned oversight of the Temple. By the time of David, they have become numerous. So, in 1 Chronicle 24, they are appointed by family name to a shift of ministering in the Temple. In this way, there will be around-the-clock availability of the Temple to God's people. In whatever manner they are arranged, this is the function of the twenty-four elders in Revelation. They provide continual worship and praise around the throne of God. They are dressed in white robes, a symbol of purity in both heart and expression. They wear golden crowns, the symbol of royalty and wealth.

From the throne come lightning and thunder. This is a reference back to Exodus 19:16, where the Israelites waited at Mount Sanai for God to deliver His law to them, and the mountain was covered in clouds or smoke. There were lightning and thunder and the sound of an immense trumpet blast. Where God is, the elements of nature respond. Around the base of the throne is a sea of glassy crystal, representing truth (transparency). Then, amongst the sounds of thunder and the sights of opulence, we begin to hear the worship.

The worship is initiated by the four "cherubim" as they fly freely around the throne room. What is a cherub? Well, in medieval art, they are often small angels with bored or mischievous looks on their faces! But that is not how they are portrayed anywhere in scripture, and certainly not in Revelation. Here, they are described as winged beasts that attend to God on His throne. They are the impetus of heavenly worship. They chant God's praise continually. John sees them as covered with eyes, front and back. They see everything and nothing goes beyond their notice. The first has the appearance of a lion, the king of beasts, and a fierce fighter.

The second has the appearance of an ox, a strong and faithful worker. The third has the face of a human (we are not told what kind of body it has, but cherubim were often portrayed with the bodies of lions or oxen.) He represents God's favored creation in God's image. The fourth looks like…well…we do not know! Revelation describes three of the four cherubim, but not the fourth! It is not even mentioned. It represents one of those elements of mystery that must always surround the presence of God. Instead, we are told that all four had six wings, and then John repeats the fact that they had eyes, but instead of "front and back," he writes "inside and outside." It is a subtle difference, but meaningful. Not only do the cherubim see everything in every direction externally, but they also see everything externally and internally. Nothing is hidden from their eyes. There are no secrets from God. They never stop – ever – chanting worship centered around God's holiness and His transcendence of time. As they chant, they motivate the twenty-four elders to fall on their faces and join in the worship! The elders also chant, but their worship is centered around worshiping God because of His power as Creator. He is the One who gave life to everything that has life, and by His will, everything has come into being! (Compare this with John 1:3)

Do not skim lightly past this section without recognizing that John is showing you the seat and source of all power in the universe! It defies description. It requires that God created some very unique angelic beings to drive the activity around the throne. It is a place from which the very laws of nature emanate and are active. It is a place where all of God's people are represented continuously, and worship never ceases. God is holy and worthy. He is forever and has created everything that has ever been created. This is the engine of absolute power. Here, everything is resplendent, yet it is orderly. On the surface, it seems boring to us. Really? This is what goes on around the throne of God, eternally? That's it? Yes. But that is enough. The throne and person of God are the source of all that power that humans incessantly try to grab through religion, or government, or politics, or war. The entire point here is that power lies, not in any of those things that look like power to us. Power lies in the presence of the Holy Creator. Read this section until you begin to understand it. Here is the engine, the source, of all the power in the universe. Allow it to capture your imagination. Understanding the source of all true power is the key to understanding the rest of Revelation, and the totality of life.

HOW MIGHT WE SHARE THIS?

Whenever I have taught this section, I have used an outline something like:

I.   God invites us to worship

II. God calls us to participate in His Holiness as worship

III. God calls us to recognize his Eternal Worthiness in worship

QUESTIONS FOR FURTHER STUDY OR REFLECTION

1. What would your response be, if Christ said, "Come?"

2. Why do you think the person of God is not described in greater detail?

3. Where did the idea of "cherubim" originate?

4. How would you define the elements of "worship?"
    This is a great opportunity to address the fact that, at least in Revelation 4:1-11, worship is not really about music or singing. It is about adoration and acknowledgment of the

attributes of God. That does not mean it cannot include music. But it means that real and intimate worship of God should focus on His attributes: His worthiness, holiness, power as creator and savior – not our feelings or needs. Worship should never come from a place of our feelings about our own worth but from an acknowledgment of God's absolute power and worth.

CHAPTER THIRTEEN

THE LAMB

IT COULD HAVE ENDED HERE, BUT WORTHY IS THE LAMB!

Revelation 5:1-14

THE TEXT:

"5:1Then I saw in the right hand of the One seated on the throne a scroll written both front and back and sealed with seven seals. 2Then I saw a mighty angel proclaiming in a loud voice, 'Who is worthy to open the scroll by breaking its seals?' 3No one was able either in Heaven or on Earth or under the Earth, to open the scroll or to look into it. 4Then I wept uncontrollably because no one was found who was worthy to open the scroll or even look into it. 5Then one of the elders said to me, 'Stop weeping. Look! The Lion of the Tribe of Judah, the descendant of David, He has conquered so that He is worthy to open the book and its seven seals.'

6Then I saw, standing between the throne and the four cherubim and the elders, a lamb, looking as though it had been slaughtered, with seven horns and seven eyes (which are the spirits of God sent out to the entire earth). [7]He came and took the scroll from the right hand of the One seated on the throne. [8]And when He took the scroll, the four cherubim and the twenty-four elders fell before the Lamb, each with a harp and a gold pan filled with incense (which represents the prayers of God's people). [9]Then they sang a new song:

> 'You are worthy to hold the book and
> break its seals, Because You were
> slaughtered, and with Your blood,
> You redeemed before God persons
> from every race and language and
> people and nation. [10]You have made
> them into a kingdom and qualified
> them to be priests to serve our God,
> and they will reign on the earth.'

[11]Then I looked and heard the sound of many angels; their number was myriad upon myriad, ten thousand times ten thousand. They surrounded the throne and chanted [12]in a loud voice, saying:

> 'Worthy is the Lamb, who was
> slain, to receive power and wealth
> and wisdom and power and
> honor and glory and praise!'

¹³ *Then I heard every created being in Heaven and on Earth and under the Earth and upon the sea, and everything is in them, saying:*

'To the One who sits on the throne and to the Lamb be praise and honor and glory and power, forever and ever!' ¹⁴ *The four cherubim responded, 'Amen,' and the elders fell on their faces and worshiped. Rev 5:1-14*

WHAT IS THE TEXT SAYING TO US?

Notice that the pace is quickening here. Rather than a paragraph addressed to a single recipient, the textual units are now entire chapters, telling of a significant vision in more massive, sweeping strokes. The details still matter, but they come faster and in a broader context. You should sense that we are rushing toward the most significant parts of John's vision. Big things are imminent! John now sees a scroll in the right hand of the One on the throne. The right hand is the one with which you shake hands and enter into covenants and treaties. Whatever is on that scroll is vital. It is also lengthy. The manuscript is written on the front and back. This means that it is essential to the One who wrote it to communicate it in one document. It is a pressing and urgent message. The scroll is sealed, not with one seal, but with seven. Every one of the spirits of God has a stake in this message. The seals can only be opened by one who possesses all seven attributes: wisdom, understanding, counsel, might, knowledge, fear of the Lord, and the Lord's very Spirit. So, a mighty angel flies through the throne room, crying out in despair, "Who is worthy?"

Now, read slowly. Attempt to feel what is going on here. The text says there was no one worthy. If the scroll remains unopened, then its pertinent message cannot be read and understood. The power it holds, the direction it must contain from the God of seven spirits, will remain locked up inside. John fears this is the end of his vision. What if it cannot be opened? Is this what God wanted him to see – that God had more to say, but no person could unlock it because all had become so unworthy and unholy? John weeps uncontrollably, for that would genuinely be a reason for despair.

Then, an unlikely speaker, one of the elders, says, "Stop weeping. The LION OF JUDAH is worthy!" Then, ready for it? Here comes the old bait-and-switch. John says he looked to see the lion, but instead, he sees…a lamb. There, amid the throne, elders, and cherubim stands a lamb, looking as though it has been slaughtered. It is not supposed to make sense. You are supposed to be caught up in all of the nonsensical elements: John turns to see a lion but sees a lamb. The lamb is standing but is so bloody it has obviously been through a slaughtering it could not have possibly survived, yet there it stands! What is impossible on Earth is not impossible in Heaven, and you already know whom the lamb represents. It is Jesus.

Horns represent strength and power. The Lamb has seven horns. His seven eyes, we are told, represent the seven spirits of God, sent out into the world all-seeing, all-knowing. Interestingly, the connection has been made. The Lamb possesses the seven spirits that correspond with the seven seals. He has what it takes to open the scroll. Our hope was slaughtered but has been raised to life by the power of Heaven! He now stands ready to reveal to us how history unfolds in our Kingdom. When the Lamb takes the scroll (in his mouth or with his hoof?), the elders fall on their faces. The cherubim cease their flying and lie on their faces on the crystal floor. They worship the Lamb.

The elders have two things now that they did not have before. Each has a small harp, the first musical instruments we have seen in the vision, and a gold pan or bowl of incense. John understands that the smoke from the incense is the prayers of God's people. Our prayers, yours and mine, are represented here beside the throne. Those who are responsible for worship in Heaven, at God's side on His throne, have our prayers in their hands. Sometimes, when I pray, it feels like I just cannot get through to God. Sometimes it seems like my prayers go nowhere. They echo back to me in shallow and hollow tones. However, the power of prayers is that they are always in front of God. They are continually lifted in the throne room of God by those charged with worship! And then, this song they sing...this new song:

> *"You are worthy to hold the book and break its seals, Because You were slaughtered, and with Your blood, You redeemed before God persons from every race and language and people and nation."*

By His blood, redemption came into the world for all people from all races and nations. What a beautiful word – redeemed.

When I was a child, my family did not have much spare cash. My parents worked hard and shopped wisely. They tried to shop loyally at businesses that gave *S&H Green Stamps*. The stamps were a kind of discount or bonus program. The more money you spent, the more *Green Stamps* you would receive. Some merchants offered more *Green Stamps* per dollar spent. If you collected the *Green Stamps*, you typically filled up little books. The books had twenty-four pages, and each page held fifty stamps. Once you had at least sixty books filled, you could *redeem* the stamps for useful items. I remember helping my mom fill *S&H Green Stamp* booklets until we had enough. Then, we would go to the *S&H* store, count our booklets, and shop for something for which we might redeem the stamps. There were toys, games, appliances, tools – all kinds of great things! You could turn in your *Green Stamps* – just little paper stamps, of no value by themselves – for valuable items you could use to make life better! That is how I learned what it meant to be *redeemed*. By shedding his blood and dying on the cross of Calvary for you and me, Christ redeemed us in God's heart and sight. He took what was literally worthless, our sinful lives, and traded them for eternal life. The *S&H* store got kickbacks from the stores that participated in their program. God got no benefit for redeeming us. He paid the full price of our sinful worthlessness and credited us with the value we could never have earned. The Lamb paid that price for us all. The Lamb paid God's part of the redemptive equation – and ours. In doing so, He earned the right to open the seals of the scroll that holds our destiny.

It is through Christ that the new Kingdom is populated with redeemed people and souls. He not only becomes the identifying factor that creates a new Kingdom out of those who believe in Him and participate in His redemption, but He also calls them to be priests. The priest was the intermediary between the common, dirty, people, and God. Without the priest, none of us ignorant, unworthy, unclean folk could have ever hoped to approach the Holy God of Heaven. Remember that, at Christ's crucifixion, the "veil" in the Temple, the dividing curtain between the holy altar (where you could approach) and the Holy of Holies (that inner place where God's Spirit resided, and you could not go) was torn open? Since Christ's death on the cross, you no longer need a priest to approach just into the vicinity of God. Since the cross, you are a priest, able to walk boldly, according to the Apostle Paul, into the very holiest presence of God Himself and present your needs directly to the Father. Christ has shattered the dividing line between God and people. Humanity has a new identity as a Kingdom in Christ and priests before God. The blood of the Lamb has crushed all that stood between! And all of Heaven – the cherubim, the elders, and angels by the tens of thousands - lays with their faces to the ground and sings:

> *"Worthy is the Lamb, who was slain, to receive power and wealth and wisdom and power and honor and glory and praise!!"*

Then, something we have never seen before happens. Prompted by the praise that is going on in Heaven, every creature in Heaven and on Earth and within the Earth and within the sea all join in the worship and sing:

> *"To the One who sits on the throne and to the Lamb be praise and honor and glory and power, forever and ever!"*

The four cherubim shout, "AMEN!" The elders fall down on their faces and worship again.

Do you feel the hope in this account? The chapter began with hopelessness – no one was worthy to open the seal. It ends with this worship that envelops all of creation. The Lamb is worthy! The scroll will be opened. Our fate will be revealed. There is hope.

Several years ago, I was called to pastor a small church of fifteen folks in the foothills of the Cascade mountains. It was a beautiful little property among towering Douglas Fir trees. Deer were often seen grazing through the yard during church. I had the privilege of pastoring fifteen senior adults in a church that was hard-pressed to see much growth in the modernistic and pagan Pacific Northwest. After a couple of years, the church was up to twenty-five folks. I met with my overseer to discuss the future of the church. I expressed to him my disappointment that I had not been able to do more for the church. He responded graciously and kindly, "Kevin, you have given them something they did not have before you came. You have given them *hope*."

Hope. It is an immensely powerful force. Without hope, people fall into despair and quit. They give up their church. They give up their marriage and family. Some even take their lives in that kind of deep despair. The winning force is hope. With hope, people will fight what looks to be impossible odds. They will overcome what appear to be hopeless situations. My friend could not have said anything more compelling to me. I was not simply a pastor. I was the agent of hope in that church. I stayed a few more years, and we saw tremendous miracles in that little church. Do you have hope today? My wish for you is that you might read this account in Revelation 5 and realize that it is about us. We were the ones without hope before Christ. We were the ones who faced certain judgment and destruction before He died for us. We were the ones who owed a debt we could never have repaid. But. Christ took our sin, our place, our unworthiness, and our destruction onto Himself in a true slaughter on the cross. God raised Him to life again, and He stands at the heart of Heaven and holds our future and our destiny in His hand. The One who loved you enough to die for you holds your fate in His hand. You can have hope amidst any terror that follows. The One who wants you to have hope is about to open the seals.

HOW MIGHT WE SHARE THIS?

Whenever I have shared this throughout the years, I have always used the same outline:

I. Heaven was frozen out of working in my life before the Lamb of Calvary

II. Jesus is the Lamb who takes away the sins of the world and un-freezes Heaven

III. Because the One who died to redeem me is in control of history – I can have HOPE!

ADDITIONAL QUESTIONS FOR STUDY OR REFLECTION

1. Why did God need a redemptive action to forgive us?

2. How many theories of atonement can you find to explain Christ's work on the cross?

3. Which theory of atonement seems to ring true with you. Which gives you the best hope?

4. In light of your identification with a theory of atonement, how might your life be affected?

CHAPTER FOURTEEN

THE LAMB OPENS THE FIRST FOUR SEALS
THE FOUR HORSEMEN OF THE APOCALYPSE

Revelation 6:1-8

THE TEXT:

"6:1Then I watched as the Lamb broke the first of the seven seals, and I heard one of the four cherubim saying, as though with a voice of thunder, "Come!" 2Then I looked, and there was a white horse, and the rider had a bow. A crown was given to him, and the conqueror went out to conquer even more.

3When the Lamb broke the second seal, I heard the second cherub saying, "Come!" 4Then another horse, a fiery red one, rode out, and the rider was given the power to remove peace from the Earth so that people might slaughter each other. He was given a large sword.

5When the Lamb broke the third seal, I heard the third cherub saying, "Come!" Then I looked, and behold, there was a black horse, and the rider held a balancing scale in his hand. 6Then I heard, as it were, a voice in the middle of the four cherubim saying, "A quart of wheat or three quarts of barley for a day's wages, but do not spoil the oil nor the wine!"

7When the Lamb broke the fourth seal, I heard the voice of the fourth cherub saying, "Come!" 8I looked, and behold, there was a pale-colored horse, and the name of its rider was Death, and Hades followed closely after him. They were given authority over one-fourth of the people of Earth to kill with the sword and with starvation and with disease and by the wild animals of the Earth." Rev 6:1-8

WHAT IS THE TEXT SAYING TO US?

We move from hope and worship within the throne room of God to the opening of the first seal and the resulting explosion of the apocalypse. The pace slows only a bit to show us the details of the vision in a more specific manner. We did not know what would happen when the Lamb opened that first seal; but, immediately, it becomes apparent that it will not be good and will likely get worse. Now, the Lamb breaks the first seal.

As soon as the seal is broken, one of the cherubim, sometimes interchangeably called "living creatures," shouts, "Come!" and a white horse appears with a rider carrying a bow. The rider wears a crown. His name is Conquest, and he rides out to conquer even more territory. Very early in history, scholars believed that this horse and rider represented Christ and the Gospel. In Revelation 19, we will see Christ riding on a white horse. Yet, here, we find elements that are negative, not positive. The rider holds a bow. The promise of Isaiah 2:4 (exactly repeated in Micah 4:3) was that people would "hammer their swords into plowshares." This rider does not come to make peace, but war. The bow is a symbol of war. Remember, when God hung up his bow in the sky and promised Noah that He would never flood the Earth again? This rider is not hanging up his bow; he is holding it high and declaring war on the world. He wears a crown, but it is not treated as a symbol of holy royalty, as it is with the twenty-four elders. This crown is just a symbol of power – of Empire. His name is Conquest, for that is what he is bent on, and he rides out to claim more of the Earth for himself.

I do not believe this is too hard to figure out. Place yourself in John's world for a minute. Where would you find the warrior on a white horse wearing a crown and raising a bow and riding out to conquer the world for the Empire? This rider represents Rome. He symbolizes the Empire known best by the churches who would read this letter. Jesus is saying that the apocalypse – the end – will begin with Empire seeking to conquer Kingdom. This could be Rome. It could be Britain. It could be the Turks and Ottomans. This could be Napoleon (an idea once popular among scholars). It could be any Empire that seeks to conquer, by any warring means, more territory or to do war with the Kingdom of God on this Earth. As I write this, my country's government is embroiled in a battle for control of its Empire. Many of my Christian brothers and sisters have chosen sides. They support parties and people and ideas that have no connection to the things we value as Christians. The battle is not a Kingdom battle, but an Empire battle that has sucked in too many Kingdom citizens. Many from the Empire are looking over at us and saying things like, "See? Christians support this guy (or that one). See? They are not deeply convicted about what they claim to believe if they can support that!" Sadly, they have a point. We have confused the Empire with the Kingdom. We have become more politically active than we are spiritually active – more conquerors than crusaders. I see the signs of the white horse in my world.

When the second seal is broken, a second cherub cries out, "Come!" Again, John looks and sees another horse; this one is red like fire. Its rider is unnamed but given a sword. He has the power to remove peace from the Earth so that its people slaughter each other. It is a very natural progression if you think about it. Conquest leads to chaos, the loss of peace, and slaughter. That has been the pattern of every conquest. Whether it was Caesar, or Hitler, the Vikings, or the Visigoths – conquest led to burning and pillaging, slaving, and slaughter. Of course, the meaning could be physical or spiritual. Still, the graphic nature of this part of the vision leads me to believe it is, often, literal. The World Health Organization reported in 2020 that around two million people die worldwide each year from violence. That's a Holocaust every three years.

Dachau opened in 1933. The last German death camp was liberated in 1945. In those twelve years, over six million Jews and dissidents were slaughtered in the Nazi holocaust. The world was horrified as the facts became known. Today, it only takes three years for the same number of people to die worldwide in violence. Add to that the fifty-six million – yes, you read that right – fifty-six million abortion deaths worldwide each year. That's like nine holocausts every single year! Slaughter, in my world? It's prevalent and, for the most significant part, tolerated and overlooked. I feel the presence of the fiery red horse in my world.

Another cherub cries, "Come." Again, John looks and sees another horse. This horse is black. Its rider carries a balancing scale (the time-honored symbol of justice). John hears a voice from somewhere around the throne, defining the price of staple foods: a day's wages for a liter of wheat or three of barley. You may be reading a Bible version that renders the price for the commodities in terms of a "denarius." In John's time, the denarius was a silver coin, roughly equal to a day's wages at most farming or labor jobs. In the interest of clarity, I have chosen to render the text as "a day's wages." Today, at a minimum wage of somewhere around ten dollars per hour, it would be worth $80 for an eight-hour day. A quart of wheat is about enough to make a loaf of bread. Three quarts of barley flour might make two loaves of barley bread. Bread was a staple of life. They would be crushing times if it took a day's wage to make two days' worth of wheat or barley bread. This rider is traditionally called "Famine." But famine is not the point here. Starvation is not introduced until the opening of the fourth seal. Yes, the grains will be expensive, but there will be grain. And the command is that the olive oil and wine are not to be harmed. Food will be costly to come by, but available. This is not about starvation.

What was it that the rider on the black horse held in his hand? Not a bow, nor a sword, but a balancing scale. You see, the grains are measured in what roughly equates to a quart, a measure, not a weight. What do the balances represent? I believe they represent justice. Look at Amos 8:

"Hear this, you who stomp on the needy, to do away with the humble of the land, saying, 'When will the new moon be over, so that we may sell grain and the sabbath, that we may open the wheat market, to make the bushel smaller and the shekel bigger, and to cheat with dishonest scales, so as to buy the helpless for money and the needy for a pair of sandals, and that we may sell the cheapest of the wheat?'" Amos 8:4-6

You see, dishonest weights and measures allow the rich to, literally, buy the poor. Economic control is the greatest of injustices because it hits the poorest the hardest. Right now, in the U.S., people are talking about enacting a production tax on manufacturers to generate enough money to provide everyone a basic income. On the surface, it seems like a good idea – tax the producers so that even the poorest can have a basic income on which to live. But there is one glaring flaw: the producers will pass along any tax as an expense in the final cost of goods. If a baker is taxed, he will raise the price of bread. Who will that affect the worst? It will be hardest on the poorest. Those with only that basic income will have to spend a more significant share of it on necessities. In turn, those will cost more because of the extra taxes placed on them to provide a basic income. The middle-class guy who gets the same basic income will not feel that pain. The poorest will.

Even the smallest economic injustice impacts the people at the bottom of the stack much more strongly than it does the folks at the top. Today, in my own country, economic injustice has been perpetrated against people of color for hundreds of years.

Through slavery, Jim Crow, and economic policies that the politicians told them were for their good – but only trapped them in urban squalor, Americans of color have found themselves trapped at the lowest level of economic opportunity. It has been pervasive and systematic. Politicians have used that system to prey on those folks and continually promise that voting for their party would result in real solutions and real opportunities. But they never came. Bills were introduced. Laws were passed. Incredibly expensive programs and projects were launched. But the people on the bottom stayed on the bottom as the politicians became millionaires. Those people were bought for the equivalent of money or shoes. The hoofbeats of the third horse are evident in my world.

A fourth time a seal is broken, a fourth cherub cries, "Come!" and a fourth horse appears. This one is described as "pale." The Greek word is chloros, and it appears only here and in Revelation, Chapter Eight. Here, it represents a pale greenish-gray color, the color of a corpse. The deathly-looking horse's rider is, indeed, Death, and he is not alone. Right on his heels is Hades. Remember Hades? It is the grave. It is that place where all the souls of the deceased are trapped and held. Some scholars say there are five horsemen of the apocalypse because Death and Hades ride together. The text says precisely that. For those without Christ, Death and the Grave come together, one harvesting, the other locking away forever. John says they were given dominion, or rule, over one-fourth of the Earth's population. They could kill them with violence, plague, famine, or wild animals.

One-fourth is a significant portion, but not a majority. As the apocalypse draws nearer, the loss of life worldwide will be on a scale that defies dismissal. In today's numbers, one-fourth would be about two billion deaths. On average, about fifty-six million people die on Earth in any given year. Two billion deaths would take a long time. Two billion deaths within a two-to-three-year time frame would indicate a severe problem. There is no death on that scale in our world today, right? Care to guess what number of people live in poverty on the Earth in 2020?

Interestingly, 1.3 billion live in abject poverty. But those who live on less than two dollars per day would be right at two billion. Those who are dying of hunger, exposure, lack of simple shelter or medication, and the lack of drinkable water – is very near two billion. He may not yet ride free, but I hear the hoofbeats of the fourth horse in my world today.

Now, a word of caution: these same factors have been seen several times in world history. Many writers, across time, could have made the same observations I just made. In truth, our world has always teetered near the brink of these kinds of disasters or events. But I believe that one day, the conditions will tip toward a significant apocalyptic event. I do not think it will be the climate. I do not believe it will be a thermo-nuclear war. As I release the final manuscript of this book to printing, the COVID-19 virus is raging around the globe. Many who know of my interest in Revelation have asked me if I believe this pandemic is related to the Book of Revelation, or the apocalypse. While I do not believe that this particular pandemic is the end of all things, I believe there are essential things to consider amid this crisis.

First, consider that the riders in this vision are not necessarily portrayed in chronological order. They may indicate a set of circumstances that beset the world all at once. In that vein, this most recent pandemic has caused me to realize that such a contagion could be bioengineered by a government to upset the eco-political balance of power on the Earth. That nation could then use that advantage for conquest, economically, if not geo-politically. Then, consider that such a pandemic has shown us that such events have the power to remove peace from the Earth. As the pandemic spread, travel between countries was banned. Suspicion broke out between bordering countries, and trade broke down. Nations began pointing fingers at other nations, blaming them for the unmitigated spread of the virus.

In an attempt to limit the spread of the coronavirus, world leaders prohibited trade and travel. Citizens around the world were ordered to stay at home. Commerce stopped. Business failed. We now see that the food supply chain was horribly impacted, and food shortages will impact the world within the next few months. The starvation of a large number of people is, indeed, a possibility. The inequities of the third rider could be terribly close as the rich can afford food, but the poor will not. The total number of fatalities is, at the moment I am writing, under 200,000 worldwide However, I suspect that at least twice that many will ultimately lose their lives as a result of the depression, domestic abuse, addiction, and food shortages that will result from this pandemic event. An event like this, which triggers all of the conditions represented by the riders of the apocalypse in John's vision, deserves prayerful consideration. I believe that one day, an event like this will trigger a tipping point of political, economic, geographic, and forceful control. We have seen how governments in Constitutional and Democratic societies have reacted to this current pandemic with the wholesale subversion of the liberties of their citizens. Though highly infectious and widespread, this contagion has been relatively mild in comparison to the death tolls of previous pandemics that have swept the world. One day, a much more deadly crisis will sweep the Earth, and a tipping point will be reached. Once the tipping point passes, the Empires of the world will rush in to take control of the lives of people, in the name of saving them. The resulting power grab will be such that those who have ears to hear will see that apocalyptic forces are at work in the world on a grander scale.

HOW MIGHT WE SHARE THIS?

Again, I have pretty much given you the text of exactly how I share this section. An outline might look something like:

I. The first horse: Empire conquers Kingdom

II. The second horse: War and the rumor of war

III. The third horse: Injustice Buys People's Lives

IV. The fourth horse: Death and Near-Death in Our World

QUESTIONS FOR FURTHER STUDY OR REFLECTION

1. Where have we seen conquest during our lifetimes?

2. Which countries are trying to expand their borders right now?

3. Which countries are trying to expand their influence and conquer economically?

4. Where are the most active war zones on Earth right now? Could they expand?

5. What are the worst injustices you see in our world today? Where do they occur?

6. Is poverty like death? How?

CHAPTER FIFTEEN

THE FIFTH AND SIXTH SEALS ARE OPENED
THE MARTYRS AND THE KINGS

Revelation 6:9-17

THE TEXT:

"*6:9When He broke the fifth seal; I saw underneath the altar the souls of those martyred because of the Word of God and because of the witness which they bore. 10They cried out loudly, saying, 'O Master, holy and true, how long will it be until you judge and avenge our deaths caused by those who dwell on the earth?' 11Then each of them was given a white robe, and they were told that they should rest a while longer until the number of their fellow servants, that is, their brothers who were to be killed as they were, would be complete.*

12Then I saw, when He broke the sixth seal, that a great earthquake occurred, and the sun became dark as haircloth, and the entire moon became as red as blood, 13and the stars of the heaven fell to Earth as a fig tree drops its unripe figs when shaken by a strong wind. ¹⁴Heaven disappeared from sight like a rolled-up scroll. Every mountain and island were shaken from their place. ¹⁵The kings of the Earth and the important people and the generals and the wealthy and powerful, every slave and free person hid themselves in the caves and in the mountain rocks. ¹⁶They cried to the mountains and the cliffs, 'Fall on us and hide us from the One who sits on the throne and from the wrath of the Lamb, ¹⁷because the great day of His wrath has come, and who can withstand it?'" Rev 6:9-17

WHAT IS THE TEXT SAYING TO US?

From the fourth seal to the fifth, there is a definite shift. We have been introduced to the four or five horsemen. We understand their symbolism. Now there is a bit of a break. Rather than follow the horsemen to Earth to observe the details of their missions, we are given more insight into what is happening in Heaven, and, this time, it involves people like us!

When the Lamb breaks the fifth seal, John is allowed to see beneath the altar of Heaven. Remember the primary function of an altar in Jewish history: it was a place where God's people offered sacrifice to God. Those of us who were raised in twentieth-century Christianity envision an altar as a wooden railing in the front of the church where people could kneel to pray or seek God. In the ancient world, it was an immense stone structure. In the case of the Great Altar of Pergamum (see Chapter 7), it was an entire building with columns and an expansive porch under the altar of offering. The people to whom this letter was written initially all knew of the Great Altar at Pergamum. It would be that type of structure they would envision in a Heavenly altar.

Inside (under) the altar in Heaven, we find out there are souls. Whose souls are these? They are the souls of all who have ever been martyred for their faith and testimony in Christ. We know from history that Rome experienced a devastating fire in 64 AD. Nero was the emperor at the time, and the people started gossiping that Nero, himself, may have started the fire. To combat the gossip and give Romans a more convenient villain, Nero blamed Christians for the fire, and persecution followed. The result was localized arrests and violence against Christians and even some Jews. The polytheistic Romans trusted neither Jews nor Christians and seemed to have confused or conflated the two often. Still, this stands as the first historical mention of the persecution of Christians within the Roman Empire. It would get much worse in the following three hundred years. Even as he writes, John knows that people like Antipas have been murdered for their Christian faith and testimony. John likely has his friend in mind as he sees these souls in the vision. The martyrs are then allowed to present their petition to God.

"How long must we wait until you avenge our deaths on the people of the world?" It is a fundamental petition of injustice. Because there are multiple souls involved, you understand that the injustice is multiplying with each martyrdom. The response from God is most impressive! They are each given a white robe. Who else in our vision of the throne room has white robes? The elders. The white robe represents purity. While these under the altar are not given golden crowns, they are given white robes in recognition of the purity and righteousness of the cause for which they gave their lives. Then they are given a very curious instruction: wait.

Note: Here is another pattern you are going to see in the Book of Revelation: each sequence of revealed actions ends with some kind of waiting time to raise your anticipation of what is going to come next! The idea of waiting is integral to the action in Revelation. Watch for it.

But for what are the martyred saints told to wait? They are asked to wait until the number of their fellow martyrs who will die for the Gospel is complete. That means it is a finite number. God has a threshold for what He will tolerate in terms of those who will die for their testimony for the Gospel – and then the end will come. A war fought in the Middle East, or anywhere else, will not be the trigger. The end will not be triggered by some political machination or event. The end will not come because the world gets so rotten that God simply gives up. The end will be triggered by the death of the last martyr who brings their number to completion. This is yet another reminder that the ultimate power behind the destiny of men rests with God. That does not make God some kind of puppet-master.

People have free will, and we choose between a myriad of options every single day. Yet, those options are seldom straightforward. They are not black versus white choices. We are so often moved to frustration by the things that happen to us politically or circumstantially in this world. Divorce breaks up families. The loss of a job threatens financial ruin. A market shift endangers our savings or retirement. There are so many events or circumstances that make it seem like we have no real power to combat the forces that influence our fortunes in this world. God wants you to know that, while those things affect you, they do not determine your ultimate destiny. They affect you, but they are not the ultimate power at work in your life. God has the power, and it is founded on the giving of lives for the testimony and work of Christ. Even if the powers of this world threaten your very life, the worst they can do is take your life and send you home. The worst they can do is add your life to the completeness of those who have given their lives for the Gospel. This world cannot truly hurt you.

When the Lamb breaks the sixth seal, there is a theophany – a reaction by the elements of Earth to the presence of God. First, there is an earthquake. We do not know if that is an earthquake on Earth or an earthquake in Heaven. These appear to be visions of how Earth will react as God and His apocalypse draw nearer. Secondly, the sun becomes as dark as haircloth (a stiff cloth made by weaving horsehair in with dense textiles.) Then the moon becomes as red as blood (many see a lunar eclipse here). The stars "drop out of the sky as a fig tree drops its unripe fruit in a gale." The fig puts on its fruit in the fall, carries the small unripe fruit through the winter, then the fruit fills and ripens for harvest in the early summer. If the winter is dry, the fruit can quickly drop from the tree. The presence of a strong wind can make the fruit fall so fast that it is alarming to those nearby.

The fallen fruit represents the loss of hope. Fallen fruit means there will be no harvest next summer. This statement carries with it a sense of loss and despair as hope falls away. The overall effect you should notice is the loss of light. Light is a constant theme in John's writing. When the light is low, something terrible is about to happen. Heaven disappears from sight like a scroll being rolled up. Throughout my career, I have spent many moments trying to imagine what this might look like! I suspect this is a device to express how the light from the sky is extinguished, and the Earth is cast into darkness. Then, in the near-pitch-blackness, the mountains and islands are displaced by the shaking of the earthquake.

All of these extraordinary occurrences serve a single purpose: to show that God is coming near, the end is at hand, judgment is inevitable. In response, people despair. Look at this list of people and see if you can identify a common theme to which we have already been introduced: important people, Generals, wealthy people, powerful people, slaves, free people. Who rules these people? Other people rule these people – Empire people. When I first realized this, I thought that everyone on this list is beholden to authority within the Empire, except free people. Then I realized, in John's day, *only* Empire citizens were free! Most cultures consisted of lesser folk ruled by superiors. Only in the Empire could you find people who lived in the freedoms granted to them by the Empire.

All of these people who depend on the Empire for their freedom now see that the Empire is not the ultimate power. Something more powerful than the Empire controls the sun, moon, stars, sky, and Earth – and it is taking them all out of their place. They cry out to the mountains and rocks, from the caves into which they have retreated for refuge, to fall on them. They cry out to be buried under rocks, rather than to have to face God who is approaching in wrath. In my mind, there is a fascinating connection here with something that Jesus says in Matthew 18:

> *"I promise you, that if anyone causes one of my little ones to stumble, there will come a day when*

he will consider that it would be better to have
a millstone tied around his neck and be dropped
into the deepest ocean than to face what I would
do to him." Mat 18:6

I have taken a bit of scholarly license in translating that verse. Still, that is the weight with which Jesus delivers that statement. He will not spare judgment of anyone who would hurt his "little ones." I do not think that He is only talking about children here. I believe He is talking about all of His children. This is one of the strongest statements Jesus ever made. I do not know why we skim over it so easily and fail to encourage folks in our churches that Jesus is committed to their protection to this extent. Again, in John's vision here in verses 16 and 17, you see this kind of strength from Christ. Notice that God's people are not included in this event. It is not that they are not present on Earth. This judgment will not be terrifying to them. They know the source of ultimate power. They know who is in control of the events of the world. There is no reason to be afraid of judgment because judgment is not for them. Judgment is against the powers of the Empire that have sought to enslave and control men and women throughout time.

A quick note: I know some of you are wondering why slaves are listed among those to whom this judgment will bring such fear. They are just innocent slaves, right? Why would God threaten them with judgment? The point here is that they are serving the wrong masters. Even as slaves, and there are slaves of faith mentioned in the New Testament, their faith should be in The Kingdom – not the Empire of politicians, generals, and masters.

HOW MIGHT WE SHARE THIS?

I have sometimes shared this textual unit in a single message and sometimes broken it into two. You should handle it according to your inspiration. I will give you two outlines that I find suggested by the text:

The Souls Under the Altar
I.   The voices of the martyrs

II. The question of the martyrs

III. The consolation of the martyrs

IV. The promise to the martyrs

The Sixth Seal – Judgment Draws Near
I.   Light and Earth melt away

II. The Empire seeks shelter

III. Are you terrified or assured by the thought that judgment approaches?

QUESTIONS FOR FURTHER STUDY OR REFLECTION

1.   Can you find the accounts of the martyrdom of at least three martyrs?

2. How does a martyr's sacrifice impact you?

3. How many recognized martyrs have there been in history?

4. Can you find other theophanies in scripture?

5. What did other theophanies signify?

6. How do you feel about impending judgment by God?

CHAPTER SIXTEEN

THE REMNANT
NO ONE LEFT BEHIND

Revelation 7:1-8

THE TEXT:

"⁷:¹After this, I saw four angels standing at the four corners of the Earth, restraining the four winds of the Earth so that no wind might blow on the Earth, nor on the sea, nor on any tree. ²Then I saw another angel ascending from the east with the signet of the living God. He cried out with a booming voice to the four angels who were empowered to harm the earth and the sea: ³'Do not harm the earth or the sea or the trees until we seal the servants of our God with the signet on their foreheads.' ⁴Then I heard the number of those who were marked; 144, 000 were marked from every tribe of the sons of Israel. ⁵From the tribe of Judah, 12, 000 were marked. From the tribe of Reuben, 12,000. From the tribe of Gad, 12,000. ⁶From the tribe of Asher, 12,000. From the tribe of Naphtali, 12,000. From the tribe of Manasseh, 12,000. ⁷From the tribe of

> *Simeon, 12,000. From the tribe of Levi, 12,000. From the tribe of Issachar, 12,000. ⁸From the tribe of Zebulon, 12,000. From the tribe of Joseph, 12,000. From the tribe of Benjamin, 12,000 were marked." Rev 7:1-8*

WHAT IS THE TEXT SAYING TO US?

Now we come to an essential thought in scripture, and in the study of eschatology (a fancy word for literature dealing with the end of time.) If you peruse the Bible, you will see that the idea of a *remnant* is very pervasive. Even just a quick scan of scripture will show you that God does not tend to wipe out everyone, ever, not even when He is furious. When Adam and Eve sinned, God threw them out of the Garden of Eden, but He dressed them first. God took the lives of perfectly innocent animals – part of His creation – to care for the man and woman who had sinned. God prefers and preserves His people. The same was true of Adam and Eve's son, Cain. He murdered his brother Abel, then tried to lie to God about what he had done to his brother. Did God wipe him out? No, in fact, at the same time that God sent him even further away than He had sent Cain's parents, He marked Cain so that no one who found him out in the unknown land would kill him. God protected Cain, even in his abject failure.

The only time God comes close to wiping out humanity is in the story of the flood. I believe the saddest verse of scripture in the entire Bible occurs only six chapters into the chronicle of human existence!

> *"⁵The Lord saw how immense the wickedness of His children had Become and that every single motive of their hearts was **only evil all the time.** ⁶The Lord God **allowed Himself to regret that He had ever made humankind on the Earth, and the heart of God Himself was saddened and broken.** Then the Lord God said, 'I will wipe from the face of Creation the entire human race and with them every animal every bird and every creature that crawls along the ground, for I am sorry that I ever made them.' ⁸But Noah found favor in the eyes of God."* Gen 6:5-8 (translation and emphasis my own)

How tragic! This is the one place in all of the Bible where you get to peek into God's heart and find that He feels regret and broken-heartedness over the sinfulness of humanity. The people of that time are so horrible that every single thought of their minds and hearts is "only evil, all the time." Do you feel the weight of that pain? It is absolutely overwhelming. Still, so strong is the love in the heart of God, so hesitant is He to unleash His total wrath, that He combs the Earth and finds one man – ONE – worth saving. Can you begin to comprehend the extreme grace in Gen. 6:8?

"But, Noah..."

Often in scripture, you will find the words, "But God..." They always express a moment of grace from God. But here, it is Noah – the one man worth saving on the face of the planet – whose salvation becomes perhaps the most incredible expression of grace until the birth of Jesus Christ. God prefers and preserves His people. God always looks to keep a remnant alive.

In the fall of the Northern Kingdom of Israel, God preserved Judah and Jerusalem in the south. When the Babylonians come and besiege Jerusalem and carry off every able-bodied person in Israel into exile, God preserved them, to one day return. You may ask why this matters, or what I am trying to get at. There is an extraordinary thought here. It runs contrary to typical thought about The Revelation and the activity of God in the apocalypse. Think about it: God is not marking these 144,000 for some kind of "rapture" event. He is not marking them to spare them going through trials or testing (tribulation). He is marking them to protect them amid those trials and tests. He is preserving them and protecting them, but not exempting them from the wrath that is about to sweep all around them.

Listen intently: throughout scripture, it is never God's way to wipe out everyone. That has never been God's desire. Whether in the Old Testament or the New, God has always worked with the leftovers. Does God change? He does not. It is imperative that you understand this point because the church of our day has come under withering scrutiny and attack in the same way that the seven churches in Revelation experienced. Some of the modern church's most visible leaders have fallen from grace in spinning, flaming-into-the-jungle spectacles. Denominations that were only one hundred years ago planting two new churches every day are now closing them almost as quickly. Worship has become nothing more than a rock concert with staging and lights (even fake smoke). Intimate worship is hard to find. Our sermons are like coaches' half-time motivational talks. The church is in crisis, and it is time we admit it and do something about it. In the midst of this crisis, I encourage you to ponder what it means to be among the remnant. If donating to the church was no longer a tax deduction, would you stay among the faithful to give? If our political climate becomes anti-Christian, will you remain among the faithful to be known as a Christ-follower? When churches become targets for those wanting to actively promote their social agenda and their next social-justice crusade; will you be among the remnant who respond in love and grace, no matter how they accuse or castigate you?

God has always worked and always will work with those who would seek deeper intimacy with Him in the trying times. Watch closely through the remainder of The Revelation and see if God wipes out His creation or redeems a remnant of it into eternity.

The text begins ominously, with an angel at each corner of creation, holding back the winds of judgment. An angel arises from the east, holding the signet ring of God, and crying out that no destruction should begin until God's remnant has been marked to be spared. There is so much here! The signet was the ring worn by the king or emperor. It was used to mark a wax seal on a document to authenticate it for whoever received or saw it. This was the king's business and was not to be interfered with by anyone until it reached its final destination and recipient. Here, it will be people, God's people, who will be marked with His seal for preservation. They are to be marked on their foreheads, just as the followers of the beast will be marked later in The Revelation. This marking for preservation hearkens back to the central story in Jewish salvation history. The story from which Israel gets her very identity, and to which all practicing Jews return every year to recount: the story of Passover. It is the retelling of that moment when the final plague against Egypt takes place. You can find the account in Exodus 12. God calls Moses and Aaron to tell the Israelites to sacrifice an animal and use the blood to mark the doorposts of their houses. God is going to pass through Egypt. In every home where the doorposts are not marked, He will take the life of the firstborn son of that household.

Yes, it is a violent act; and one we have trouble attributing to God in our day. But Pharaoh (the king of Egypt) had enslaved God's people and ignored God's miraculous signs and wonders intended to impress him to set them free. The final plague was designed to break Pharaoh so that he would free God's people. Since that day until this, Jewish people observe this as Passover – the night when the Spirit of God passed over their homes and preserved them so that they would escape the bonds of slavery in Egypt.

The idea of the remnant is deeply ingrained in the salvation history of Jews and Christians. Here, it appears in The Revelation as God calls the angel to mark 12,000 members of each of the twelve tribes. The numbers are significant: twelve is the number of the tribes (families descended from each of the sons of Jacob/Israel). It is the totality of God's people. 12,000 is an unfathomable multiple of that entirely complete number – a perfect multiplication of perfect totality. In our twenty-first-century culture, we hear astounding numbers all the time. Our federal budget items are in the billions of dollars. Our national debt is in the tens of trillions. For a moment, put yourself in the place of the culture to which John writes. They had no calculators, no computers. To them, a number in the hundreds was hard to manage. The thousands were astounding. To quote a number in the tens of thousands was simply saying, "More than you can count or imagine."

When God calls for the marking of 12,000 from each of the twelve tribes, He's including everyone possible. That's all. The 144,000 is not meant to be a limiting number, but an all-inclusive totality. Every single person who belongs in the family of God will be marked to be spared from the judgment that will come when those angels stop holding back the winds of wrath that are to come. No one who belongs to God will be left behind…not one. God's people will be safe in the midst of all that may come against the people of Earth. As God preserved Noah and his family, He will once again preserve His people. They are going to endure great hardship. They are going to endure an unimaginable measure of pain. They are going to shed a tremendous number of tears. But they will not be left unprotected. God will not forget them.

HOW MIGHT WE SHARE THIS?

Through the years, I have sometimes treated this chapter as a single unit and entitled the message or study, "The Remnant and the Redeemed." Other times, I have separated the two into individual lessons under the same, but separate titles: "The Remnant" and "The Redeemed." Both are such significant and meaningful thoughts that I have separated them here and shall treat them this way in the future. I would outline "The Remnant" something like this:

I.   God withholds judgment from His people – every day, and in the end.

II. God knows those who belong to Him – every last one of them.

III. In the Kingdom of God – no one who knows God gets left behind.

QUESTIONS FOR FURTHER STUDY OR REFLECTION

1. Can you think of other times in the Bible where God has worked with a remnant?

2. Have you ever felt like you were one of the leftovers, the remnant?

3. As part of the remnant, how do you construct a positive view of the future for the church?

4. How might we prepare to be part of a remnant if the church falls out of popularity in our culture?

CHAPTER SEVENTEEN

THE REDEEMED

THE UNSEEN UNFORSAKEN CHURCH

Revelation 7:9-17

THE TEXT:

"⁷:⁹After this I looked and was amazed to see a huge crowd which no one could even begin to number, from every nation and tribe and people and language group, standing before the throne and before the Lamb, dressed in white robes. They had palm fronds in their hands. ¹⁰They cried with a loud voice, 'Victory belongs to our God who sits upon the throne and to the Lamb.' ¹¹All the angels, who had been standing around the throne, and the elders and the four cherubim fell prostrate before the throne and worshiped God, ¹²saying, 'Amen, praise and glory and wisdom and thanksgiving and honor and power and might to our God forever and ever; Amen.'

¹³One of the elders said to me, 'Who are these people dressed in white robes, and where did they

come from?' [14]I replied to him, 'Sir, you know.'
He then responded to me, 'These are those who
came out of life-long tribulation. They washed
their robes and made them white by the blood of
the Lamb. [15]For this reason they are before the
throne of God and serve Him day and night in His
temple. The one who sits on the throne will shelter
them. [16]They will neither hunger any longer nor
thirst any longer; neither will the sun fall on them
nor any scorching heat, [17]because the Lamb in the
midst of the throne, will shepherd them and guide
them to the springs of life. And God will wipe
away every tear from their eyes.'" Rev 7:9-17

WHAT IS THE TEXT SAYING TO US?

Now, there is a sudden shift in the location and action of the vision. God has just marked everyone on Earth that belongs to Him for preservation from the coming wrath. When, suddenly, this tremendous crowd of people is seen before the heavenly throne in white robes, waving palm fronds, and declaring God's ultimate victory. At their proclamation, worship breaks out in Heaven. All the angels, and the elders, and the cherubim return to their face-down-on-the-crystal-floor positions and begin chanting or singing God's praiseworthy attributes. You may notice that here, their worship begins and ends with "Amen" – let it be so! Then one of the elders asks John a question: "Who are these people dressed in white robes, and where did they come from?"

There is a fascinating parallel here with an event in the Old Testament. In Ezekiel, Chapter 37, you will find the story of "Ezekiel and the dry bones." If you grew up in the church, you might remember the account from Sunday School. If you have never heard of it, it goes like this: Ezekiel is a prophet who, like John, gets a message through a vision, not unlike the one John is having in The Revelation. In the portion of that vision recounted in Ezekiel 37, God shows the prophet a vast valley, the floor of which is covered with bleached and dried human bones. God asks Ezekiel the same kind of rhetorical question that the elder asks John in Revelation 7:13: "Son of man, can these dry bones live again?" Now, make a note here.

As you and I read either account, we likely can put ourselves in either Ezekiel's or John's place. Were we asked either question, "Can these dry bones live," or "Who are these people?" our first answer would be, "I don't know!" But see the subtle difference in either prophet's response? Ezekiel says, "Sovereign Lord, only you know." John says, "Sir, you know." Neither says, "I don't know" because that would leave them answering what they cannot answer. Each says, "You know" because that opens the way for instruction. This is a rabbinical device for educating young people in Jewish *yeshiva* school. The Rabbi often teaches by asking questions. Each question has an appropriate answer. As the children learn the response that corresponds with each problem, they can give it as proof of their learning. But the first time they are asked a given question, their answer is to be, "You know, Rabbi."

I recently used the same kind of response in a job interview. The interviewer asked me to describe their business offerings. I responded, "Perhaps it would be better if you described them to me." He later approached me and expressed his delight with that answer. He said it showed him that I was aware of the things I did not know and was a humble expression of my willingness to be teachable. Truth be told, I was simply trying to provide a smarter and more open-ended answer than, "I don't know!" I believe the lesson in both Ezekiel and Revelation is clear: be teachable when God asks you something you do not know. John's answer leads the elder to explain who the great crowd of people are, and how they came to appear in white robes before the throne of God. The elder explains that this host of people are those who have come through the great testing, or tribulation.

Are you ready for some steak? Here is one of those sacred cows of The Revelation. Much has been written about the "Great Tribulation." People have tried to figure out if it is a single event, a multi-year event, or a more sweeping section of history. Folks have engaged in theological contortions and scriptural gymnastics to try and explain or shape this simple term – tribulation. The fact that the word "great" appears alongside the term for "tribulation" makes it more tempting to try and fashion "the great tribulation" as some single significant event. But the language simply does not push us in that direction.

There are two Greek words at work here. The first is the word *"megalès."* Take a second and look at that word. See anything that looks familiar to your English-speaking brain? Mega, as in megaphone. In fact, this is the exact word used when Christ cries out from the cross in a "loud voice," or *"phonè megalès."* It is the same word used in Matthew 24:31 to describe the "loud trumpet sound," with which God's angels will descend to Earth. When The Revelation speaks of the "great tribulation," it is not a reference to a particular event. It is only a reference to the idea of the challenges we all continuously face while living in a world where our faith in God makes us foreigners. Job says,

> *"Man, born of woman, lives only a few days, and those days are full of tribulation." Job 14:1*

Psalm 34 tells us,

> *"Many are the tribulation of the righteous, but the Lord delivers him from all of them." Ps 34:19*

The thought that God helps His people endure trials and testing appears throughout scripture with incredible consistency. Jews have always believed that it is the place of God's people to suffer in this world for the sins of everyone else. That is why they have such a hard time seeing Christ as Savior. Did he die for the sins of the world? Of course, He did. That is what any good Jew would do! This concept of suffering is precisely how the Jewish community has coped with the slaughter of 6 million of their brothers and sisters in the holocaust. They call it "redemptive suffering." By the suffering of righteous people, redemption is released into the world for the unrighteous. After centuries of persecution, the concept of "redemptive suffering" has allowed the Jewish community to survive and prosper in a world on which they might, otherwise, have given up. From John's Jewish perspective, trials and suffering are the very avenues through which redemption comes into the world.

I know it is a rather tricky concept to latch onto. Perhaps it even harder if, like me, you were raised with the teaching that this "great tribulation" was some kind of seven-year event. Let me share with you one more perspective before we move on. In 2 Timothy 3, Paul writes:

> "*¹But be alert to this: The last days will be terrible times: ²People will be lovers of self, lovers of money, braggadocious, opportunistic, abusive, disobedient to their parents, ungrateful, unholy, ³unloving, unforgiving, slanderous, without self-control, brutal, not lovers of the good, ⁴treacherous, reckless, conceited, lovers of pleasure rather than lovers of God — ⁵making a show of godliness but having none of its power.*" 2 Tim 3:1-5

Boy, won't it be rough to live through the tribulation of those last times? I am certainly glad we do not live in those times, aren't you? But wait. That description absolutely fits our times. Then again, that description absolutely fits the time in which Paul wrote it, and every day in human history since. That description fits Adam, Eve, Cain, and every moment on this Earth since the Garden of Eden! That is the exact description of human existence for the thousands upon thousands of years for which we have inhabited this planet. That is a great deal of testing. That is a great tribulation.

The fact is that you and I live in a world that exactly fits that description. We live amid evil, murder, struggle, and temptation. If we keep our faith from day to day, it is because we intently focus on trying to be the man or woman that God has called us to be in this wicked world. Friends betray us. Enemies ambush us. Leaders fail us. Politicians abuse us. Families fall apart. Businesses fail. Sickness comes upon us suddenly and without warning. Loved ones die unexpectedly. This world is a rotten mess most days. As Job said, we only get a few days, and those are full of tribulations.

Who are these people that John sees? They are those who have come through life-long trials and heartbreak but held onto their faith. They did not just now arrive in Heaven – we simply had not seen them before this moment. They are the multitude of souls in Heaven who lived on this Earth and died with some element of faith in God in their hearts that caused them to be redeemed in Heaven. They are the "great cloud of witnesses" from Romans 12:1. They exist eternally before the throne of God, and they worship him continually. In return, just as He protects His remnant on Earth, God protects his redeemed in Heaven. (See the connection?) God "shelters" them from hunger or thirst. He keeps the sun from beating down on them and scorching them. He leads them beside the cool and refreshing springs (Compare with Psalm 23:2). God cares for them so intently, the Lamb shepherds them so gently, that all of their trials, testing, suffering, and loss is forgotten. Every tear is wiped from their eyes.

I must confess, every time I read this, I am deeply moved by that promise. If I knew nothing more of Heaven, this one statement would make me long to be there. Now, it is only fair to be transparent enough to let you know that I cry at TV commercials! I have always been easily moved. As a child, I used to listen to the stories of missionaries – OK, even as an adult – and

I would find myself overwhelmed with tears and terrified that God was going to tell me I had to go to Africa! But, if we are honest, those are not tears of pain or trial. Instead, they are joyful and hopeful tears. My life has brought plenty of the other kind of tears. I have known enough of the hot, painful tears of loss, grief, or pain. Because I am easily moved, I cry a great deal. I almost always try to wait until I am alone. I do not like to appear hurt or anguished. I do not like for others to see me crying in pain. Those tears of anguish are, to me, a private expression of shattering pain and failure. They represent loss and losing to some harmful evil in the world. They represent the most profound grief, even despair, that my heart can know. I do not like those painful tears. In fact, there is a real sense in which I despise them. I would gladly never have to experience them, and the associated pain, again.

That is the exact promise of Revelation 7:17: that God will take away every one of those tears from my past, my present, and my future. He loves me so immensely that, once in His presence, my heart can know the kind of absolute joy and love that overcomes all pain, all grief, all loss. The same God who marked me as His while I live on Earth will claim me as His when this life is over, and I stand in His very presence. I was once asked why I did not preach more about Hell. I replied that I was convicted that, if I could not preach on Heaven convincingly enough that people wanted to go, I should never preach on Hell. If I knew only one passage from which to preach the hope of Heaven, it would be this one. If I could know a place and time where there were no more tears forever, I would want to be certain that I was headed there.

HOW MIGHT WE SHARE THIS?

Anytime I have shared this in a sermon or lesson, I have used an outline something like this:

I. The God who protects His remnant also protects His redeemed

II. If I really understood what it meant to be redeemed, my worship would be different

III. The one thing I look forward to most in Heaven – no more tears, ever.

QUESTIONS FOR FURTHER STUDY OR REFLECTION

1. Why are the redeemed shown in white robes, but the martyrs were given white robes?

2. What do you believe we must do to be considered among the redeemed in Heaven?

3. What are the things that cause tears in this life? What would it mean to you if those things were absolutely healed in your life until they caused you no more pain?

CHAPTER EIGHTEEN

THE SEVENTH SEAL AND FOUR TRUMPETS OF WRATH

SILENCE BEFORE THE STORM

Revelation 8:1-12

THE TEXT:

"⁸:¹When he opened the seventh seal, there was silence in Heaven for about thirty minutes.

²Then I saw the seven angels (the ones who stand before God), and seven trumpets were given to them.

³Another angel came and stood before the altar of incense with a golden censer. A great amount of incense was given to him to offer upon the altar, before the throne, as a complement to the prayers of all God's people. ⁴The smoke from the incense, mixed with the prayers of God's people, went up from the hand of the angel before God. ⁵The angel received the censer and filled it with some glowing embers from the altar of incense and threw them upon the Earth, and there were thunder and rumbling and lightning and an earthquake.

⁶The seven angels with the seven trumpets got ready to sound them.

⁷The first angel sounded his trumpet, and there were hail and fire mixed with blood, and it was thrown down to the Earth with the result that a third of the earth was burned up, and a third of the trees were burned up, and all the green grass was burned up.

⁸The second angel sounded his trumpet, and something like a great mountain blazing with fire was cast into the sea with the result that a third of the sea became blood, ⁹and a third part of the living creatures in the sea died, and a third part of the boats were destroyed.

¹⁰The third angel sounded his trumpet, and a huge star fell from Heaven burning like a torch and fell on a third of the rivers and on the springs of water. ¹¹Now, the name of the star is Apsinth, and a third of the water became bitter like wormwood so that many people died as a result of the water because it had turned bitter.

¹²Then the fourth angel sounded his trumpet, and a third of the sunlight was darkened, and a third

of light of the moon and a third of the stars with
the result that a third of them were darkened and
a third part of the daylight was extinguished and
the night lights in the same way." Rev 8:1-12

WHAT IS THE TEXT SAYING TO US?

Now we come to a significant break in the action. In my mind, this is the midway point in The Book of Revelation. After this point, the vision begins to accelerate to the end of Creation and the New Jerusalem. The symbolism after this point becomes much more prevalent and more difficult to decipher. To this point, it was simpler to translate the meaning of what we saw. Either the text simply told us what a character or symbol represented, or they were straightforward enough that we could reason them out. That is all about to change. Something more ominous is coming. All of Heaven is aware of what is to come, but as you and I read the letter, we are not mindful of what lies ahead. We waited through the sealing of the 144,000 faithful of God. Then, we were diverted to Heaven to observe the great multitude before the throne in white robes. Both groups are waiting along with us for whatever is to come when the seventh seal is finally opened. Then the Lamb breaks the seventh seal, and we get…

Silence.

Thirty minutes of silence. Again, you see the devices by which God, through Christ, through John builds expectancy and tension into this account. There were only seven seals, right? The last has to be the final word. God's judgment has to come by the time the seventh seal is broken; does it not? Yet, when the seventh seal is broken, there is nothing. Wait. What? That cannot be! Yet it is. But as my friend, Reuben Welch used to say, "When nothing's happening, something's happening."

We move from this Heaven where everything is active, thundering, quaking, flying around chanting and singing, falling on their faces and worshiping, people appearing and making the worship louder...to absolute silence. The effect should be chilling. It is as though the entire host that we just saw, crying out with all of Heaven in worship, suddenly go silent, and all turn their faces toward Earth, where judgment will now fall.

But why thirty minutes? I have a friend who reminds me that Peter points out:

> *"To the Lord, a day is the same as a thousand years, and a thousand years are the same to Him as a day." 2 Pet 3:8*

My friend points out that, on that scale, this silence could be twenty years in earth-time. The point here is valid: in Heaven, there is no time or space limitation. A moment in Heaven could be years on Earth. Heaven has all of eternity to work with; a few minutes are not even noticed. Thirty minutes, therefore, is a significant time on Earth, but the blink of an eye in Heaven. It's time for God to draw a breath, while for us, it is enough time to understand how ominous it is that all of Heaven goes quiet. This kind of silence in Heaven is not unprecedented.

Between the final prophetic utterance from Malachi in the

Old Testament and the Opening statements of The Gospel of Matthew, four hundred years transpire. Our Roman Catholic friends have Biblical books in between, but those are mostly historical accounts. The voice of God is silent. Can you imagine four hundred years without a word from God? Has He forgotten us? Is He angry? The last thing that happened in Malachi was that the prophet called for the doors of the Temple to be nailed shut until people could worship with pure hearts and motives. So, it looks like God could have been angry at the end of the Old Testament. We know when a friend is silent to us that something is wrong. The effect at the end of the Old Testament should be that our friend, God, has gone silent. Something is wrong, or something incredibly significant is coming. Then Matthew opens, and we realize, Christ is coming!

Bear in mind also, that one of the major recurring themes in John's writing – whether in his Gospel, his letters, or The Revelation – is the theme of the Word of God. In his Gospel, he opens with words that sound very similar to the Genesis 1 creation story:

> *"¹At the very beginning, God created Heaven and the Earth, ²and the Earth was shapeless and void of life, and darkness enveloped the surface of the waters, and the Spirit of God nestled down into the chaos. ³And, the Lord said, 'Let there be light!' and there was light." Gen 1:1-3*

> *"¹At the very beginning was the Word, and the Word was there with God and, at the same time, the Word was God. ²The Word was with God*

from the very beginning. [3]By the Word, all things were made, and without the Word, nothing came to be that has come to be." John 1:1-3

God creates by speaking. His Word is His creative power. With just a Word, He can speak light, or air, or beasts into existence. As long as God is speaking His Word, creation continues. But now, there is silence in Heaven. God has stopped speaking. His creative action has abruptly ceased. There is about to be judgment, and then de-creating...destruction.

There is a brief interlude where we get a look at what happens in Heaven before the trumpets are sounded. An angel stands before the altar in Heaven, and he holds a censer. What is a censer? Well, if you grew up in the Roman Catholic church, you are very familiar with this item. It is a device, typically a metal box or container that usually hangs from a chain. Inside is burning incense that represents our prayers or God's presence. At different times in the mass for worship or as a sacrament, the priest waves it about to show us by the smoke that God hears us, or that God is present. But observe this: when the angel is handed a large amount of burning incense, representing the prayers of God's people on earth, he does not put it in the censer. He holds the burning prayers of God's people in his bare hand! Then, he takes the censer and fills it instead with burning coals from the fire of the altar. The symbolism here is straightforward: God will continue to hear the prayers of His people, but the time for judgment of Earth has come. While His people are protected, the rest of the world is going to receive His fiery wrath. The censer full of glowing coals is hurled to the Earth, and there is a theophany – thunder, rumblings, lighting, and an earthquake. Remember, the theophany represents the reaction of the natural elements to the approach of God.

Trumpets are the instruments of an announcement. They herald the approach of royalty or a particular event or time of day. The judgment that they are announcing here is not the final judgment, but the beginning of God's wrath on the world. It will not be the end, but it will be the beginning of the apocalypse. As the seven angels with the seven trumpets step forward to be ready to sound them, you should feel a bit of anxiety or dread. God's judgment is about to be announced, and it will not be easy to hear.

The first angel sounds his trumpet, and three things are flung from Heaven to Earth: hail, fire, and blood. Two of these three: hail and blood, hearken back to the first and seventh plagues brought on Egypt as Pharaoh refused to release the children of Israel to Moses. The first plague was the turning of the water to blood. The seventh plague was hail. Here, each of these items of judgment represents some particular element in the wrath. Hail represents pain. I do not know if you have ever been caught outside in a hailstorm, but I have! Large hailstones can severely injure a person, but even tiny pea-sized hail stings horribly. The pelting is constant and inescapable. As we discussed previously, fire represents both purifying and destruction. The point is clear: that which will not be purified by God, He will destroy. Blood represents death. John tells us that the result of the first trumpet is the destruction of a third of the trees and grass on Earth. From the destructive force of the recent fires in Australia, I can imagine the awful effect of losing a third of the fruit and habitat trees and all of the grazing grass on the face of the Earth. Death will undoubtedly result.

The second angel blows his trumpet, and again, we are reminded of the first plague on Egypt. Something the size of a mountain, but on fire, hurtles into the sea. Most scholars suggest a meteor here, and that does not seem too far-fetched. The water, as it did in Exodus 7:17-18, turns to blood. The result is that a third of the life in the sea is terminated. A third of all vessels on the sea are destroyed. The result, again, will be tragic. Death will ensue as the balance of creation is terribly disrupted. Those who rely on the oceans for food will suffer massive shortages, as well as a diminished capability to bring that food in from the water.

The third angel sounds his horn, and a flaming star falls from Heaven and into the rivers and streams – the sources of fresh drinking water. It is named "Apsinth," which is likely a reference to the plant known as absinth, or wormwood. Absinth is an ancient medicinal herb. It is very bitter and even toxic in sufficient quantity. Because it turns the water so bitter, people refuse to drink it. The result is not inferred here but rather spelled out clearly: because they refuse to drink the bitter water, people die. The destruction begins to compound.

When the fourth angel sounds his trumpet, we again see the common theme of light used to illustrate the undoing of creation. Just above, we quoted the very first act of God in creation as He spoke light into being. Now, we witness the corresponding act of "uncreation." There is no object flung to earth with the sounding of the fourth trumpet. The lights simply go down. The light of the sun, moon, and stars are each reduced by a third. The day and night both grow darker. God is withdrawing His creative energies. Those lights which once ruled the day and the night are dying. Without the light of day, things will begin to die. Without the lights of the night, people will lose guidance. The light of life and the light of guidance are both dimming. Pain prevails. Suffering is ongoing. Hope is dying.

HOW MIGHT WE SHARE THIS?

My first thought is, "Must we share this?" It is not a happy section of The Revelation. There might be some kind of message about husbands understanding that when they get the silent treatment, fire is about to fall? But that is not a real positive message either. I try not to linger here, but there is no avoiding the truth of this passage. Hit it head-on:

I. When God is silent, it is about to get real (bad)

II. When the Creator becomes the un-Creator

III. What would the world be like without light?
   (I have reworded and reworked these in many ways)

QUESTIONS FOR FURTHER STUDY OR REFLECTION

1. What happens to people who endure extended silence?

2. Have you ever encountered total silence? How did your body react?

3. What kinds of feelings or thoughts do you experience as the trumpets sound, and judgment descends from Heaven?

4. Does the Bible ever say why God is taking His wrath out on the world in Rev. 8?

5. "Why do you think God is beginning to take out His wrath on the world in this passage?

CHAPTER NINETEEN

THE FIFTH TRUMPET OF WRATH
LOCUSTS FROM THE ABYSS

Revelation 8:13-9:12

THE TEXT:

"8:13I looked and heard an eagle flying in mid-heaven crying with a loud voice: 'Woe, woe, woe to the residents of the Earth because of the remaining bursts of the trumpet which the three angels are about to sound!'

9:1 Then the fifth angel blew his trumpet, and then I saw a star which had fallen from Heaven to Earth. He was entrusted with the key to the shaft of the Abyss. 2He opened the shaft of the Abyss, and smoke arose from the shaft like smoke from an immense furnace so that the sun and sky were darkened by the smoke from the shaft. 3Out of the smoke, locusts descended upon the Earth, and they were given authority as scorpions have authority over the Earth. 4But they were ordered not to harm the grass of the eEarth nor any plant nor any tree but were sent against people who did not have the seal of God upon their forehead. ⁵They were commanded not to kill them, but to torture them for five months (their torture was like the torture of a scorpion sting to a person). ⁶In those days, people will seek death but not be able to find it; they will desire to die, but death will elude them.

⁷The locusts looked like horses armored for battle. On their heads were something like gold crowns, and their faces were like human faces ⁸with hair like that of women, and their teeth were like those of lions. ⁹They had thoraxes like iron breastplates, and the sound of their wings was like the sound of many chariots with teams of warhorses rushing into battle. ¹⁰They have tails with stingers like scorpions so that with their tails, they have the power to harm people for five months. ¹¹Their king is the angel of the Abyss, whose name in Hebrew is Abaddon, and in Greek, he is named Apollyon.

¹²The first disaster has occurred, but watch: two more disasters will come after these things." Rev 8:13-9:12

WHAT IS THE TEXT SAYING TO US?

The first four trumpets sound and saltwater, freshwater, life, and light are affected. Then there is a clear break. The interlude starts with one of those statements to which you are, by now becoming accustomed. "I looked, and heard an eagle flying..." He looks with his eyes, but his ears hear the eagle before he sees it. Of course, John is not talking about actually hearing the eagle fly but hearing the message it speaks. The eagle is a typical royal symbol in many cultures. It represents a message from the King of Kings. The eagle flies through "midheaven." The Jews believed in different levels of Heaven. The highest Heaven was where *Yahweh* lived. Midheaven was space – where the sun and moon and stars existed. The lower heaven was the atmosphere – the air around Earth. This eagle flies through where the planets and stars exist and declares "Woe" over all the lower creation. The eagle repeats "Woe" three times because there are three trumpets yet to sound. Two of them will unleash pain and suffering. As you have already likely anticipated, the final trumpet will not unleash punishment but will usher us into the next portion of the vision.

Then, a star falls from Heaven to Earth. This is not Satan, but an angel – a messenger. The ancient Jews believed that stars were angels, "heavenly beings," as it were. Falling stars were seen as bad omens as if an angel had come from Heaven to bring a message to the Earth. Do not read too much into the identity of this angel: it serves only the purpose of using the key with which it comes. The Jews in John's time believed in a three-storied universe. On the top floor were the Heavens, and as we just discussed, they had three levels in and of themselves. The second tier was the Earth on which life existed. The third tier was the underworld.

The word "Abyss" actually means "bottomless pit." It was envisioned as the place where all manner of evil dwelt. In Revelation, it is the place from which the Beast is going to rise, and the place where Satan lives. God has spared Earth from these influences until this point because The Revelation portrays the Abyss as locked up behind a door. The demonic and evil forces of the Abyss have not been allowed to invade the Earth-tier. That is about to change. The fallen angel opens the door to the shaft that leads down into the Abyss, and black smoke belches from the shaft and further darkens the sun.

An interesting historical aside here: Vesuvius erupted in 79 AD, just fifteen or sixteen years before The Revelation circulated through the churches. There is clear historical testimony from Pliny and Cassius Dio that the eruption darkened the sun until it seemed to be night for several consecutive days. That most of the audience had heard stories of the eruption of Vesuvius or experienced the effects, gave them a comparison to imagine. Also, worth noting are historical references to locust swarms darkening the sky. There are even modern videos on the internet in which you can observe grasshopper swarms so dense that the sky looks dusky in their midst. That may be more of what John has in mind, given what is about to emerge from the pit.

Out of the smoke come "locusts," but you must be aware from the outset that these are not insects. These are demons from the Abyss. I understand that this is a passage that has been widely abused by many modern writers. Along with you, I have read that these are battle tanks, or armored helicopters, or A-10 Warthog aircraft. I have heard televangelists exclaim, "Stingers! They have stingers! We even call our missiles 'Stingers!'" Take a deep breath and remember that the Abyss is an ancient depiction of a spiritual place, in much the same way that more modern Christian culture depicts Hell. It is not a physical place, so physical things do not emerge from it. It is a spiritual place of darkness. It belches darkness into the world of light. What emerges from its depths is evil and demonic. Trying to literalize these demonic things is to over-simplify them and minimize the evil they represent. Bear in mind; they are just the first thing belched out of the Abyss. It will get worse soon.

These are demons, for their leader is the angel of the Abyss, Abaddon (verse eleven). Locust plagues are mentioned several times in the Old Testament as plague or pestilence. They were the eighth plague on Egypt. They were the feared judgment of the prophet Amos. The insect variety from the Old Testament could strip plants, trees, and crops and leave total devastation in their wake. But these are weird, demonic creatures. Unlike the insects, they are not here to target plants, crops, and trees – but people! They do not threaten with biting or eating, but they have the power, even the authority, to sting with their tails like scorpions.

There is something innate about the fear that people, and even many beasts, have of scorpions. That is what John means when he says the demons were given the "same authority as scorpions." The arachnid version crawls on the ground. They are not fast, but even horses and dogs jump away from them. Imagine how devastating they could be if they could fly! My second daughter was once stung on the foot by a scorpion one Sunday evening in the yard of a church where we served. She collapsed with the instant burning pain, and I saw the little critter scurry into the grass along the sidewalk. I scooped the three-year-old up into my arms and headed across the street to the fire station, knowing that one of our friends was the EMT on duty that evening. My little daughter looked at me through tears and asked me, "What stung my foot, daddy?"

I replied, "It was a scorpion, honey. Don't worry; the firemen will help us."

She pulled back slightly and looked at me with nearly over-whelming fear in her big green eyes. "People die from scorpions, don't they?" she asked. It was then that I questioned the wisdom of letting my children watch all of those missionary videos in children's church.

I assured her that Oklahoma scorpions were no worse than a bee sting and that she would be fine once Mr. Brad at the fire station washed her wound and put a band-aid on it…and so she was. But you understand, yes? The terrestrial variety of the bug is intimidating! That is the "authority" that John means to convey here. The demonic variety has that same power of intimidation, terrorization, and tyranny.

Then, there are thoughts conveyed here that I hate to point out. Verses three through five contain passive verbs. Passive verbs mean that the action was directed by someone unseen. They use words like "was given," and "were instructed." The "angel of the Abyss" leads these demonic creatures. Yet, who sent them to cause pain to those who do not know God? The implication is that God has granted them authority, at least freedom, to terrorize those who have refused to acknowledge and worship Him. It is God who forbids them from harming grass or tree or crop. So, it must be God who allows them to torment people who do not have the mark of God on their foreheads, those not marked as belonging to God when the 144,000 were marked for protection. Still, the demons are constrained to an extent. They are not allowed to kill those they torment and terrorize. God is still in control. His protected people are still on the Earth. Even the terrible demonic attack force has boundaries.

The demons are given a deadline, a timeframe in which they can torment people. The time limit is five months. Just as insects hatch in spring and die at the end of summer, so the terror has a life cycle – a season. Further, the number five is commonly used in both the Old and New Testaments to signify a small amount. We might use the term, "a few." Five is more than three, which is a sort of minimal group in scripture, but it is short of an entire that would be signified by numbers like seven or twelve. This is a trial with limitations, a sort of tribulation lite.

The effect of the tyranny of suffering and terror is that people will despair to the point that they will want to die rather than endure any more suffering. There is a very applicable and instructive parallel here in the words of Jesus in Matthew 24. Take a moment and read the account that Christ gives us in that chapter concerning the final days. Go ahead, then come back to this point. Did you catch verse 22?

> *"If the sum of those days had not been cut short, no one would have survived. Yet, for the sake of the chosen, God will place a limit on the suffering." Mat 24:22*

The people tormented by the demonic forces are driven to despair. They get caught in this hopeless cycle where they "seek death, but it runs away from them." They call for death, but it does not answer. Yet, Jesus tells us, for the sake of God's people still on Earth at the time, the season will be cut short.

Then, John returns to further describe the demonic force. This time, he likens them to horses – a direct comparison Jewish folk would recognize from Jeremiah 51:27 where horses of battle are compared to a swarm of locusts! But these demonic beasts are as robust and fast as horses, they have armor, and wear golden victor's crowns. They have human faces, which symbolize that *they can communicate with the human mind in a language it understands.* They have the teeth of lions. If you grew up in a land where there were any lions, you would know the fear you feel at seeing a lion bare its teeth and roar at you. They have long hair like women, but it is not for their glory. Their hair is messy – a sign in Hebrew culture of poverty or demonic possession. The overall depiction here is that these demons are indestructible. There is no defense against them. No offense will deter them. They are unstoppable and, with those teeth, deadly. Some of their attributes are repeated. This serves as a reminder of their power. It also provides a reminder that they have a limitation of five months in which to do their harm.

Naming their leader serves to differentiate him from any of the other characters who are going to appear later in The Revelation. He is not Satan, nor is he any of the beasts that are to follow in the vision. He is an angel; a simple messenger sent to bring a message or perform a single task. His name means "destroyer." When his task of destruction is complete, he will exit the stage and, if you can imagine, worse will come. There are still two trumpets to sound.

HOW MIGHT WE SHARE THIS?

I always attempt to share this account with an eye to the fact that, in creation, God brought order from the chaos. In the Noah story, God allows just a bit of that chaos to fall back into creation as the water, over which His Spirit nestled in the earliest passages of the creation narrative. (See Genesis 1:2) This trumpet heralds the beginning of allowing the world to melt back into chaos. This is the beginning of the end – the starting point of the destruction of creation. It should feel ominous.

I. Heaven pauses, but for Woe, not silence

II. When God stops holding back the demons, we are not sure we believe in

III. Terror has limits, but despair can be overwhelming

IV. The children of the King are still being protected

QUESTIONS FOR FURTHER STUDY OR REFLECTION

1. What is meant by a statement of "Woe?"

2. Why would God unleash a spiritual attack on those who refuse Him?

3. Even in the passive sense of "allowing" this attack, are you okay with God doing this?

4. If God is going to allow this attack, why might He put a time-limit on it?

5. If any of these who are subject to this torment were to repent, how do you believe God would respond?

CHAPTER TWENTY

THE SIXTH TRUMPET OF WRATH
THE SPIRITUAL BATTLE BREAKS OUT

Revelation 9:13-21

THE TEXT:

"*8:13Then the sixth angel blew his trumpet, and I heard a voice from the horns at the corners of the golden altar of incense that sits in the presence of God, 14announcing to the sixth angel with the trumpet, 'Release the four angels bound at the great river Euphrates.' 15Then the four angels who were prepared for that very hour, that very day, that very month, and that very year were released to kill a third of humanity. 16The number of horse soldiers was tens of thousands times tens of thousands (I heard their number).*

17The horses and their riders I saw in my vision looked like this: they had breastplates that were fiery red and blue like hyacinth and yellow like sulfur. The heads of the horses looked precisely like the heads of lions, and from their mouths

*belched fire and smoke and sulfur. ¹⁸A third of hu-
manity was killed by these three plagues; by the
fire and the smoke and the sulfur which poured
from the mouths of the horses. ¹⁹For the power of
the horses is in their mouths and in their tails, for
their tails, which resemble snakes, have heads,
and with them, they inflict deadly injury.*

*²⁰The rest of humanity, those not killed by these
plagues, did not repent of the products of their
own manufacture; that is, they did not cease to
worship the demons, or idols, made of gold and
silver and bronze and stone and wood, which
cannot see, hear, nor walk, ²¹and they did not
repent of their murdering, or sorcery, or immorality, or their thefts." Rev 9:13-21*

WHAT IS THE TEXT SAYING TO US?

The fifth trumpet released a force that had been pent up in the
Abyss. So, the sounding of the sixth trumpet leads to the freeing
of an equally terrifying force bound on Earth. The sixth angel
sounds his trumpet. John hears a voice from the protrusions, or
handles, at each of the four corners of the altar. The voice calls for
the releasing of four angels that have been bound. These are likely
the same angels mentioned in 7:1-3. In that passage, those angels
are called not to release any harm until God's people are marked
for protection. I believe these are the same angels for two reasons:

1. Both of these groups of angels are spoken of as being re-strained, or "bound."

2. There simply are no other mentions, of which I am aware, of a group of four angels anywhere else in The Bible!

The fact that they have been bound, or restrained, seems to indicate that these are not holy angels, but evil. Still, it is essential to note that while rebellious or evil angels do not follow God, they must always obey His commands. Just as the demonic spirits portrayed as locusts in the last section were not holy messengers, they could not have harmed without the authority to do so. Compare this to the story of Job in which Satan has to have God's permission to harm Job.

The bound angels are released at the Euphrates River. Trouble often comes from the east in Biblical apocalyptic or prophetic writings. It makes sense – to the west of Israel is the Mediterranean Sea, to the south the Negev Desert. The Assyrians had attacked from the north in 721 BC, but real trouble like the Babylonians came from the east. The Euphrates was the far eastern boundary of the glory days of the Kingdom of Israel under David and Solomon. It was a significant border of the Assyrian, the Babylonian, the Persian, and the Parthian Empires. In Jewish history, it was the site of the first humans, the first sin, the first lie, and the first societal rebellion against God (the Tower of Babel). Some scholars have suggested that either group of four (nations or list of firsts) may be behind the fact that there are four angels represented here. Again, I would warn against trying to tie these symbols to personalities or entities we know, because doing such oversimplifies them drastically. In Revelation 7:1-3, these angels were instructed not to release harm onto Earth until God's people had been marked for protection. Neither of those enumerations could possibly account for that constraint. I believe the fact, in chapter 7, that the angels stand at the four corners of the world, illustrates that when they are allowed to unleash violence, it will be upon the entire world. The fact that they release the destruction from the Euphrates is merely symbolic of the fact that trouble, sin, and judgment started in the region along the Euphrates and that the final dreadful spiritual attacks will come out of that same kind of spiritual place.

We are told that these angels have been bound into this place, restraining this evil for this hour, day, month, and year. That does not necessarily mean that this exact moment in time was predestined at a particular point. Still, at the least, it means that this point was foreseen and would come to pass within the sequence of events at whatever point it was time. Now it is time. There is a confirmation that these are not holy angels because their mission has always been defined: to kill humanity. The effect of reading that gives one a sense of dread. When they are unleashed, one-third of the people on Earth will perish.

We then come to one of the more confusing points in The Revelation. The trumpet was blown, the voice called for the loosing of the four angels, they have been released and are going to slaughter one-third of humanity. Then, with no explanation, we are given a general number of soldiers. Beware Biblical math problems! This phrase is anomalous. It might read, "twice ten thousand times ten thousand." This phrase could mean twenty thousand times ten thousand; or, it might mean ten thousand times ten thousand times two. It also might be translated ten thousand times ten thousand (one hundred million) to the second power. Some texts read two-hundred million. But, as we discussed previously, numbers past about 10,000 were just about impossible for people in that historical frame to even envision. As a result, "ten-thousand" was a general descriptor for "a big, huge army!" The city of Rome was the largest city known to humanity at the time – and it was around one million by the best estimates. The entire population of the Roman Empire was somewhere around four or five million. I think the best way to translate this number is, as I have here, "tens of thousands *times* tens of thousands." It's an unimaginably and unfathomably immense number. So unbelievable would it have been to readers of John's time that he affirms that this is the number he heard.

Now John goes on to describe the millions of demonic horsemen he sees. They wear breastplates – again showing invincibility. The colors of the breastplates are red, blue, and yellow to coordinate with the fire, smoke, and sulfur that they exhale. The demonic steeds have the muscular body of a horse, the ferocious head and mouth of a lion, and a tail like a collection of snakes with heads which can inflict deadly venomous wounds. They belch fire, smoke, and sulfur. These are not like the plagues sent against Egypt but are many times worse. These are beasts from Hell itself. Only the final plague against Egypt brought death, and that in a silent passing spirit. Here are millions of demonic apparitions, bringing violent and terrible death. Imagine, a beast with no vulnerability – armored in the center, a lion's jaws with which to rip their adversaries to shreds at the front and venomous snakes to bite at the rear.

A typical horse-borne warrior is threatening enough! He and the horse both have eyes to the front. They can avoid attack from the front, or answer it with sword, spear, or bow. The rider is up higher than foot soldiers, with the ability to see clearly over the battle to the left and right. The rider's only vulnerability is usually to the rear. But not in this case. These riders are shielded to the rear by a tail of writhing and poisonous snakes. There are millions of them. Such an attack force would be absolutely devastating. They exhale the atmosphere of Hell, and they take the lives of one-third of humanity. Where the locust-like demonic force tormented, intimidated, and terrorized humankind for a season – this force comes with but one aim – to wipe out anyone in their path.

I understand that many authors of much greater wisdom than myself have made efforts to connect both the locusts and the cavalrymen to natural, physical beings, vehicles, or nations. But as you read only the text, it seems clear to me that these are demonic forces. In fact, both were unleashed. Do you see that? One was locked in the Abyss, and the Euphrates restrained the other. Bear in mind that, in the Biblical creation story, the world starts out as "chaos." In just the second verse in the entire Bible, the text says God "nestled down" into the chaos. The word evokes the thought of a bird that settles down over her eggs. In Genesis, God is about to create. He is about to hatch a universe. To do so, He speaks boundaries into place. He speaks, and there is light that creates a boundary from the darkness. He speaks again, and the dry land appears, which creates another boundary with the water. So then, the entire story of creation is about God defining the boundaries of the chaos. As I mentioned earlier, in the story of the Flood of

Noah, God allows the water above (a boundary set in the creation story) to fall from where it had been constrained. It represented God, allowing a bit of that primal chaos to creep back into the world.

At the end of that story, God promises never to destroy the world with water. To this point, as God has shown John what the apocalypse will bring, you have seen the loss of the boundary between light and dark – the darkness beginning to creep back into creation. At the sounding of the fifth and sixth trumpets, God does something even more terrifying. He takes away the constraints that have held back the chaotic spiritual forces in Hell and on Earth! Those who do not serve God lack any resources to combat such demonic warfare. They will be tormented first, and then they will die. There is no natural way to accurately describe these two horrific prophecies because they extend so far beyond anything that physical forces could accomplish. I have read other writers who have speculated that the locusts represent physical sickness. In contrast, they believe, the horse cavalry represents mental anguish. I would submit that either of these interpretations is an over-simplification of the evil we are meant to sense here. These are the forces of Hell – one arising from the smoke and sulfur – the other breathing the breath of Hell into humanity's faces. We are meant to read this and feel a measure of soul-terror. This is what it will be like as the world is de-created, and chaos streams back into the creation.

But how will those who do not know God react? They will not repent. If you read this with any concept of God, your response has to be something like, "How could they not?" I remember when I first read this account, with any adult understanding, being totally bewildered by the lack of response from those who did not know God. But now, it makes perfect sense. They did not repent of their murder, sorcery, immorality, or theft precisely because they never stopped worshiping the idols and demons. Did you catch that? They were attacked by the very things they worshiped. The stench of Hell was not foreign to them. They daily lived in it. Why is war not absolutely repugnant to the people of Earth? Because we walk in it every day of our lives.

In the Enlightenment of the late 1800s, people fancied themselves becoming so enlightened that they would solve all the world's maladies and problems within a couple of generations. Disease would be conquered by science. Conflict would cease to exist as folks became more educated and more capable of statesmanship and the craft of peace-making. Utopia lay just a few years ahead. But, at the height of Enlightenment, came World War I. Because of humanity's technological capabilities and scientific skill, it was the most brutal war the world had ever seen. New armaments, new battle weapons, airplanes, and chemical weapons now made it possible to massacre men at a rate never known in history. When it was over, the Enlightened called it an aberration. Now, surely, humanity had gotten that out of their systems. They called it "The War to End All Wars." With their tattered Enlightenment barely surviving, they pressed on not even twenty years until the world descended more deeply into World War II. The Enlightenment died among the savagery of five empires tearing at each other for the life of the planet. The world learned that science could now produce even more horrific weapons, and the casualties could number in the tens of millions within days.

But we never learned. In almost any time-period since then,

there has been a war in one place or another on Earth. Some have been tiny; some have been massive, but we never learned. We never repented. We have never stopped killing each other and fighting and manufacturing new weapons of greater destruction to use on each other. We breathe the atmosphere of Hell so that Hell simply does not seem that strange to most of us. We live with the demons of hatred, prejudice, depression, anger, and blame. We rip each other to shreds with our mouths. We poison each other with venomous attitudes. When the four horsemen rode out to bring the apocalypse, I said something like, "I hear the hoofbeats of the horsemen in my world." Now, nine chapters deep in this book, I have just read the account of the most awful demonic terror that could be unleashed. I have to ask myself, "Do I smell the sulfuric reek of Hell in my world?" Can we detect, at least, the beginnings of the loss of boundaries and the advent of chaos in the world in which we spend every day?

Sometimes I am afraid to answer my own questions.

HOW MIGHT WE SHARE THIS?

I have always used the same basic outline in sharing this section:

I. When God Stops Holding Back

II. When Evil Is Unleashed

III. When Men are Too Darkened to Repent Any More

Often, as I have taught these last two sections, I have ended my lesson stating that, though I loved everyone in the room, there was no reassurance in this chapter of The Revelation. The only hope was that we belonged to those sealed away from spiritual attacks like this. I have always explained that this chapter exists expressly for the purpose of allowing each of us to sense some dread and to take that "fearless and searching moral inventory" that our friends in Alcoholics Anonymous live by. Before you take on any other questions for reflection, may I ask you to honestly reflect on this one, most important question? "Do you know Christ? Are your heart and mind safe from the worst the enemy can unleash on you?" If your answer is "yes," then I celebrate you as my brother or sister and ask that you help me and all you can reach to know that assurance. If your answer is "No" or "I don't know," might I encourage you to seek out a Christian friend you trust? Share with them what you have read here and the questions it has caused you to ask, and ask them to share with you where their faith comes from? Then the writing of this book will truly have been worth anything it has taken or cost.

QUESTIONS FOR FURTHER STUDY OR REFLECTION:

1. Why is the River Euphrates significant in Bible history?

2. How can angels be evil?

3. How would you imagine the size of an army of 200 million?

4. What kind of impressions do you sense as you read this account?

5. Do you think the world is yet so lost as portrayed here by their unrepentance?

6. What does it mean to repent?

7. Do you feel the need to repent of anything right now in your own life?

8. With whom might you share your spiritual reflections and questions? Why not get in touch with them now?

CHAPTER TWENTY-ONE

THE ANGEL WITH THE TINY SCROLL
INGESTING GOD'S WORD CAN LEAD TO STOMACH UPSET

Revelation 10:1-11

THE TEXT:

"*¹⁰:¹Then, I saw another mighty angel descending from Heaven, wrapped in a cloud with a rainbow encircling his head, and his face was like the sun and his legs like pillars of fire. ²He held a tiny open scroll in his hand. He placed his right foot in the sea but his left on the land. ³Then he cried with a loud voice like a roaring lion. And when he roared, the seven thunders spoke their own response. ⁴When the seven thunders spoke, I was about to write down their words, when I heard a voice from heaven saying: 'Conceal the words of the seven thunders; do not even think about writing them down!'*

⁵Then the angel, whom I saw standing on the sea and on the land, raised his right hand to the heavens ⁶and everything in them, the Earth and everything in it, and the sea and everything in it:

'There will be no more waiting, [7]but in the days
when the seventh angel blows his trumpet, then
the secret plan of God will have been fulfilled, as
he announced to his servants the prophets.'

[8]The voice, which I heard from heaven, again
spoke to me and said, 'Go, take the tiny scroll
which lies open in the hand of the angel standing
on the sea and on the land.'

[9]Then I went to the angel and asked him to give
me the scroll. He said to me, 'Take it and eat it,
and though it will upset your stomach, it will be
sweet as honey in your mouth.' [10]Then I took the
scroll from the angel's hand and tasted it, and it
was as sweet as honey in my mouth, and when I
swallowed it, my stomach became upset. [11]Then
I was told, 'You must again prophesy against
peoples and nations and languages and many
kings.'" Rev 10:1-11

WHAT IS THE TEXT SAYING TO US?

Now, as you likely have become accustomed to expecting, there is
a pause before the final trumpet sounds. Once again, this device
serves to heighten your expectancy and hold your attention. It
works, doesn't it? In the interlude, John sees a "mighty angel."
This term is only used twice in The Revelation and serves to

connect the two angels who both deal with scrolls or books. The first was in 5:2. In that verse, his question concerned finding one who was worthy to open the first scroll, printed front and back, and sealed with seven seals. This angel is described in much more detail. He is a titan! In fact, it is entirely possible that the people to whom John is writing knew of the Colossus of Rhodes and, likely, had seen its ruins. This intention behind this image may well be to invoke that very same immensity in their minds. The colossal angel is descending from Heaven, the direct presence of God, enveloped in a cloud. The cloud here, as in the depiction of Mt. Sanai in Exodus 19:16, indicates the immediate presence of God. A rainbow-colored halo encircles the angel's head. The rainbow is the sign of God's promise to Noah but also denotes, as it did around the throne of God, the immediate presence of the promise-maker. The angel's face shines like the sun, just as Moses' face was alight with the presence of God after he stood in God's direct presence in Exodus 34:29. Do you notice a pattern? The angel's legs appear to be ablaze, like pillars of fire. Again, the reference is to the pillar of fire in which God wrapped himself, during daylight hours, to lead the Israelites out of bondage in Egypt. (Exodus 13:21) The implication and connection are clear: this mighty angel comes directly from the presence of God. The residual effects of having been in God's direct presence are all over and around His messenger.

The angel brings something – but it is not what you might expect in the hands of such a colossal angel. In his left hand (since v. 5 tells us that his right is about to be raised to Heaven in an oath-taking gesture), is a tiny scroll. It lies open, unsealed, which means someone has been reading it, or it is in the process of being written. He assumes a stance that spans land and sea, fitting because he is about to swear an oath to the God of land, sea, and heavens. Then the angel cries out with a voice like that of a roaring lion!

I do not know if you have ever experienced the sound of a lion's roar, but it is awe-inspiring. I remember a time when my children were small that we took them to the zoo for the day. We spent that beautiful sunny day roaming the zoo and seeing all of our favorite animals. I have always accused my children of having a particular affinity for the monkeys...but that is a topic for another time. Around mid-afternoon, we had just emerged from the reptile building, when we heard a sound like none of us had ever heard! It was deep and earth-shaking and loud! The kids immediately ran toward it, and adults followed.

As we drew nearer, the sound only intensified. We could clearly sense the resonance in the ground. It was the lions. For whatever reason, they had joined in a chorus of roaring. One after another, they took turns, as though in some kind of kingly contest to see who could roar the loudest. And roar loudly they did! I remember the looks of delight on my daughters' faces to simply stand in the power of that sound. The lions carried on for five or six minutes with their successive roaring, and then abruptly stopped. My oldest daughter looked at me in amazement and exclaimed, "Wow! I never knew a lion's roar was THAT loud!" I had to agree. It was a sound that, were you to encounter it in the wild, would make your hair stand up and your insides turn to gelatin. To this day, it is likely the most impressive sound I have ever heard in person produced by a living being. A colossal angel crying out in that kind of voice would undoubtedly have every bit of my attention.

This is the only place in The Revelation that an angel speaks, but John does not record any words. It is as if the angel simply roared, but so impactful is the voice of the angel that it elicits a response from "the seven thunders." The thunders have not been previously enumerated, and there is certainly a reference to the voices of the seven spirits of God. It is as if the entire person of God answers back to the mighty angel. The implication is that the thunders are interpreting the cry of the angel. Still, John is forbidden to write down the interpretation. I believe there is a straightforward explanation to what the angel cried out, what the thunders uttered, and why John is prohibited from writing it down: it is the name of God.

Jewish writers have, from the earliest times, refused to write the name of God. In the Old Testament, you may find the phrase "the name of the Lord" in place of the actual name. In Hebrew scripture, you will find the "four lines" that represent the consonants of the name of God. Even in modern Jewish blogs or religious articles, you will often see the attribution as G--D. To the Jewish mind, the name of God is far too precious to reduce to writing. It is an expression of sheer reverence not to utter the name. I read Revelation 10 as an almost guttural and reflexive cry on the part of the angel – crying out the name of God in response to having been directly in His presence. Because it is THE NAME, he cries out. The thunders cannot help but respond in worship and adoration – and they, too, thunder out the name of God. In Revelation 19:12, Christ is said to have a name that no one knows but Himself. That name is never revealed. I believe it is that name that the angel cries out, and the thunders repeat in peals of worship. As John goes to record it, he is stopped cold. The words are strictly prohibitive: "Don't you even think about it!" Christ is so holy that He, indeed, has a name that is "above all names" and so sacred that no one is qualified to utter it.

Then, the angel swears an oath. There will be no more waiting (while we are, in fact, waiting). The seventh angel will blow his trumpet, and the final judgment of God will come. Then, as you would expect, there is going to be a bit more waiting. The angel presents the scroll to John. Great! Now John can read what the scroll says, and he can write it down, and then we will know this grand final plan of God, right? No. Keep waiting. It is snack time! The voice commands John to go take the tiny scroll from the angel, so John approaches and asks for it. The angel gives John the scroll and tells him to…eat it. Wait. Are we not supposed to read books, not eat them? (Though, in second grade, I once got in a lot of trouble for eating paper torn from the pages of my books. I must have had some kind of wood pulp deficiency.) We read books, yet John is told to ingest this one. The angel warns him that it will be sweet as honey in his mouth (compare with Ezekiel 3:3) but will make him sick to his stomach. Listen to the words of Psalm 19:

> *"⁷The law of the Lord is perfect: it brings re-*
> *freshment to the soul. The teachings of the Lord*
> *are trustworthy; they make the simple person*
> *wise. ⁸The precepts of the Lord are righteous;*
> *they give joy to the heart. The commands of the*
> *Lord are radiant; they give light to the eyes. ⁹The*
> *fear of the Lord is pure, it endures forever. The*
> *decrees of the Lord are certain, and all of them*
> *are righteous.*

> *[10]They are more precious than gold, even the pur-*
> *est gold; they are sweeter than honey, even the*
> *honey straight from the comb." Ps 19:7-10*

In both Ezekiel 3 and Psalm 19, the Word of God is likened to honey. Ezekiel 3 is almost an exact parallel of the scene in Revelation 10:9-10. A hand offers a scroll, the prophet is told to eat the scroll, and that it will be sweet in his mouth like honey. Is that not exactly how the Word of God is? It is sweet to us! We long for the spiritual nourishment it gives us.

I remember coming back to the faith in my early twenties. As mentioned before, I had drifted from my childhood faith when I went to college. In some ways, I had been rebellious to the faith in which I had grown up, but in most ways, I simply put it on a shelf and did not carry it in my heart. Once I left college, the faith began to call me back from many directions and from many voices. I began to sense a call to ministry in 1984 and was deeply moved that I needed better Biblical knowledge. I purchased the entire Bible on cassette tapes with commentary on every single passage by a well-known Bible teacher of the day. For weeks, every night when I got home from work, I would plug in a tape and start taking notes in my Bible. I was hungry for every word. Every lesson was sweet new food for my soul. I clearly remember the evening I was listening to the words of the Prophet Hosea, and the recording came to Hosea 13:5:

> *"I fed you in the desert, in the land of burning*
> *heat. But when I fed them, they became satisfied,*

> *when they were satisfied, they became proud;*
> *And in their pride, they forgot me."*

I remember highlighting and memorizing that verse. It described how, even as I had departed from my faith, God had watched over me and fed me. Still, I had fancied myself independent and having outgrown my need for God. I became arrogant and proud. I had forgotten God, and this verse spoke directly to me. Like honey in my mouth, it brought me energy despite my youthful pride and selfishness.

Eight years later, on a crisp and lovely Fall Sunday morning in Minnesota, I found myself sitting on the platform of the church I pastored. The worship was rich that morning. A young man who attended a local private college had happened into our church. A very talented pianist, he had started playing in our worship service. What a blessing! That morning, he had helped pick the hymns and songs for worship. Everyone's faces shown with their joy at sensing God near to us in our fellowship. The ushers collected the offering as the young man played a beautiful number on the piano. When he had finished, I stepped up and opened my Bible to preach the message I had prepared.

Now, only two or three times in thirty-five years has anything like this happened to me. But that morning, as I opened my Bible, God clearly spoke to me.

"Preach Hosea 13:5-6."

I froze in my spot. I sensed the voice again, very clearly.

"Preach Hosea 13:5-6"

That could not be God, could it? Our service had gone so well up to that point. Everyone looked to be enjoying God's presence in the service. These were not hard-hearted folks; they were dear people. Their church had, only a few years earlier, dwindled down to five people. The bishop that oversaw that state had prayed fervently, kept the church open, and called a church planter. These people had sacrificed and worked and believed that God would raise up their church. These were not lazy people. God had raised up their church! God…had…fed them. Now the church was… full. It was…comfortable.

I opened my Bible and asked the congregation to turn to Hosea. I remember thinking that, if I had a moment to run to the restroom, I would throw up before having to read this passage to these people. I was more than nervous, more than anxious – I was terrified. I understand that you do not know me, but I do not get nervous in front of a crowd. I have the innate gift to make being in front of even very large crowds smooth and easy. But that morning, in that place, with that message, I was sick to my stomach. I read the passage. When I was done, I remember their faces looking back at me – as though I had slapped them. Yet, God gave me the words to exhort them. He gave me guidance to provide assurance that they were blessed by God, but not for comfort. They had been blessed and filled in order to press on. As they filed out of the church, many shook my hand or hugged my neck and said, "Pastor, I could tell that was hard for you. But that was exactly what we needed to hear this morning."

Honey in our mouths. Bitterness and anxiety in our stomachs. It is the prophet's way, perhaps the curse of the prophets. All of us, whether laypersons, teachers, or preachers who know God, understand that God may call us to share something sharper than a double-edged sword into the lives of others. We may have to take

the very words that were honey in our mouths, and share them out
of that sickening feeling that they may be too heavy for our loved
ones to bear. Yet that is the call that we all answered. Paul says to
his young protégé, Timothy:

> *"Preach the Word of God; be ready when it is
> easy and when it is not; Patiently correct, strongly
> rebuke and lovingly encourage—with extreme
> grace and careful instruction." 2 Timothy 4:2*

I believe that Christ, through John, in Revelation 10, takes this
interlude to speak to us.

In the same way that I have, at times in this book, taken an
aside to speak to you of something I want you to see or understand,
so John takes us all aside here. The message is simple and clear:
what lies immediately ahead is going to be heavy and real. John is
not delighting in laying it on us. He believes with all his heart that
it is the nourishing and sweet Word of God; yet, he knows it will
be difficult to hear and understand. The Word may bring convic-
tion to our hearts. Parts of what we are to be told may bring fear,
sadness, or make us feel like we have failed at our mission, but it is
going to come to us anyway. God trusts us with this message. God
believes in us to take it to heart and hear His calling amidst the
wonderful and awful things we are about to be told. We, listening
to this message, are the living. We are the church! God, Himself,
has addressed these words to us through His Apostle because we
have the power to do something with them. God trusts us to either
change the direction of the lost parts of this world or to interpret
them to the people we love in the coming calamity. It may not be

easy, but it will be sweet. It may turn our stomachs, but it is why we were born into this moment in time.

Along with John, we are told, "Now that you understand the nature of the message, you must once again prophecy to nations, races, and power." You must, again, speak truth to power. Now preach!

HOW MIGHT WE SHARE THIS?

I love the fact that, in some cases, the textual unit is a neat and entire chapter. This is an aside that allows for encouragement after the hefty demonic visions of the last two trumpets. I have always attempted to share it as such – as encouragement, and a refreshing break before the vision hits us with renewed energy. I have allowed the chapter to dictate the outline in something like this form:

I.   God Sends a Mighty Angel

II. The Mighty Angel Brings Us God's Word

III. God's Word Nourishes Us and Stirs Us to Preach On

QUESTIONS FOR FURTHER STUDY OR REFLECTION

1.   Compare and contrast this mighty angel with the one in Revelation 5:2.

2. Why do you think this angel is clothed in a cloud, and not descending on one?

3. What parts of God's final plan might you find in the words of the Prophets?

4. How do you perceive God's call in your own life? What has He called you to do?

CHAPTER TWENTY-TWO

THE TEMPLE AND GOD'S TWO WITNESSES
THE CHURCH AND THE WORD

Revelation 11:1-14

THE TEXT:

"11:1Then I was given a reed, like a measuring stick, and was instructed: 'Go and measure the Temple of God, including the altar area, and count those who worship within it. 2But do not measure the courtyard outside the Temple, for the Gentiles will be permitted to keep the holy city under siege for forty-two months. 3I will empower my two witnesses to prophesy 1,260 days clothed in sackcloth. 4These are the two olive trees and the two lampstands which stand before the Lord of the Earth. 5If anyone tries to harm them, fire comes from their mouths and wipes out their enemies; if anyone should wish to harm them, they will certainly die in such a way. 6They have the power to shut up the heavens so that no rain will fall while they prophesy. They also have power over the waters, that is, to turn them to blood,

and to strike the Earth with any type of plague whenever they wish.

[7]When they complete their witness, the beast which ascends from the Abyss will wage war on them, that he might conquer them and kill them. [8]Their bodies will lie in the public square of the great city, which is called, prophetically, 'Sodom' and 'Egypt,' where their Lord was also crucified. [9]And some of the peoples and races and languages and nations will see their bodies for three-and-a-half days, but people will not permit their bodies to be buried. [10]The inhabitants of the earth will gloat over them, and they will celebrate and will exchange gifts with one another, for these two prophets tormented the inhabitants of the Earth.

[11]Now after the three-and-a-half days the breath of life from God entered into them so that they stood on their feet, so that great fear fell on those who saw them. [12]The witnesses heard a loud voice from Heaven, saying to them, 'Come up here.' Then they ascended to Heaven on a cloud while their enemies looked on.

[13]And in that hour there was a great earthquake so that a tenth of the city was destroyed and seven thousand people were killed so that

the survivors were terrified and gave glory to the God of Heaven.' [14]The second disaster has occurred; watch, the third disaster will come shortly!" Rev 11:1-14

WHAT IS THE TEXT SAYING TO US?

I believe that understanding this section of The Revelation depends on not losing sight of where the passage begins. There has been a great deal of speculation about what God is saying here, who the witnesses might be, and what might be the motivation behind this chapter. Look carefully at where it starts: In John's vision, he is handed a measuring rod. This is a direct parallel to Ezekiel 40:3-42:20, in which Ezekiel has a vision very much like John's and is called to measure out the Holy City. The specified length of the rod Ezekiel is handed is about ten feet. By measuring an area, one defines it. By measuring the inner court, and counting those who worship therein, God is calling on John to determine the extent of His holy household. He is identifying those who are in and those who are out – we would call them His "Church." John is forbidden to measure the outer court, which was known as the "Court of the Gentiles." In the temple in Jerusalem, there had been an outer court, into which anyone could enter and mingle. Then, there was an inner court into which only Jews could enter. This was the area where Jews prepared to enter into the holy portion of the temple to offer sacrifices to God. It was the inner area of the temple that defined them and set them apart from the rest of the people of the world.

In the same way, John is called to measure the inner court, which will define the boundaries within which God's people will be preserved. The implication is, again, that God is protecting those who belong to Him. His real Church is inside and spared the judgment and wrath, which will befall those on the outside.

The outer courtyard is to be trampled by the outsiders for forty-two months. That is three-and-a-half years. Please note how often this number appears in the coming chapters. What does it mean? Again, remember our previous discussion on numbers in the Bible. Seven is a number of totality. Three, seven, twelve, and forty are all numbers that signify that something is whole or complete. To state that anything happens for three-and-a-half days, weeks, months, or years is to say that it happens for a partial time, an imperfect time. In the timeframe of God, holy things happen in complete seasons. Unholy things happen in an abbreviated season. Otherwise, they might not be survivable. God does not let his people undergo a siege or a test to the point that they are entirely broken or defeated. As you read in The Revelation, please pay attention to the fact that you will never see a reference to seven years. I know, I'm slicing a steak off of a sacred cow here. So, rather than simply make the assertion, I am asking you to watch and see if a time reference of seven years ever appears in the book. At some point, I may make a suggestion as to why that is. For now, I am much happier if you come to your own conclusions. Here, the outsiders will attack God's church – His holy city – for only a season. Those who have devoted their lives to God will remain protected and safe inside his holy court.

At the same time that God's people are under attack by the outsiders, John sees two witnesses. They are claimed as God's own witnesses, and they will be empowered to prophesy to the world for 1,260 days. How many months is that? Oh, it is forty-two months – or three-and-a-half years. What does it mean? It means that as long as God's people are under attack from the world, God will have a witness in the world to support, guide, and protect them. Please get this message; it is vitally important to you today. No matter what seems to be overwhelming right now in your life, no matter what is thrown at you from the outside, God has the opposite and greater force at work on your behalf. The real power is inside the holy place where God's people are preserved. The noise outside is not real power. The chaos outside is not real power. The threats and the violence, the murder and the bloodshed, are sometimes terrifying – but they are not the real power in your life. Remember the words of Christ:

> *"I have told you all these things so that in trusting me, you will be unshaken and confident, deeply at peace. In this godless world, you will frequently experience trouble. But take heart! I have overcome this world!" John 16:33b*

God's two witnesses are "empowered" to prophecy for 1,260 days, all the while clothed in the garments of repentance. This is a roughly woven fabric, similar to the rough fabric that I remember feed sacks were made from in my childhood. We called them "gunny sacks." They were burlap bags that were so rough you would never want them next to your skin. They were cheap. To be clothed in sackcloth is a sign of poverty and repentance. In the Old Testament, sackcloth was the typical garment for one who was grieving. The two witnesses wear it as a spiritual symbol of their yielded spirits and their call to repentance.

The two witnesses are referred to as "the two olive trees and the two lampstands." Herein lies the key to telling you exactly who they are. Think with me for a moment. This reference of olive trees does not appear anywhere else in The Revelation. Nor is anyone anywhere in the Bible referred to as an olive tree. But it is not a hard riddle for a person of Jewish background. What do you get from olive trees? Olives. If you live in ancient Palestine or Rome, what do you get from olives, other than only eating them? You get olive oil. Now, for what two uses is olive oil most employed in ancient Palestine, or Rome. There are two different answers, depending on whether you are talking about the Empire or the Kingdom. In the Empire, olive oil is used in lamps to bring *light*. Notice the Johannine theme. In the Kingdom, olive oil was used for anointing. It symbolized the presence of God as it was poured over a person's head and allowed to run down through their beard. (Psalm 133, for example) It was fragrant and nourishing.

The reference to a lampstand is much more immediate to the Book of Revelation. We saw them right away in Chapter 1:12-13. Their meaning was definitive, and it has not changed. What did they stand for? They represented the churches to whom the letter was written. Now, you have the tools to understand who the two witnesses are. I know, many scholars have said they are Moses and Elijah, or Moses and Enoch, or Moses and Jesus, or Jesus and John, or James and John. But you and I promised to stay inside the witness of this letter. You are sitting in your meeting room, and the leader of your church is reading this letter. The only references you have are this letter and the Jewish background from which your church was born.

To my mind, it is evident that the two witnesses are the Church and the Word of God. Look how deeply this symbolism runs: they are both lampstands. They are light. In Isaiah 49, God calls his people a "light to the gentiles." In Matthew 5:14, Jesus says to his disciples,

"You are the light of the world."

The Word of God is a light, as well. Psalm 19:105 says,

"Your Word is a lantern to my feet and a light on my path."

No other two things in scripture are so clearly called light.

Olive oil is for anointing. In 1 John 2:20, the Apostle says of the church,

"But you are anointed by the Holy One, and you all know the truth."

Scripture repeatedly shows God's Word as anointed, such as in Jeremiah 23:9, where the prophet says he feels like his heart is broken and his bones are shaky and weak because of the anointed words of God he must speak as a prophet of God.

These two things are anointing and light: God's Word and Christ's Church. You cannot kill the Word. Neither can you kill the Church. Earthly rulers have tried to kill both. Those rulers are long dead. Empires have tried to end both. They have fallen. Every influence that has ever made war with the Word and the

Church has been destroyed. Who has the power to shut up the skies so that no rain falls? God's Word and God's people are the only ones with access to such power. Only God can control the rain, but God's people can call on Him and, by His authority, shut up heaven. Elijah did in 1 Kings 17:1. Who has the power to bring plagues on the world? God's Word and God's people have access to such power. He has brought them himself, and He has brought them through His people, like Moses in Exodus 7 through Exodus 11. But the Church and the Word are not immune from attack.

Now you get a bit of a preview of what lies ahead. To this point in The Revelation, all that has come up out of the Abyss are the locusts. But there is going to come up, out of that horrible place, a beast. Remember that the Abyss is a spiritual place. If the Abyss is symbolic, then so is the beast that comes out of it. If the beast is a symbol for a spiritual force, then so must be the two witnesses. We make trouble for ourselves in interpreting this book when we try to mix the symbolic with some literal person or thing. That is why trying to interpret the two witnesses as literal historical figures breaks down. There are no two who were ever attacked by the world, murdered in the public square, and resurrected. But here, the beast from the Abyss – that is Satan – the one who was, then was not, but then will come back, attacks the witnesses, and appears to murder them.

Remember the idea of the "event curve?" It is the depiction of God's Word as a straight line through history. In contrast, history is a waveform that intersects the Word at different times. How many times in history has an Empire tried to squash the Church and the Word? The Roman Empire attacked Christians on multiple occasions. The Soviet Union attempted to outlaw the

Church and God's Word, so did the Communist regime in China. Modern culture continually tries to put an end to both by portraying them as unpopular or outdated. In 1882, German Philosopher Friedrich Nietzsche proclaimed, "God is dead." But God thought differently. My own culture has repeatedly tried to define itself as "post-Christian," yet God and the Church are still here. I only know my own lifetime and experience. To me, it seems like God and His Church have never been under such vicious attack as they are today. But then, I am fairly sure that the Christians in those tiny churches in The Revelation would have said the same. I am just as sure that Russian Christians in 1919, under the cleansing pogroms of the Bolsheviks, would have said the same.

You see, this is not simply a one-time event. The three-and-a-half years symbolize an imperfect time, but not a single instance. In each imperfect cycle, Empires have attacked the Kingdom to wipe it off the face of the Earth. Over and over, one Empire after another has gloated. The text refers to the great city as Sodom, Egypt, and Jerusalem – but says that this is what they were called "prophetically." Yet, when John writes these things, Sodom, the Egyptian Empire, and even Jerusalem no longer exist. These names are code for Rome. Remember, John uses apocalyptic symbolism to protect the Christians to whom he writes. His letter might fall into the hands of the Roman Empire and invite persecution on his friends. Here, the code is for Rome, in particular. Yet, it also serves as a reference to any Empire where the Church and the Word have ever been and ever will be attacked.

In Sodom, the people chose sexual immorality over God. In Egypt, Pharaoh chose slavery over God's people. In Jerusalem, the crowd chose crucifixion over God's Son. In Rome, they chose to worship the Emperor over worshiping God and Christ. Empires have repeatedly believed they have silenced the witness of Christ. They have gloated at silencing it and celebrated that the Christian witness will no longer be present to preach against the sinfulness of the Empire. Yet, every single time, the witnesses have been resurrected! Every time the Church seems to be ended. it is only for an imperfect interval of time. The demise is never complete. The Spirit breathes resurrection life into His Word and His Church, and they rise again. Not only do they come back to earthly life, but they exhibit ascended power that lifts them to Heaven in the eyes of the world.

The response of the world is fear and awe, for the world has no such power from any source. Creation reacts to the power of God at work in His Word and His Church. There is a mighty earthquake – because God commands the elements, not Baal, not Mammon, not Satan. Unlike the unrepentant people when the plagues struck Egypt or those who endured the sounding of the sixth trumpet, the survivors of the earthquake who witnessed the power of God's Word and His Church praised and glorified God. The true agents of repentance in this world are only two – God's Word and God's Church. You have more power than you know.

HOW MIGHT WE SHARE THIS?

Each time I teach or preach this section, I use a very similar outline:

I.   What You Measure, You Define and Protect

II. The Two Witnesses – The Word and The Church

III. The Indestructible Witnesses – The True Power in This World

QUESTIONS FOR FURTHER STUDY OR REFLECTION

1. Why do you think John does not give us the measurements of the Temple, nor the headcount of the believers? Does it matter?

2. What other symbolisms might make sense for the two witnesses?

3. How would you describe the witness of God's Word in this world?

4. How would you describe the witness of God's Church in this world?

5. How many cultures can you think of, or research and find, that have tried to stop the witness of the church in the world?

6. Why do you believe, if you do, that the witness of the Word and the Church are indestructible?

CHAPTER TWENTY-THREE

THE SEVENTH TRUMPET OF WRATH
THE TIME HAS COME

Revelation 12:15-19

THE TEXT:

"*¹¹:¹⁵Then the seventh angel sounded his trumpet, and there were loud voices in heaven, saying: 'The kingdom of the world has become the Kingdom of our Lord and of His Messiah, and He will reign forever and ever.'*

¹⁶The twenty-four elders who were seated before God on their thrones fell on their faces and worshiped God, ¹⁷saying:

'We thank you, Lord God Almighty,
who was and who is, because You
have exercised Your great power
and have instituted your reign.

¹⁸The nations are enraged, and Your
wrath has been poured out on them.

> *Now the time has come for judging the*
> *dead, and for rewarding Your servants*
> *the prophets and Your people who*
> *revered Your name, both the famous*
> *and the common – and for the destruc-*
> *tion of those who destroy the Earth.'*

> *[19]Then God's Temple in Heaven was opened, and*
> *within His Temple could be seen the ark of His*
> *covenant. Then there came flashes of lightning,*
> *and rumblings, crashes of thunder, an earthquake,*
> *and a torrential hailstorm." Rev 12:15-19*

WHAT IS THE TEXT SAYING TO US?

After two interludes, the seventh angel sounds his trumpet. The expectation was that it would bring "Woe," but it does not. It brings a proclamation, worship in Heaven, and confirmation of the place of God's residence in Heaven. After the horror of the fifth and sixth trumpets, the break is welcome. Since the sixth trumpet sounded, we have seen the mighty angel bring the tiny scroll to John to ingest, the measuring of the temple, and the revealing of the two witnesses and their murder and resurrection. You may have almost forgotten that there was yet one more trumpet to sound, but here it is. After the account of the two witnesses, the seventh trumpet may tend to feel a bit anticlimactic. Still, it gives us essential insight into God's place and presence before we are thrown back into some extraordinary events in John's vision.

After the trumpet sounds, John hears loud voices. They are exclaiming in chorus. God has conquered. What was previously the worldly kingdom (Empire) has become the Godly Kingdom. All of creation has been reunited under God's rule. This is the answer to Christ's prayer, the one we call "The Lord's Prayer:" It states,

> *"May Your Kingdom come to Earth, May Your will be done, on Earth in the same way it is in Heaven." Mat 6:10*

The original design of creation was a perfect place under the supervision and protection of a perfect God. Sin disrupted that created order. When the man and woman sinned against God, they created a separation between themselves and God. When Cain sinned and murdered Abel, his sin caused him to be further cast away from God's presence, and greater separation resulted. Each successive sin created an even greater separation. Generation by generation, person by person, sin by sin humankind grew exponentially further from God. When the wickedness was so pervasive that the Bible says the thoughts of humankind were "only evil, all the time," God decided to wipe out creation with a flood: but he spared Noah and his family and a remnant of all of creation. God, in effect, started completely over with a new "Adam." Then, what was the first thing Noah did after the Ark landed on dry ground? He got hammered and passed out naked. I can just imagine God rolling His eyes and shaking His head. You and I are meant to understand that nothing had changed. Wickedness would come roaring right back. Within just two chapters in the

Book of Genesis – from Genesis 9 when the Ark lands to Genesis 11 – God's created people are building a tower in an attempt to storm Heaven. More eye-rolling and head-shaking on the part of God, as He scrambles their languages and scatters them across the Earth so that they cannot so easily plot against Him.

But here, in the closing verses of Revelation 12, creation returns to the way it should be, once again, unified under God's Lordship. To those who are Christian, depending on the traditions in which you were raised, this might be an odd thought. Has God not always been in charge? Has He not always been Lord? You are asking exactly the right question. From a Jewish perspective, the answer is "no." Sin caused separation and the loss of the relationship between God and humanity. If there is no relationship, there cannot be a covenant. Without a covenant, there can be no lordship, except by force; and God created people for fellowship, not force.

That does not mean the story is over. The elders fall on their faces and worship – it is what they do. In their worship, they proclaim that God has exercised His right to reign. The nations rose up in anger, and God's wrath was poured out on them. Now comes the time for the judgment of all humankind. The elders affirm that there are rewards for the prophets and the faithful followers of God and destruction for the finally disobedient. Does that mean it is over? No. There is still nearly half of the Book of Revelation to come, but this small interlude sets the stage for what is to come. The rest of the book is going to be dedicated to explaining where the power behind evil comes from, how it has behaved, the results it causes, and how it will be ended on Earth.

The most important part of this small defining point in the

vision is the final few verses. While this entire textual unit has involved John seeing what is happening in Heaven, the first sentence of verse 19 is the single most important phrase in this section. Heaven is opened. That is a very interesting reminder that, while John is seeing what is going on in the throne room of Heaven, he does not see all of Heaven. The reference here is a Tabernacle or Temple reference. In Exodus 26:33, God gives Moses instructions for building the wilderness Tabernacle, which will be the traveling home of God's presence as the Israelites move from slavery in Egypt to residence in the Promised Land that will become Israel. In the deepest part of the tent is a room, separated by a heavy woven curtain. In that fifteen cubic foot space is only one thing – the Ark of the Covenant. The Ark of the Covenant is not Noah's ark. It was a chest, gilded in gold. It held a few iconic items from the desert journey, and it was the container for the presence of God. One person was allowed to enter this holiest of holy places, and he could only enter once per year to do penance for the sins of all of God's people. When the Israelites settled in Jerusalem and built a permanent Temple for God, the Holiest of Holies was situated on the far western end of the Temple. So holy was the place, that when the High Priest went in on his annual mission, legend tells us that they affixed bells to the hem of his robe and tied a rope around his ankle. That way, if God struck him dead, they could hear the bells as he hit the floor and pull him out without having to desecrate the space by sending someone else inside. If you think about it, that likely means just such a thing happened at least once!

This glimpse into the Holiest of Holies in Heaven is remarkable. This vision makes it clear that the instructions for the Holiest of Holies on Earth were an exact replication of the holiest place in Heaven. God does not merely have a throne in Heaven; He has a home. His covenant with His people is not only an Earthly covenant, but it has its home in the center of Heaven. The Ark is referred to as the "Ark of the Covenant" because God's presence is a constant reminder that He lives among His people in fulfillment of a promise He made to Abraham in Genesis 17 (a verse or two after God had changed his name from Abram):

> *"And I will establish a covenant between you and me, and your descendants throughout every generation: an eternal covenant, to be God to you and to every generation after you." Gen 17:7*

The message is clear: God is the power at the center of everything John sees happening in this vision. Behind it all is this covenant relationship in which God will be the God of all who will be His people. While God will not force anyone to follow Him or believe in Him, He will be God for every generation and every person who will live in covenant with Him. What are the bounds of that covenant? In the Old Testament, it was keeping the Law of Moses. In the New Testament, the covenant moved from the Law to grace. Sin had continually and increasingly separated people from God. If there was to be a remedy, God would have to provide it because people could not. God knew it would be this way, so He made that covenant with Abram in Genesis Chapter 15. God told Abram that he would become a nation and have offspring more numerous than the stars. Abram asked how he could know that God was sincere.

In Genesis 15:9-20, we find the account of God's sealing

promise to Abram. God invites Abram into what scholars call a Suzerainty Treaty. In the typical treaty ceremony, two landowners would cut animals into halves and lay them out to define a pathway or virtual bridge between their properties. Each would stand on the other's property, and one would take a smoking firepot and walk between the halves of sacrificed animals onto his own property. As he walked, he would say something like, "If ever I violate this treaty, may what has been done to these animals be done to me."

Then, he would hand the smoking pot to his neighbor, who would pass over onto his own property, waving the fire pot and repeating the same promise. But in Genesis 15, God has Moses cut up the animals – a heifer, a nanny goat, a ram, a turtledove, and a pigeon. He lays them out to create the lane through which they will walk. Then, Abram lays down and falls asleep. When he awakens, he sees the smoking firepot passing through the halves of sacrificed animals. God is taking his part of the covenant. God's part would have sounded like the above recitation: "If ever I break the bonds of this covenant, may what has been done to these animals, be done to me."

But then, something remarkable happens. The firepot passes back the other direction. God is taking Abram's part of the covenant on Himself! The implied recitation would sound something like, "If ever you break the bond of this covenant, may what has been done to these animals, be done to ME!" Wait, that is not how this is supposed to go. Abram must have some responsibility, mustn't he? No. God knew Abram and his descendants would fail. God had already experienced generations of separation from His creation on account of their sin. So, in just the fifteenth chapter of the Bible, God extends grace to every person who will ever descend from Abram on the face of the Earth. That includes you and me.

When humankind had murdered and stolen and worshiped idols and forsaken every promise they had ever made to God and each other – when people were completely without hope of ever being redeemable to God – He sent Jesus Christ. In this Old Testament sense then, Jesus Christ takes the responsibility of Abram's (and our) half of the treaty. God fulfills His promise to bear both sides and allows Jesus to uphold the treaty and to be slaughtered on the cross, as an animal led to the sacrifice. That is how much God loves you. Amidst an Empire that battles other Empires, in the middle of a life experience that threatens to steal your peace every time the news comes on, God wants to assure you that your debt is paid. The covenant is still in place. Christ paid the price God promised He would pay if you could not.

At the very center of Heaven is the place in which God resides forever. It is the center of authentic power. No matter what the world around you throws at you – sickness, death, grief, depression, loss – you are connected to the source of eternal creative power. The Holiest of Holies has not moved. It will not change. The constant and preserving power of God emanates in a continual stream from the heart of Heaven on your behalf. You have nothing to fear...not one thing.

HOW MIGHT WE SHARE THIS?

I.   The Seventh Trumpet Sounds – But No Wrath Comes

II. God Switches the Power On and Takes Charge

III. We Get a View Inside the Holiest Place in Heaven

QUESTIONS FOR FURTHER STUDY OR REFLECTION

1. Why do you think there is no wrath released with the sounding of the last trumpet?

2. What do you think it means that, "The Kingdom of the Lord and His Christ has come?"

3. Is this the announcement of the final judgment?

4. Is this the "last trumpet" mentioned in 1 Corinthians 15:52?

5. Why is there no mention of any fear when the very heart of Heaven is revealed?

CHAPTER TWENTY-FOUR

THE WOMAN, THE BABY, AND THE DRAGON
YES, VIRGINIA, THERE IS A DRAGON IN THE BIBLE

Revelation 12:1-17

THE TEXT:

"12:1A great omen then appeared in the heavens, a woman clothed with the sun; the moon was under her feet, and on her head was a crown of twelve stars. 2She was pregnant and cried out in the pain of labor, in the moment of childbirth. 3Then another great omen appeared in the heavens. And behold, a great red dragon with seven heads and ten horns and seven crowns upon his heads. 4His tail swept down a third of the stars of Heaven and cast them down to the Earth.

Now the dragon stood before the woman who was about to give birth, so that when she gave birth, he might swallow her child. 5Then she bore a son, a male child, who will shepherd all the nations with an iron staff. But her child was caught up to God and to his throne. 6The woman then fled into the wilderness where a place had been prepared for her by God, that she might be protected for 1,260 days.

[7]There was a battle in Heaven. Michael and his angels fought with the Dragon. The Dragon and his angels fought back [8]but were defeated, as a result, there was no longer any place for them in Heaven. [9]Then the great Dragon was thrown down, the ancient serpent, who is called Devil and Satan, who leads the whole world astray; he was thrown down to the earth, and his angels were thrown down along with him.

[10]Then I heard a loud voice in heaven saying: 'The victory and the power and the kingship of our God and the authority of His Messiah have now begun, because the accuser of our brothers and sisters was thrown out, the one who accused them before our God day and night.

[11]They overcame him through the blood of the Lamb and through the word of their testimony, for they did not love their lives to the point of death. [12]Therefore rejoice, O heaven, and those who dwell in Heaven. Woe to the earth and the sea, because the Devil, who is very angry, was thrown down to you, because he knows that he has only a short time.'

¹³And when the Dragon realized that he had been thrown down to the Earth, he hunted the woman who had delivered the male child. ¹⁴Then the woman was provided with the two wings like those of a large eagle that she might fly to her sanctuary in the wilderness where she will be taken care of for a time, times, and half a time from the presence of the Dragon. ¹⁵Then the Dragon spewed water like a river from his mouth in the direction of the woman that he might wash her away. ¹⁶Yet the Earth helped the woman, and opened its mouth and swallowed the river of water which the Dragon spewed out of his mouth. ¹⁷And the Dragon was angry because of the woman and left to wage war with the rest of her children who kept the commandments of God and maintained their witness to Jesus." Rev 12:1-17

WHAT IS THE TEXT SAYING TO US?

With the account of the two witnesses, you may have noticed a shift in the symbolism in The Revelation. Beginning with that account, the symbolism gains depth and breadth. Where before the account of the two witnesses, the vision had moved fluidly between Heaven and Earth and the literal and figurative, with the two witnesses, the text moved into a much more consistently symbolic voice. In Chapter 12, the narrative moves to an exclusively symbolic perspective. It does not return again to any significant expression of literal historical imagery. This shift is confusing if the reader does not keep their eyes on the symbols that are fairly easy to interpret. If we take our eyes off of the straightforward pieces, then all of the symbols begin to make less sense. You can easily see that this happens to even the best of scholars by simply reading a few sources with ideas on who the woman, the child, and the dragon of Revelation 12 might be. This is the point at which most casual readers tend to give up. Stick with it. The possibilities are incredibly diverse, but the rewards are tremendous.

Please allow me to share a quick perspective that I gained on the Bible in the earliest days of preparing for the ministry. I was called into ministry out of the world of public-school education. I was a music teacher. I had no formal religious training, no background in the Bible or theology. I was a relatively new Christian, and everything in the Bible was new and fascinating to me. My friend group consisted primarily of committed Christian business and church people. These friends also had no formal religious or theological training, but who had hearts deeply devoted to God. We would often sit around a table in one of my friends' businesses and "study" the Bible together. The endeavor we most enjoyed was speculating on what some phrase or image from the Bible might mean. We would often ask each other, "Well, do you think this *could* mean…?"

When God called me to ministry, I understood that calling came with a deep need to go back to school and improve my religious, theological, and practical ministry training. I resigned from my teaching job and enrolled in a nearby private liberal arts Christian university. I felt called to earn a master's degree and fulfill the requirements for ordination in the denomination in which I was serving. On the very first day, I had a class at 7 AM entitled "The Minor Prophets." A brand-new Ph.D. in the Old Testament taught the course. He had worked hard to earn his doctoral degree and seemed determined that we would be working just as hard! He wasted no time in throwing us into the deep end of the prophetic pool. We started that morning, in the Book of Hosea. We had not gone far before I felt inspired to interrupt to inquire about the meaning of one of the passages the professor had just read.

"Do you think that might mean_____?" Whatever I asked, I thought it might be a brilliant insight. But the professor explained to me that my idea, while fanciful, was not at all what Hosea was saying. He read on.

In a few more verses, I was once again inspired. My hand shot up. "Dr., might this passage be speaking about_____?" I was sure that, this time, I had landed on a particularly meaningful insight. The professor put down his Hebrew text. He looked at me for a long furtive moment. Then, he said, "Mr. Hopkins, these verses – in fact, any verses anywhere in the entire Bible – *might* mean just about anything. Our pursuit in Biblical scholarship is not to discuss what any verse *might* mean, but to attempt, through responsible scholarship, to determine what it actually *does* mean."

The other students, many who have gone on to become life-long friends, snickered at me that day. It was not that they might not have asked the exact same question, only that I had asked it and been the one who got the gentle chastisement of the professor. But, that day, I remember my simple approach to wondering what the scripture might mean became a thirst to find out what it meant to those to whom it was first spoken or written.

With Revelation 12, we are entering a world where the symbols might mean many things. Indeed, a quick review will show you that many theories and ideas exist of what might be portrayed in this chapter and the following chapters. Some have considerable historical credibility; others are as wacky as ideas can possibly be. As I have up to this point, I will share with you my opinion on what John sees and what it means to us today. Of course, I could be absolutely wrong. Again, I affirm that I am your servant and that my perspective is always subject to whatever confirmation or denial my thoughts have within your heart and mind. Hopefully, your spirit will resonate with what I bring forward - at least to the end that you find something useful in my thoughts.

The two great omens, or constellations, that John sees here are the woman and the dragon. The word used to describe them can be rendered "signs, omens, or constellations." I have chosen to use the reference to them as omens because I believe that is consistent with the core word meaning here. But, by calling them by this name – which could mean "constellations" – John is making it very clear to you and me that these figures are as big as the sky in symbolism. They are not simple historical figures, but larger-than-life protagonist and antagonist in this story. Do not lose sight of their immensity.

The woman is wrapped in light, walks on the moon, and wears a crown of 12 stars on her head. This is not nearly as hard as many scholars make it out to be. I believe the woman is Israel. She was meant to be a "light to the Gentiles." (Isaiah 42:6, 49:6, 52:10, 60:3, etc.) Being clothed in the sun is a reference to the fact that she was intended to be God's light to the world. She walks, travels, on the moon. The Jewish calendar months are based on the lunar cycles. Israel literally travels through the year on the cycles of the moon! The stars in her crown are the 12 tribes of Israel. When we meet her in this account, she is at the moment of giving birth to a baby boy.

The other great omen is a dragon. He has seven heads, ten horns, and seven crowns. Now, try to draw that thing on paper and figure out how many horns go on each head! Some will have one horn; some will have two. What in the world can this dragon be? We know from the text in verse 9 that this dragon is Satan, the Devil. So, why does he have seven heads, ten horns, and seven crowns? Let's break the symbols down:

As we have mentioned along the way, seven is the number of completion or wholeness. Seven heads indicate that the Dragon is entirely evil. He never sleeps. There is nothing he does not see or hear. He is formidable and terrible in his entirely evil form. Horns are the symbol of power throughout the Bible. The fact that the dragon has more horns than heads to put them on is a device to show how over-powering he is. Anyone who is foolish enough to take him on in a power-against-power battle is most likely to lose. His power is even greater than even his thinking or perceiving powers. He has a crown on each head. This serves to show that he has dominion and kingship, at least over the kingdoms he controls. He has, at the least, the appearance of authority. He will use his power and influence to create the illusion that he has dominion. God has not granted any authority to him. He is frightening and terrible, but remember, he is a false power.

The dragon assumes an aggressive stance in front of the woman. Apparently, he is not able to harm her, or he would. He waits for her to give birth so that he can devour her child – presumably to keep the child from doing whatever it is being delivered to do. The child is born, the Devil lunges, but misses! At this point, I want you to keep in mind that the woman and the dragon are heavenly representations – omens or constellations. They represent spiritual forces on the Earth, not literal persons. Some have taught that the woman is Mary, the mother of Jesus. She is not. Some have taught that the baby was Jesus Christ; it is not. Neither of the omens is given the recognition in the text that Mary or Jesus would receive. Who are they? We have already discussed that the woman is Israel. The baby is the Christian Church.

From where did Christianity come? It came from Judaism. Jesus was never a Christian. He lived and died as a Jew. His disciples were Jews before they became leaders of the fledgling Christian Church in the New Testament. John, who writes The Revelation, grew up a Jew and was called by his Rabbi, Jesus, as a Jew. It is likely that every one of these churches to whom John writes his Revelation was born out of Jewish synagogues in their community. The leaders in each of them were, most likely, converted Jews. We know this is true of Ephesus, where Paul taught in the synagogue until the Jews kicked him out. We know he attracted and converted many Jews in Ephesus to be Christians. It seems highly likely that the same pattern would repeat itself in cities across the Roman Empire. Judaism was the mother of Christianity. We continue to include their scriptures with ours: The Old Testament Jewish scriptures and the New Testament Christian Scripture. God did not snatch Jesus up as soon as he was born to protect him from the enemy, but He has protected the Church from the Devil from the day it was born! Even though it might not always seem that you live in a protective relationship with the Father, you most certainly do.

I was recently discussing the fact that there is no doubt in my mind that I have experienced divine protection from harm at different times in my life. There are clear instances where I heard about some calamity. When I thought about the timeline and location of that calamity, I realized I had been delayed by some odd distraction just long enough to not be in that place at that time. Because I know from experience that this is true, I am aware that there must have been times in which the same kind of dangers were headed my direction, and God stopped them. I suppose we will not know of these instances until we stand in Heaven and can see all of time and space as if it all happened at the same moment. But I tell you, as surely as I know anything in this life, I know that God has protected you and me. Will He always? I do not believe so.

There is an old story once told to me by a history teacher. It involves a general in the civil war. As the story goes, the general was involved in a fierce battle, yet remained atop his horse. At one point in this battle, the general's adjutant begged him to come down off of his horse in the face of withering enemy fire. "Sir," the general is said to have responded, "I serve the one true living God. Until my time in His service is completed, I consider myself to be invincible. And when that time shall come, no power in Heaven nor on Earth can keep me from answering His call to the next life." Now, the story may be legend or myth; but it defines my attitude to God's keeping grace perfectly. Until the moment God calls me home, this world cannot harm me. In the moment God calls me heavenward, no force in creation can stop me from going.

I believe my interpretation of this account is supported by the time for which John is told that the woman will be protected from the dragon. It is a familiar timeframe for us: 1,260 days. That is 42 months or three-and-one-half years. Again, it is that season – that imperfect period of time – not indefinitely. You will see in the next couple of paragraphs why Israel would need God's protection from the dragon. The child has escaped into the presence of God, and the woman has been sheltered in the wilderness. The Devil is about to come to his first judgment.

The scene remains in Heaven, but abruptly we are told that there was once a battle in Heaven. Be aware that this battle account does not have to chronologically follow the previous account. This is a spiritual accounting for what happened to make the Devil what he is. This is a theological account, not a historical account. We are told that the battle involved the Devil and his angels. They are the one-third of stars that his tail swept from Heaven in verse 4. They fight the archangel Michael and his angels. The Devil has the smaller force and is overcome. Because of their rebellion, they cannot be allowed to stay in Heaven with God, and so there is separation. The Devil and his followers are hurled out of Heaven onto the Earth. Then John hears a voice in Heaven proclaiming the Devil's defeat and more.

The voice proclaims that all power and Kingship now belongs solely to God because the Devil and his followers are gone from God's presence. The one who accused the brothers in front of God is gone. This is a clear connection to the idea that Satan lived in God's presence. You can find this Old Testament thought clearly portrayed in the story of Job, found in the Book of Job. Twice, the Devil is shown as happening through God's throne room. Twice,

God asks him about the faithfulness of Job; and twice the Devil asks permission to hurt Job in increasing increments. God allows the testing both times. The story of Job is a story that I may, well, one day write another book over. Suffice it to say for now that you should read the Book of Job bearing in mind the entire time that it was the Devil who struck Job, not God. Here, I only cite the story to show you how the character of the Devil was thought of in ancient Jewish times. After God casts him to the Earth, the Devil can no longer accuse you and me in God's presence.

Look at verse 11: "They overcame him through the blood of the Lamb, and the word of their testimony" – the Church and the Word. Who is defined by the blood of the Lamb? His Church is made up entirely of those who have been "washed in the blood of the Lamb." The Lamb's shed blood was the price of the Suzerainty Treaty. The blood defined the new covenant under which the Church would live in God's grace. Because of their identity as God's people, they fight using God's Word. Their testimony is not simply their account of the things that have happened to them, but it is the fact that their faith and trust and mission in God's Kingdom are all based on His Word. That is how the Devil is overcome, then, now, and forever. The Church and the Word are the overcoming power of God at work in Heaven and on Earth.

Oh, yes – Earth. In the next verse, the angel cries out a word of woe upon the inhabitants of the Earth because the angry Devil has been thrown down onto Earth. But, the key to his defeat has been defined. He is defeated by the Blood of the Lamb and the Word of God's testimony in the lives of His Church. The Devil seems to be temporarily knocked-out, for he comes to his senses and realizes he has been hurled to Earth.

Realizing that he cannot get to her child, who has been taken into God's presence, the Devil goes hunting for the child's mother – Israel. What in the world does this mean? I believe it is God's way of showing John an explanation for the fall of Jerusalem to the Roman Empire in 70 AD. Only about 25 years before John's vision, the Romans had grown tired of the Jews' obstinance and of trying to manage them in Palestine, at such a distance from Rome. The Jews had mounted a rebellion against Rome. In response, Roman legions under the command of Titus, who would eventually become Emperor, attacked and conquered the city. To squash the rebellion for all time, the Romans demolished the city. They dispersed the Jews throughout the Roman Empire – an event we call the *diaspora*.

But the Jews survived. They were taken from their Holy City out into the…wilderness, as it were. They were removed to cities and towns where they were strangers. They were forced to start over. Yet, they held their faith and continued to worship God. They built synagogues and schools, where the fledgling Church would find fertile ground to sprout. The eagle's wings are God's way to describe how the Jews flew into the wilderness, to all of the places into which they were scattered, but alive. The vision then says that the Devil was not happy. Israel remained alive. He spewed out a flood of water to try and overtake her because he was unable to reach her directly. This is a reference back to the chaos that ruled creation, about which we have already spoken in Chapters 20 and 22. The dragon's last resort at harming the woman is to spew chaos at her to cause some destruction of the created order. But he fails. Acting to maintain creation, the Earth itself opens up and swallows the water and protects the woman from the Devil's scheme. Having failed to injure the spiritual foundations of Israel, and being unable to touch her child, the Church, the angry Devil resigns himself to trying to reach her children on the Earth. He will do battle against those who keep the commandments of God and hold to the testimony of Christ. He is coming for the Church, for you and me. Remember that the angel cried woe over us? We are about to see why.

HOW MIGHT WE SHARE THIS?

I would propose an outline something like:

I.   The Woman, the Baby, and the Dragon

II. The Dragon is Defeated in Heaven

III. The Dragon is Foiled at Taking Out Jews or Christians

QUESTIONS FOR FURTHER STUDY OR REFLECTION
(THE SKY IS THE LIMIT HERE!)

1.   Why does John call the woman and the dragon "constellations?"

2.   Does it make sense to you that the woman is Israel? Can you build a case that she represents something or someone else?

3. The text tells us that the dragon is the Devil. How do you typically think of the Devil?

4. Does it make sense to you that the child is the Church? Can you build a case that he represents something, or someone, else?

5. Who is Michael? Is he the only archangel described in scripture?

6. What does it mean if the Devil and his followers are on Earth?

7. How does this story make you feel about your place in the Church, in God's plan, or in the world?

8. Describe a time when you are aware that you were protected from harm.

CHAPTER TWENTY-FIVE

THE FIRST BEAST
THE DECEPTION OF THE PEOPLE OF EARTH

Revelation 12:18-13:10

THE TEXT:

"*¹²:¹⁸Then the Dragon stood on the edge of the sea. ¹³:¹I saw a beast rising up out of the sea, with ten horns and seven heads, and on its horns were ten crowns, and each head were blasphemous names. ²The beast which I saw was like a leopard, and its feet were like those of a bear, and its mouth was like that of a lion. The Dragon gave him his power and his throne and great authority. ³One of the heads of the beast appeared to have been fatally wounded, but the mortal wound had been healed. The whole Earth was astonished and followed the beast. ⁴They worshiped the Dragon because he gave authority to the beast, and they worshiped the beast as well, chanting, 'Who is like the beast, and who is able to war against it?'*

⁵The beast was given haughty and blasphemous things to say, and it was given the authority to be active for forty-two months. ⁶It uttered blasphemies against God, it blasphemed His name and His abode, and it blasphemed all those who live in Heaven. ⁷And it was permitted to make war against God's people and conquer them, and it was given authority over every tribe and race and language and nation. ⁸All the inhabitants of the earth will worship him, everyone whose name was not written since the creation of the world in the Lamb's Book of Life, that is the Lamb who was slaughtered.

⁹If anyone has an ear, let him hear:

¹⁰If anyone is to go into captivity, into captivity he will go; If anyone is to die by the sword, with the sword he will be slain. This will require great endurance and faith on the part of God's people."
Rev 12:18-13:10

WHAT IS THE TEXT SAYING TO US?

Unable to exercise any authority in the spiritual realm and, having been thrown out of Heaven and onto the Earth, the Dragon looks for ways to cause harm to the believers still living on the Earth. Remember, the Dragon is a spiritual omen – a constellation – while he has been flung down to make his residency on Earth, he has no earthly form or substance. He is only a spirit. If he is going to make mischief on the Earth, he will need some sort of physical representation. John sees the Dragon, standing on the shore of the sea, raising up an earthly reflection of himself. Look at how closely it parallels him in appearance. It has the same seven heads, the same overabundance of horns (more strength than brains), rather than seven crowns on its heads, it has ten crowns on its horns. The subtle difference is significant. Its followers will reign simply by power, not by wisdom or reason. On each head is displayed some blasphemous name.

This beast is likely an earthly portrayal of the beast suddenly introduced in Chapter 11. In that chapter, he came up "out of the Abyss." You will notice that no beast described in the rest of The Revelation comes up "out of the Abyss." This first beast rises up, however, out of the sea. The ancients considered the sea to be bottomless. They believed it harbored all manner of horrible monsters in its depths. One such creature is what the Old Testament refers to as the "leviathan." While the leviathan is mentioned several times in the Old Testament, I think the most significant is Isaiah 27:1:

> *"On that day, the Lord with His sharp, strong, and giant sword will punish the fleeing serpent, Leviathan the twisting serpent, and He will kill the dragon from the sea."*

Jewish folks in the churches to which John addresses his Revelation would be well-aware of this passage from Isaiah. They would immediately make the connection between this first beast and Leviathan – the twisting sea monster. You and I should connect him to the beast in 11:7 and understand that the sea and Abyss might well be the same. John then gives his readers, including you and me, greater detail and insight into exactly how this beast will show himself in our world.

I believe the beast represents "Empire," as perpetually opposed to "Kingdom." Specifically, I think this beast represents the Roman Empire. The seven heads do not represent different emperors – there is no way to make that count work. Remember, seven represents an entirety…a completion. The beast represents the Empire, Roman or otherwise, in all of its evil. The horns bear crowns – both horns and crowns are symbols of power. The Empire always seems more immediately powerful than the Kingdom. The Empire imposes taxes, regulations, laws, penalties. The Empire can kick down the door of your home and carry you off into incarceration. The Empire can tell you what you can say or not, what you can print or not. The Empire can even dictate what or who you are allowed to worship! The Kingdom allows you freedom and latitude. The Kingdom does not dictate your life to you, nor tax you, nor tell you how you must worship. Because it gives you flexibility and autonomy, the Kingdom can seem weaker. It is not. Remember – the beast is a portrayal of power, but he is only an earthly image. He has no real power of his own.

On his heads are blasphemous names. I believe these are names from the Imperial Roman Cult: king, lord, majesty, grace, beauty, ruler, god, etc. It is imperative to bear in mind that the Empire is never truly the source of any power. Further, it is essential to remember that the Dragon behind the beast on Earth is also a defeated enemy – powerless. The only strategy left for them is to attempt to mimic real power. The titles are blasphemous because they claim for the beast the authentic power that only God possesses.

The description of the beast is a combination of the four beasts in Daniel 7. The purpose here is to show that this beast is the epitome of all earthly empires across time. This beast has the body of a leopard. Think about the leopard: they are exotic and beautiful – exquisite in appearance. They are sneaky and patient – they stalk their prey until they spring on it to kill it. They are cruel and ferocious – they grab their prey by the throat and use their rear claws to eviscerate it alive. They are amazingly swift and can overtake the fastest prey. By likening the beast to a leopard, the Bible gives it all of these attributes. The feet of a bear are large and powerful. The bear has long claws with which it slashes its enemies. It can move quickly but makes hardly any sound as it rambles through even the densest woods. The mouth of a lion is terrible and frightening. It not only crushes its prey in one biting motion, but it roars loudly and intimidatingly. In Daniel, it is widely accepted that the three beasts represented Greece (leopard), Persia (bear), and Babylon (lion). In Daniel 7, there is mention of one more character that does not appear in Revelation. It is a small horn that arises and takes over the three others. It may easily be interpreted to be Rome. Here, in Revelation, it is vital to remember that this beast is not meant to represent one dynasty, but the concept of the human "Empire" in any generation.

Now, we see the most terrifying part. The beast was given blasphemous things to say. These likely came from his spiritual mentor, the Dragon. The devotion to any Empire becomes the worship of the spiritual force behind it. Blasphemy is to utter those things that should belong to God in praise of anything, or anyone, else. The ultimate praise of any Empire is that it has become invincible. No one is as great as our Empire. No one could defeat us in a war.

The wounded head is a reference to the Roman Empire and Caesar Nero. In 69 AD, Nero was an adopted son of Claudius Caesar, his great uncle. As a result, Nero ascended to the throne in what many Romans saw as an illegitimate climb to power. His mother guided him until he had her put to death. He steeped himself in excess and presented himself as a master-of-all-trades being, at different times, a poet, an actor, a musician, or a charioteer. The political leaders in Rome felt that he was less than distinguished and harmed the esteem of the Emperor's office. Uprisings started within Rome; Nero fled and was tried *in absentia* and sentenced to death. Rather than return and face trial, he committed suicide. Civil war ensued as the Roman Empire crumbled, and differing factions fought for control. Ultimately, Vespasian prevailed and preserved the Roman Empire. The wound was healed, and the Empire resurrected.

What is it that astonishes the people of the Earth? Power is genuinely all that most people understand. Look at our current world: people look to political leaders, whom they hope can bring prosperity. People follow those who offer them greater autonomy or freedom. The world runs after the leaders who promise peace, an end to war and strife, and a better environment. As I write these words, there are even political leaders claiming that they can control the weather, if only people give them enough money. Politicians are vying for power and pandering for donations around nothing but hatred in my country right now. People follow them like sheep, motivated by hatred for "the other side" and hoping to grab power for their own causes. My own time, probably like any other time in history, is a dismal portrayal of exactly what John sees in this vision. The world runs after the Empire because it appears to have such great power over everything that hurts them.

The vision now reminds us that adoration quickly becomes worship. The pursuit of power that the Empire can afford us constitutes worship of the spiritual power behind it. I am sure you are aware that this kind of worship is, most often, totally unintentional. In fact, there are a great number of people in my own culture who believe that God is somehow behind the power of our Empire. They attribute any good thing that comes to our nation as "God's will." But our political machine can trample human rights, healing arts, and religious freedoms. Our leaders constantly make shady, even immoral decisions while people who support any side of any debate call on the name of God as affirming of the political machinations. In political campaigns, both sides of any issue call on God as the witness that they are the ones doing what is right. Still, God is not a God of division and chaos, but a God of unity. I fear that what many of my countrymen acclaim as God's clear guidance is, truly, the influence of the Dragon in all of our lives.

Then, it was given "authority," which only comes from God, to exercise its influence for – you got it – forty-two months (three-and-one-half years). For this season, the beast blasphemes all that is Godly – His Name, His Heaven, His people, even His very existence. It is allowed to make war against all of God's created people. Be careful not to think that this is only those who are devoted to God. The term here seems to take in people as an entire group. The beast gets to make war against everyone who does not have the mark of God on their lives. So overwhelming is his power that everyone on Earth who does not belong to God will worship him.

How many nations on Earth today claim to be "post-Christian?" In how many nations does the government claim to meet the needs of its citizens from the cradle to the grave? I even hear in my own country, things like, "Well, the governments of other countries provide_____ to their citizens! Why can't we?" Now, think for a moment, where does any power or service or provenance come from in any government? It comes from the people themselves. Nothing is free. If something is to be provided to citizens, they ultimately have to bear the cost of any such program. The power of Empire is the power of self-sufficiency and self-rule. What is the nature of sin? Self-promotion, self-aggrandizement, self-reliance – these are the nature of all sin because they deny our basic need for God. Thereby, they are, by their very nature, *blasphemy*.

Those with ears are not only encouraged to hear but to understand what happens anytime people depend on Empire over The Kingdom. It always turns out the same. Those who blindly follow political or governmental power are setting themselves up to be ruled by that same force. Because of the world's reverence and desire for power, people will follow the pursuit of Empire power until they are its captives. The pursuit of power can only lead one place – to being hostage to the things that provide that power. This is easily seen in the typical lifecycle of any politician in my own country.

In my lifetime, I have watched repeatedly as a man or woman with great intentions, and strong convictions ran for public office.

They wanted to "make a difference." They wanted to do great things to bring progress and help to the people they were asking to serve. Once elected, they face the reality of political power: you must play along with the power structure to get to where you might ever do anything for your constituency. Still wanting to do what was good for others, these politicians start to look for power swaps that can get them to where they believe they need to be. Votes on particular issues are traded for favors. Favors are traded for appointments to caucus leadership positions or committee chairmanships. Clout in our system accrues over time, so politicians prioritize those actions and trade-offs that keep them in office for more extended periods.

After a few years, that bright-eyed person who ran for office to make a difference has lost all sight of the reasons for which they ran for office. They become more a part of the problem than the solution. They answer, less and less, to their constituents and more to the national organization of power which they serve. Certainly, there are exceptions. But you can likely cite several more instances where the above scenario has played out as people pursue what they thought was the power to do good. The power of the Empire mimics the power of The Kingdom, but at its core, it has the purpose of accruing power, not using power for good. Ultimately, that power carries off all who pursue it into the captivity of pursuing power – a vicious cycle that it is nearly impossible from which to escape. If people pursue that power to the extreme – it costs them their lives. The old adage says, "Live by the sword, die by the sword." It is exactly that thought at issue here. The power of the Empire is the power of strength and influence. It is the power of the sword. The person who pursues that power takes the sword in order to exercise that power. By wielding that power against others, that person endangers themselves to the extent that they may well sacrifice their own life to living with the sword – until they die with it, or by it.

The wisdom with which we must read this section requires that we be patient and wise. Suffering will come to anyone who lives under an Empire. That Empire will make war on enemies it would have been wiser to have left alone. The Empire will institute taxes that will cost all of its people – Kingdom citizens included – great amounts of money or resources. The Empire will enact laws and regulations that will take resources away from all of its citizens, even Christians. The Empire will, without fail, pursue power based in everything except Kingdom priorities and wisdom. You will be dragged along for the ride. You will have to withstand the political wars between parties and sides as they compete for power and control. I am not saying that everything any government does is wicked, or that God cannot use governments to accomplish His purposes – the Bible clearly says He can and does. I believe that the trajectory of any Empire is, ultimately, always at odds with the priorities of the Kingdom. Be aware with which system of power you are connecting your life. Understand that, in the end, what you pursue with all your heart is that which you worship. Living your life in order to conserve your relationship and citizenry in the Kingdom might look socially liberal, even permissive, to the world around you. You may have to bear criticism from those who call themselves "Christians" but are yielding to control by the Empire. You will seldom, if ever, take the popular course when you stand up for the pursuit of Kingdom principles. Stand up anyway. If you do not, the beast will conquer everyone and everything.

HOW MIGHT WE SHARE THIS?

The text might seem to suggest an outline something like this:

I. What the Devil Can't Do in Heaven, He Will Try to Accomplish on Earth

II. False Power Always Mimics Authentic Power

III. Empire Rule versus Kingdom Rule – Where Do We See the Difference?

QUESTIONS FOR FURTHER STUDY OR REFLECTION

1. Why does this beast arise from the sea?

2. What does it mean if this beast is the combination of Babylon, Persia, and Greece?

3. What kind of powers do you see in your own culture that attract people to follow?

4. What detriments do you see in your own world as a result of people chasing power?

5. How might Christians combat or cope with the detriments of "power-chasing?"

CHAPTER TWENTY-SIX

THE SECOND BEAST

THE MARK OF THE BEAST

Revelation 13:11-18

THE TEXT:

"*12:11Then I saw another beast rising from the Earth, and it had two horns like a ram, but it spoke like a dragon. 12It exercised the full authority of the first beast, on its behalf, and compelled the earth, that is, those who dwell on it, to worship the first beast, whose mortal wound was healed. 13It performed impressive miracles, even causing fire to fall from the heavens to the Earth before peoples' eyes. 14It deceived those who dwell on the Earth through the miracles it was permitted to perform on the authority of the first beast. He forced those who dwell on the Earth to fashion a cult statue in honor of the beast who was wounded with a sword but lived. 15It was permitted to give life to the cult statue of the beast that the cult statue of the beast might speak, and cause whomever did not worship the cult statue of the beast to be executed. ¹⁶It forced everyone, the unimportant and the important, rich and poor, 'free and slave, to take a brand on their right hand or on their forehead, ¹⁷so that no one could buy or sell unless he had the name of the beast or the number of its name branded on him.*

⁸This requires wisdom. Let the one with under-standing calculate the number of the beast, for it is a number referring to a person, and the number of that person is six hundred sixty-six." Rev 13:11-18

WHAT IS THE TEXT SAYING TO US?

The first beast rose out of the sea – the Abyss. The second beast arises from the Earth. Notice that the text does not say from "out of the Earth," but "rising from the Earth." If you read this passage as "rising from among earthly men," it could be an indicator that this beast is truly a fleshly servant of the Dragon and the first beast. Since he is later called the "false prophet," I think this is the best approach to take. In Genesis 2, you may remember that the first man, Adam, was made from dirt. I view the succession of evil in Revelation 12 and 13 this way: The Dragon is the spiritual real-ity of all evil. The first beast is often equated with the antichrist, but not called by that name anywhere in The Revelation. It is the earthly manifestation of that general Evil that we have expressed in terms of Empire versus Kingdom. The second beast (often called the "false prophet") represents the practical and fleshly presence of Evil on the Earth. As the first beast is a mere copy of the Dragon, so the second beast is a weak copy of the first.

The earthly beast has only two horns. Thus, it is evident that he lacks the power of the Dragon or the first beast. He looks like a normal sheep. I see a strong connection here between this beast and Jesus' warning about false prophets as "wolves in sheep's clothing" in Matthew 7:15. This could lend credence to the reference to this earthly beast as the "false prophet." I believe his identity is meant to be more representative of the entire group of such figures – more like all the false prophets who will ever come to earth. He looks like a sheep – but he speaks like a Dragon. While he seems innocent, even Godly, when he speaks, it is the hissing blasphemy of the Dragon that comes out. This beast is the mouthpiece of the first beast. He speaks of the first beast's power and how it was resurrected. In urging people to worship the miraculous Empire, the earthly beast performs apparent miracles. He even goes as far as to call of fire down from Heaven. By doing such wonders, he hopes to astonish the people and create belief in them that the Empire can provide them the things that God provides.

From the viewpoint of the seven churches to whom The Revelation was initially written, it is easy to see the Dragon as the Devil, the beast from the Sea as the Roman Empire, and the earthly beast as the Roman Imperial Cult. There is even language in this paragraph to indicate that such a portrayal is precisely at work here. The application in our lives in the twenty-first century is not the worship of the Roman Imperial Cult. However, it is still a valid application in the more general sense. When the earthly beast commands the people of the Earth to fashion a cult statue of the first beast, I do not doubt that the churches of Revelation understand this is a reference to the Roman Empire, Domitian, and Roman Imperial Cult worship.

Before Nero, most Imperial Cult worship centered around Julius Caesar and Caesar Augustus. While during their lives, they had discouraged their subjects from worshiping them as gods, the cult around them grew robust after their deaths. The Roman Empire accepted as normative that Emperors were revered as deities after their death, but not during their lives. Nero pushed for a change in this custom. There is, in fact, some evidence that Nero even persuaded the Roman Senate to pass a law ordering, and provide funding for, a colossal statue to Nero to declare him a deity while he was yet alive. This may have been part of the Senate's distaste and disdain for Nero. When he committed suicide, civil war broke out, Vespasian prevailed and reunited Rome. Vespasian led the Romans to return to worshiping only Julius Caesar at first. There is evidence that he removed the head of the colossus of Nero, and had it refashioned into the head of the Sun god. This may well be what is behind the language of The Revelation that says one of the heads had a fatal injury that had been healed but, be warned that I am speculating here.

Still, the explanation of Vespasian's refashion of Nero's colossus does not explain the next scene. The earthly beast causes the cult statue to speak and to bring about the penalty of death on anyone who refused to worship the statue of the first beast. In John's vision, there is a definite element of magical arts being involved in animating the image. This thought could also be a figurative way to represent the ways in which worldly governments tend to recruit authority from previous rulers, whether living or deceased, to add credibility to whatever program the current ruler is trying to accomplish. For example, think about how often in our own government some reference is made to John F. Kennedy, Abraham Lincoln, or even George Washington in reference to the importance of some action for which contemporary leaders are trying to engage citizen involvement.

There is also undoubtedly some parallel here with the story of Nebuchadnezzar found in Daniel 3. Nebuchadnezzar makes a very fitting prototype for the authoritative hierarchy described in Revelation 13. If you think about it, the Dragon is the spiritual force behind evil in the world. The beast from the sea/Abyss is the evil motivation behind Empire, like Nebuchadnezzar's Babylon, the Empire that will continue to serve as the prime example of earthy Empire in the remainder of The Revelation. The beast of the Earth, the puppet of the beast, and the Dragon is, typically, a ruler like Nebuchadnezzar. In Daniel 3:6, he orders his subjects to worship a cult statue that he had commissioned his artisans to fashion from gold and had erected in a prominent place out on the plains. When the trumpets sounded, anyone who refused to bow down to the ground and worship the cult statue was to be thrown into a fiery furnace. The lesser beast in Revelation 13, often called the "false prophet," issues just such a proclamation, but then goes a big step further.

So oppressive in his pursuit of power is the second beast, that he orders all subjects of his Empire to submit to branding! That is the actual word here – branded, on the forehead or the right hand. Think about this for a moment, because the branding plays a particular role in worship that you need to recognize, to better understand what is at work here. The worship of the image of the first beast is a public act of worship. Accepting a brand, mark, tattoo, or any other kind of identifying image on one's body in order to express devotion to anyone or anything is a very private act of devotion.

If I was preaching this message right now, we would pause and talk about folk who tattoo each other's names on their bodies in conspicuous places, only to break up a few years later and have to figure out what to do with that person's name indelibly "branded" in their flesh. Entire cable television series have been launched on how people have sought to cover up the regrettable tattoos they have taken with someone else's name. It can be hilarious to watch, but the original reason that anyone would mark their body with the name of another is a very personal and private statement of loyalty and devotion to that person. People may say anything, may represent themselves at all manner of levels of devotion, when they are complying with public opinion or peer pressure.

Most people choose their devotional alliances much more carefully in private. The point here is that the power of the Dragon, the Empire, and the ruler are so intense that they not only inspire public devotion but the kind of private devotion that would cause someone to accept a brand to prove their allegiance. So brainwashed are these subjects that they will permanently and painfully mark their bodies to prove their allegiance to the Empire and the ruler, who care so little for them that they would have that citizen murdered, simply for not doing what the ruler ordered of them.

As you reflect on this passage, I want you to weigh two factors. First, I want you to consider your value to God. His Word calls you a treasure (1 Peter 2:4), says that God carefully created you in His own likeness (Genesis 1:27), promises that God will never forget you (Isaiah 48:15), and affirms that even though you were broken – Christ died for you (Romans 5:8). Over and again, scripture describes how God loves you and how He has chosen and called you. Christ speaks in stories we call "parables." Parables are teaching stories that tell about how He would leave 99 secure sheep to search for you if you were lost. Another shows how God welcomes back His children if they make poor choices and run off to a far country in rebellion. To God, you are the treasure. You are His beloved child.

Then, consider how much you mean to the Empire in which you live. As long as you file your tax return, they remain relatively happy with you. Still, you are no treasure to the Empire. They do evil things, and you are expected to support them. They force you to be represented to the world by their platforms, policies, and campaigns. In the greater scheme of what the Empire wants to accomplish, you matter only as a number, if that. You are grist for the mill. Take a number. Have a seat. Bring us your papers. Do as your told. If you cost the Empire more than you are deemed to be worth, it will discard you. Your life does not matter in this Empire until you are old enough and capable enough to make some material contribution. When you are too old or broken to make a continued material contribution, your life matters so little they may even withhold necessary medical care so that you die sooner.

That is how much you mean to the Empire under which you toil – even in the twenty-first century. You bear its number: XXX-XX-XXXX. You deal in its currency and coin. You pay homage to it every April fifteenth. Every week, your homage is withheld from your check. Try and stop it. You pay homage to the

Empire on your home, your car, your properties, even your laundry detergent requires a tribute. (Taxes used to be referred to as "tributes.") It is a distraction of the enemy to have you waiting for some particular name or number, or computer chip, to consider yourself as having taken the "mark" of the governmental beast. Remember, these are symbolic issues. The "mark of the beast" is a symbolic marking – an attitude, a compromise, or just trying to get along in the system.

I continually hear my Christian brothers and sisters talking about what it will be like, one day when the government forces them to take "the mark of the beast." My social media feed buzzes at least weekly with some discussion about whether or not "the mark of the beast" might be a chip or a tattoo. But the truth is, the Empire has already marked you. Truthfully, you are marked, and the influence of the Empire is indelibly printed in your life right now. It is nearly impossible to conduct any business without the marks of the Empire. Your social security number, your driver's license, your permit number, your cell number, your fingerprint on the scanner, your retinal scan, or your face in the facial recognition reader - are all ways in which you have already been marked. Reflect for a moment.

You gave up your fingerprints for quick access to your bank account. You gave those and a retinal scan to bypass security at the airport. You have handed out your social security number to all kinds of entities that are not the government, for whose purposes it was issued. To more quickly access your latest smartphone, you allowed it to map your facial recognition parameters. You cannot escape and go "off the grid." Your mobile phone sends a signal to the nearest tower, even when you turn it off! Any officer who contacts you can run your driver's license, or your car license plates, and gain instant access to your entire legal history. Any financial entity – a bank, an apartment rental office, a car dealership, a finance company – can lock up your ability to buy anything with credit. It only requires them to go to the effort of a few keystrokes. John says that people will not be able to conduct business without the mark. Consider this: you cannot buy a house, rent an apartment, buy a car, or even open a bank account or credit card without a social security number.

Crush your cell phone, burn your identity cards and passport, try to live off the grid. You are still identifiable by your facial recognition profile any time you walk past any of the millions of cameras that watch you every day. Make no mistake about it, you are already marked, in multiple ways, by the beast of Empire in your world. I have illustrated how deeply the tentacles of the Empire entangle your daily life. John hints at who the lesser beast, the antichrist, was to churches of The Revelation.

In verse 18, John says, "This requires wisdom." That means, though, that it can be done. The beast can be calculated. His effect in our lives can be revealed. Who is he? Verse 18 says his name has a number: 666. I know, many different calculations have been offered. Some are way out there: the Catholic Church, the Pope, Richard Nixon, Adolph Hitler, etc. Think about the people to whom this letter is written. If they exercise some wisdom, John affirms, they can figure out this puzzle. Unlike the Romans who might intercept this letter, the Christians have Jewish people, Aramaic speakers and writers, in their ranks. Those who grew up Jewish were taught Aramaic in school to be able to read the scriptures. Aramaic would be like a secret language in the Roman Empire. Only those with a background from Israel would understand it! The one thing that Greek (the language of the Roman Empire) and Aramaic have in common is that, in both languages, letters also have numeric values.

So, it stands to reason that if a name is to have a number, it would be the sum total of the letters of that name. Many names might come close, but this puzzle is very specific. The first person that would come to anyone's mind when looking for the epitome of a mad and corrupt ruler would be the name of Nero. But those four letters do not come close to adding up to 666. But wait. Nero is an abbreviated form of his name. With his royal title, he is Caesar Nero. In Greek, it would look something like *"Neron Kaisar."* Adding up the total of those letters will not get you to 666. Wisdom is required. If you took those Greek letters and assigned them each the equivalent letter in Aramaic, you would form nonsensical letter combinations in Aramaic. Still, the sum value of the numerical values of those letters would be 666. The beast of the Empire could be Nero! But wait, there is another fascinating possibility!

The emperor Domitian had a long title. In English equivalents to the Greek letters, at least the best I can provide you, Domitian's full title would look something like: *"Autocratos Kaisar Dometianos Sebastos Germanikos* (my apologies to those of you who are more skilled at Greek than myself!) That is quite a title! In the Roman Empire, each emperor re-struck the coinage of the Empire during his reign. In many instances, in order to do business within the Roman Empire, you had to use the coins with the current emperor's picture on them. Did you catch that? Without the "mark" of the current emperor, you were not able to conduct business. Coins are not the largest artistic canvas in the world. They are rather small. The space on which one can strike an image and a title is minuscule. Domitian's lengthy title had to be abbreviated to fit on his coinage. You can find coins from Domitian's reign among ancient collectible coins. They are engraved with the abbreviation, *"A KAI DOMET SEB GE."* (Aune, 52B, p. 1,433) Anyone care to venture a guess at what you will come up with if you use the Greek numerical equivalents to that abbreviation to get a sum? If you guessed 666, you would be right! That answer does not even require conversion into Aramaic.

What does it all mean? The meaning is the same, either way. The earthly leader that requires you to worship him as a deity is the false prophet and the second beast. Not just Nero, or Domitian, but every earthly ruler who sees leadership as a power barter, who sees the means of his leadership as control and accrual of power – is a false prophet and a personification of the second beast. You can list the historical versions of such beasts – Attila, Genghis Kahn, Stalin, Lenin, Mussolini, Hitler, Hirohito, Mao, Amin, Pinochet, Hussein, Khomeini, Assad, Gaddafi – they all qualify. I could make commentary here on American political leaders, but I will leave those equivalencies to you. The key point is that any leader in the pattern of Nero or Domitian, who accrues power through force, who subjugates people to perform service to themselves rather than their fellow citizens, is part of the influence of the Dragon and his beasts in your world.

Were you waiting for some modern-day political superhero to appear on the world stage so that everyone could proclaim,

"There is the beast!" or "There is the antichrist!?" I believe that is one of the greatest deceptions that the enemy has ever orchestrated. It has lulled generations of Christians into believing that the Revelation was portraying someone far into the future. It took our eyes off of the power structures in our own world that undermine the witness of the Church and the power of God's Word in each day. John had already tried to warn us and, for the most part, we missed it:

> *"Dear children, this is the last hour. I know you have heard that the antichrist is coming. But you need to know that already many Antichrists have come. This is how we know that this is the last hour." 1 John 2:18*

Wake up! The Empire has already marked you. The question is: Whom do you serve?

HOW MIGHT WE SHARE THIS?

I. The Misleading Leader

II. The Power of the Mark

III. The Pattern of the Deceivers

QUESTIONS FOR FURTHER STUDY OR REFLECTION

1. In what ways does the secular government rule your life?

2. In what subtle ways are you marked by the secular world? (think broadly)

3. Do you believe it would be possible to throw off all the markings of the world?

4. If you cannot throw off all the markings, how do you express your devotion to Christ?

CHAPTER TWENTY-SEVEN

THE REMNANT BECOME REDEEMED
FEAR GOD

Revelation 14:1-12

THE TEXT:

"14:1Then I looked, and saw, the Lamb was standing on Mount Zion and with him a group of 144,000 with His name and the name of His Father written on their foreheads. 2I heard a sound from Heaven like the roar of the sea and like the sound of loud thunder. The sound which I heard was like that of many harpists playing their harps. 3Then they sang a new song before the throne and before the four cherubim and the elders.

No one could learn the song except the 144,000 who had been redeemed from the Earth. 4These are those who have not sullied themselves with women but have kept themselves pure. They follow the Lamb wherever He goes. They are the ones who have been redeemed from humanity, servants devoted to God and the Lamb, 5and

'in their mouths no deceit was found." They are
blameless.

⁶Then I saw another angel flying in midheaven,
with an eternal message to proclaim among those
who dwell on the Earth and among every nation
and tribe and language and race, ⁷proclaiming
with a loud voice,

'Fear God and give Him glory, because the hour
of His judgment has come, and worship the one
who made the heavens and the Earth and the sea
and the springs.'

⁸Then a second angel followed, saying, "Fallen,
fallen is Babylon the Great who gave all nations
to drink of the wine which represents her immoral
passions."

⁹A third angel followed them, proclaiming with
a loud voice, "If anyone worships the beast and
his cultic image and receives the brand on his
forehead or upon his hand, ¹⁰then he also will
drink some of the wine, which is the fury of God
poured undiluted into the cup, that is, His wrath,
with the result that he will be tormented in the
pit of fire and sulfur before the holy angels and
before the Lamb. ¹¹The smoke of their torment
ascends forever. Those who worship the beast

and its cultic image, or receive the brand of its name or number, will have no rest day and night. [12]This calls for patient endurance on the part of God's people and calls for keeping the commands of God remaining faithful to Jesus.' Rev 14:1-12

WHAT IS THE TEXT SAYING TO US?

John looks and sees the Lamb that we met in Chapter 5, and with Him are His 144,000 sealed faithful followers. Well, this is a familiar group! We first saw them in Chapter 7 when the Lamb marked them as His for preservation. Notice the number is still the same. You may remember that we said that this extreme multiple of 12 represents the totality of believers in Christ. Seven chapters, four or five horsemen, seven seals, seven trumpets, two witnesses, a woman, a baby, a Dragon, and two beasts ago God promised to keep them to the very end. Now, they stand on Mount Zion, that is, in Jerusalem, with the Lamb – every single one of them. You may remember that our concluding point when we discussed Chapter 7 was that none would be left behind. Now we see that history has worked out exactly that way. God is good to both His word and His Word. John hears a sound coming down from Heaven (notice that this affirms that the 144,000 are still on Earth – the sound comes from Heaven, where they are not.)

The sound is a thunderous roar like…many "harpists harping on their harps!" Wait. Harp Thunder? My ancestry is Scottish. If he had said bagpipe thunder, I would totally get this! But harp thunder? That would take an incredibly huge chorus of harpists.

The alliteration here is apparently intended: "harpists harping on their harps." It sounds as funny in Greek as it does in English! I believe John intends to challenge our aural imagination here, just as his visual descriptions of Heaven's throne room challenged our visual imagination. How many millions of harps would it take for the little kithara to sound like thunder? Yes, millions, indeed.

Now the vision shows us that what is spoken or sung on Earth impacts Heaven at the same time. While the remnant stands on Mount Zion in Jerusalem, they are also seen from the throne room of Heaven. What are they doing in this place with their feet on Earth, but being heard from Heaven? They are singing a new song – a song never heard in Heaven, nor on Earth, before. In my career, I have used this verse of scripture whenever someone complained about doing some form of "new music" as part of a worship service. The complaint would be something like, "I don't like that new song."

My response was always something along the lines of, "Well, you may not like Heaven very much."

"Why is that?" was the usual follow-up.

"Because," I would say, "Revelation 14:3 says we are going to stand in Heaven and sing a *new song!*" I know, but I think I am funny sometimes! What does it mean to sing a new song? The implication here is that singing this song is a privilege reserved for the saints of God. The angels cannot sing it. The elders cannot sing it. The cherubim cannot sing it. It is the song of the redeemed remnant. Only the lips and spirits of those who have dedicated their lives to serving God may sing the song.

Several years ago, I was at a concert put on by an *a capella* Christian group. Halfway through the evening, they taught the audience a new song that would come out on their upcoming album. It was just a simple, repetitive little 8-line song. Once the audience had taken up the song and was singing it with good energy, the artists began to leave the stage. They departed one at a time until the stage was empty, and we were all left singing the song. Realizing that the artists had left us unsupervised, we began to delight in our starring roll! The song grew louder and more robust. Harmonies began to appear and enrich the melody as singers took them up. For probably 15 or 20 minutes, we just sang at the top of our lungs and with all our hearts. Few were trained singers. Some could only make a "joyful noise!" But it was absolutely enjoyable. As they had left the stage, the artists returned one at a time. They took up the song with us and then proceeded to finish it out. When they ended the song, the place erupted in shouts and cheers! The man sitting next to me had tears streaming down his face. I asked if he was okay. I will never forget the look on his face – glowing – as he said, "Oh, yes, Sir! I am better than okay. I just believe that is what it will be like in Heaven for eternity!"

The concert went on another 45 minutes, or so. When the artists thanked the audience and took their final bow, someone in the audience again started singing the chorus they had taught us. People took it up as the artists walked off the stage. Again, it grew louder and louder until 15 minutes later, the artists rejoined us, and we sang for another 20 minutes together. A new song... with brothers and sisters I had never seen before and will not see again until we stand before the throne. If the song is half as good as that one, that will be some chorus.

There is this interesting statement that these are those who have "not sullied themselves with women." I have tried to use gender-inclusive language whenever possible in this book, but there is just no way to get around this one! What in the world can he possibly mean here? Are women a terrible sullying force in creation? Obviously, that is not the point of God, Christ, or John here. From this remark, it is clear that the 144,000 sealed were likely men. In John's culture, women did not have the freedoms and status that they enjoy in my culture. When I come to points like this in the Bible, it reminds me to be grateful for Christian women from John's day until now. They have led in Jesus' church and have stood up for their place in society, ministry, and the workplace. In the sealing of the 144,000, the Bible is not trying to say that only men are called, sealed, or protected by God. The remark about getting sullied by women is simply a remark about living a pure life. That would mean they had lived a life without committing adultery or without engaging prostitutes. In our culture, it could include not engaging in pornography or the exploitation of women through cultural pursuits that encourage objectifying women or trafficking women and girls. It would be just as fair to see these saints as women who had not been spoiled by bad men! The crucial point is that male or female; they follow the Lamb wherever He goes.

Now, Christ redefines the 144,000. They are no longer the remnant, but the redeemed. They do not lie. They do not practice deceit. They are blameless. Does that mean they are perfect? In God's eyes, yes. You see, there is only one standard that matters, and that is God's standard. It is different from ours because the love of a father drives God's standard. I was talking to a parent a few years ago as her two-year-old slept next to the table in his car seat. I knew that child. He had a voice that could raise the hair of a lion's mane and frighten fully-grown grizzly bears! His energy level was such that, when he came to my home, my cat would run and hide, and we would not see her for hours. That little sleeping bundle by the table was a weapon of mass destruction! His mother looked at him adoringly and said, "He is just such a perfect child."

I bit my tongue very hard. I thought to myself that we must not be thinking of the same child – and I was right. You see, she was looking at that baby through her mother's lens. I was looking at him from the outside. God looks at us through his Heavenly Father's eyes. If you look at my life from the outside, you would never call me "blameless." There are many things you might call me, but that is not one of them. The Bible says everyone has sinned, and none is perfect. These must not be real people if the Bible says they were blameless, right? But wait. The Bible does not say they were perfect. The Bible says they were blameless. That does not mean they never sinned, only that there was no one to blame them – to charge them with sin. You understand the difference, yes? There is only one in all of creation who is fit to judge. The Father has given to the Lamb, the one who was slain, all authority to judge. Why was He slain? To purchase redemption, to cleanse from sin, and to change our status before the Father.

> *"God reckoned Him who had never known sin, to be sin on our behalf, so that, in Him, God could reckon us as the very righteousness of God." 2 Corinthians 5:21*

Another angel flies through the heaven of planets and stars to proclaim to all creation: "Fear God!" His presence and message mean that there is still a chance for people to repent and acknowledge Christ as Lord. The evangelistic task is not yet over, but the judgment is imminent. God will not wait any longer, but neither will He pronounce a final judgment without allowing one final call to repentance. A second angel follows the same path and proclaims that Babylon the Great has fallen. A third angel follows quickly, proclaiming that anyone who worshiped the beast or accepted the beast's brand will suffer the same judgment as did the beast himself. He will endure torment in the fire and sulfur of the Abyss, in full view of all of Heaven. Those who refused to have faith in Christ will know no end to suffering.

The final admonition is that we are to understand that judgment is surely coming. We are to have faith that rewards are surely coming. God will set the record straight in the end, and holding onto that belief will require "patient endurance on the part of God's people."

In fact, the requirements are three: keeping God's commands, remaining faithful to Jesus, and patient endurance. I pray you are ready because I am going to carve off the largest piece of sacred cow porterhouse steak in the entire sit-down-full-service-restaurant of God's Kingdom. Take a deep breath, please? Now think about this. You just saw the beginning depiction of God's judgment on humanity. The proclamation of the judgment comes with a blatant warning to all who are reading or hearing it. Understanding this truth requires keeping God's commands, being faithful to Jesus Christ, and patient endurance. What was John told repeatedly throughout the messages to the churches?

> *To the church at Ephesus, he wrote: "To the one who prevails..." To the church at Smyrna,*

he wrote: "To the one who prevails..." To the
church at Pergamum, he wrote: "To the one who
prevails..." To the church at Thyatira, he said:
"To the one who prevails and keeps My works
until the end..."

To the church at Sardis, it was: "The one
who prevails to the end..." To the church at
Philadelphia, it was: "As for the one who pre-
vails to the end..." Finally, to the church at
Laodicea, he wrote: "And the one who prevails
to the end will be allowed to sit with me on my
throne, just as I also prevailed and sat down with
my Father on His Throne."

To "prevail" is to be victorious. When is victory had, or lost? At the very end of the contest. The Greek word for "prevail" in every one of those verses that applies to us, is *"vikown."* The word means "victorious in the end." You see, there is no rapture in the Book of Revelation. In fact, the word "rapture" never appears in the Bible – not once. I invited you to look. Have you seen a single instance in The Revelation where any period of testing or protection was defined as being seven years in length? You have not, because there is never a period of seven years of tribulation defined in Revelation, ever. So, where did those thoughts come from?

Well, the Bible uses the word "tribulation," and The Revelation mentions "great tribulation." But it was not until the mid-1700s that preachers started to talk about "The Great Tribulation," as though it were a particular event. Those preachers used that

"Great Tribulation." They portrayed it as happening at that very time or coming right around the corner. They used the idea to frighten people into the faith or, as one evangelist so fittingly put it, to "hold(s) you over the pit of hell." (Edwards. "Sinners in the Hands of an Angry God" 1741)

As you can imagine, after 70 or 80 years of that kind of preaching, people began to question what kind of God would do such a thing. It is a very pertinent question. Were we to serve the kind of God who would toy with us, dangling us over the fire of Hell until He seared us into repentance? When folks read the Bible and saw the Christ of grace and healing and forgiveness, this angry God looked cruel and capricious. In about 1830, an Irish preacher and spiritualist by the name of John Nelson Darby suggested what he believed to be an inspired fix. Before any "Great Tribulation," which sinners certainly deserved, God would yank away from the world, all of those who believed in Him! He called that event, the "rapture."

Darby would later become known as "The Father of Dispensationalism," the idea that history can be divided into sections according to the events and grace that God "dispensed" during a given time. One of those timeframes is called "The Dispensation of Grace," which Darby said, runs from the Cross to the Rapture. You see, he would need this idea of a "rapture" to define his view of how God works through history. This was all wrapped up in the mystical explorations of fringe Christian groups and leaders in the 1700s and 1800s. You can study modern mysticism for years to come. Suffice it to say here, that the idea of a "rapture" is a 19th Century creation – not a Biblical concept. It was a reactionary idea to the overly zealous revivalist extremists of the 18th Century.

When I read through The Revelation for the very first time, I went to one of the most insightful preachers I had ever known. I asked him why I could not find a "Great Tribulation" or a "rapture" in The Revelation. I remember that his response shocked me. "Well," he said, "that's really very simple. They don't appear in The Book of Revelation."

I asked him to explain, and he did. He showed me the connections that people tried to make in Daniel and in Zechariah, to shoe-horn Revelation into events and portrayals in those books. He told me, "Kevin, they simply have it backward. Revelation references those symbols, but it is telling a completely different story."

I pressed him on the issue of the "Great Tribulation" and the "rapture." Did they have any place in eschatology – in a truly Biblical view of the end times? Again, his response was hard to take, "No, Sir," he said, "in fact, some have gone as far as to call them a hoax."

That is a big step, and I do not know that I want to go that far, but very close. Please, hear me out. I believe the enemy of your soul has used these concepts to deceive you. He has misled people for over two centuries with the belief that they did not need to get serious about faith until they saw the signs of this "Great Tribulation." Then, preachers started talking about a "rapture" that would not happen until half of the "Great Tribulation" had taken place. Well, that would give us even more time to get right with God! We could pretty much live as we please until we saw those terrible signs that the "Great Tribulation" was on us, and repent before we got beamed up to Heaven, right?

In the mid-1970s, my friends in the evangelical movement in

the United States went one better. They produced movies and showed them to those of us in youth groups across the nation. The films portrayed a "rapture" that just might leave some of us behind! There was a song we sang each week in our youth group that said things like, "Two men walking up a hill, one disappears, and one's left standing still – I wish we'd all been ready." The movie showed that those who got left behind after the "rapture" would be beheaded for believing in Jesus! If you think about it, that was kind of weird. Why would I ever believe in Jesus if it might get me killed one day? Those attempts to frighten us into faith were very little different than the fiery preaching of "dangling us over hell" from the mid-1700s. Having survived such "evangelism," I had to try and help people sort it out, as a popular televangelist of the mid-1990s brought it all back, complete with scary movies!

Honestly, that is simply not the story of The Book of Revelation. In Revelation, God protects His people *through* any trial or trouble they will face in these wicked final days. The promise is no less. You may even lose your life for your testimony, but it is not this life that matters. What matters is overcoming, being victorious, prevailing until the end. Whether Jesus comes to you, or you go to Him, does not really make a difference. Either way, on the day that you stand face-to-face with Christ, the end has come. Judgment will take place. Rewards and punishments will be decided. Throughout my ministry, I have tried very hard not to argue these things with people, but simply to point to the end of our lives as the moment we each must, inevitably, face. We will stand before the Lamb. We will be accountable to God, who, thankfully, sees us with Father's eyes.

What about 1 Thessalonians 4:16-17, or 1 Corinthians

15:51-52? Are those not truth? Of course, they are truth. But nothing in either of those verses indicates that they take place at any other time than the very end. Take a look, 1 Corinthians 15:52 expressly says that the event it describes (which is the Apostle Paul's relating of the same event) happens, "...at the last trumpet." It occurs at the very end, at judgment time.

Finally, I want to leave you with an assuring thought; because I always remind myself of this truth anytime I am studying the end times. First, this most helpful question: of all the people in the Bible, who would know best about the end of time? Jesus would be the expert, right? So, my next-most-helpful question is: how does Jesus portray the role of His people leading up the end? My faith is assured and helped by Jesus' words in Matthew 24:

> *"And the Good News of the Kingdom will be proclaimed to the entire world as a witness to all the nations of the Earth, and when that is done, the end will come." Mat 24:14*

I pray those words are as encouraging to you as they are to me. I have a task to accomplish in this lifetime. Will the end of the world come in my lifetime? I do not believe so, but I know that at the end of my life, my end will come. Until the day I go to Christ, or He comes for me, I have one task – to share the Gospel, the Good News about the forgiveness and love I have found in Jesus Christ. Jesus tells us that when that task is complete, and all the nations have heard the double witness of the Church and the Word – the end *will* come.

HOW MIGHT WE SHARE THIS? (LET ME COUNT THE WAYS!)

Sticking to only the obvious outline that might be suggested by the text, I would propose:

I.   The 144,000 Reappear

II. Remnant to Redeemed

III. Where will You Be in the Final Moment?

QUESTIONS FOR FURTHER STUDY AND REFLECTION

1. Where is Mount Zion? What is its significance to Jews? To us?

2. What does it mean to you to think about being "unsullied?"

3. Why do you think that worship here is expressed in singing a new song?

4. What elements of response from Heaven are missing in regard to the worship here?

5. Do you believe we will be judged immediately after our death? If not, when?

6. What do you believe is needed in order for us to stand blameless at the last moment?

CHAPTER TWENTY-EIGHT

THE HARVEST OF THE EARTH
"THE GRAIN AND THE GRAPES"

Revelation 14:13-20

THE TEXT:

"14:13Then I heard a voice from heaven saying, 'Write: "How fortunate, indeed, are the dead who die in the Lord," says the Spirit, "that they might rest from their labors, for their works follow after them."

14Then I looked and saw a white cloud, and upon the cloud was seated one like a human being with a golden wreath upon his head and a sharp sickle in his hand. 15Then another angel came out of the Temple, exclaiming with a loud voice to the one seated upon the cloud, 'Swing your sickle and harvest, for the hour to harvest has arrived, because the harvest of the Earth is ripe.' 16The one sitting upon the cloud swung his sickle across the Earth, and the Earth was harvested.

17Then, another angel came out of the Temple in Heaven, and he had a sharp pruning knife. 18Yet another angel emerged from the Temple (the one from the altar of fire) and called with a loud voice to the one who had the sharp sickle, 'Use your sharp pruning knife and gather the clusters of grapes from the vineyard, which is the Earth, for its grapes are ripe.' 19Then, the angel swung his pruning knife across the Earth and gathered the vintage of the Earth and threw it into the great winepress of the wrath of God. 20The winepress was trodden outside of the city, and blood flowed from the winepress to the height of the bridles of the horses for a distance of 180 miles." Rev 14:13-20

WHAT IS THE TEXT SAYING TO US?

After we see the Remnant-become-Redeemed, there is a brief statement that is very important, because it serves as something of an anchor for all of Chapter 14. A voice from Heaven delivers what most of us would consider to be a very odd message. Fortunate are those who die? It is not our way to consider dying a fortunate circumstance. You have likely already noticed that I left out the qualifying, "in the Lord," to treat separately. That is because this short message tells us at whom we are looking in Chapter 14: those who die in the Lord. The 144,000 that defined the total of the remnant becomes the sum total of the redeemed, as they pass from this world into Heaven. The harvests you are about to see are not meant to be seen simply as specific historical events. They are broad and general eschatological truth. By that, I mean that they are representative of the harvesting of Earth in both a final event and the harvest that happens every moment, as souls pass from Earth to Heaven. Bear in mind that there are two harvests: one for the grain, and another for the grapes.

John sees a white cloud, and a being sitting on it who appears just like a human being. He borrows language from Daniel when he says, "like a son of man." However, in Daniel, that language is often used to describe an angel or some foretelling of the Messiah. In the Gospels, that language is appropriated to speak, almost specifically, of Jesus. But those connotations are not implied here. With the variety of creatures that John has portrayed in his vision, he is clarifying that this being looks just like a human being – one born of humankind. On the being's head is a golden crown, signifying that he serves God. In Matthew 13:30, Jesus says it will be "the servants" who gather the harvest. Nowhere does the Bible show Jesus doing the harvesting of souls himself. This should not be construed to be Christ, but an angel who stays in direct contact with the Father. Yet another angel comes flying out of the Temple in Heaven – out of God's immediate presence – and gives the command to swing the sickle and harvest the Earth. The angel on the cloud swings his sickle, and we are told that the Earth was harvested. Notice, however, that there is no indication that this is the final harvest, nor the only harvest of the Earth. That is not the point here. The point is that this is the harvest of the grains. Grains are harvested and stored. There is a great deal left unsaid here. People from an agricultural economy as diverse as the region to which these words were written would have understood perfectly that the grain harvest goes into storage.

I am at a bit of an advantage here, having grown up on a wheat farm. Every summer, we would cut the wheat. I learned to drive at the age of thirteen, driving a wheat truck from the field to the elevator. The grain elevator is a set of huge storage tanks or bins. We would dump the truck into a collecting bin under the floor of the elevator, and it would be augered, or elevated, to the top of the storage bin dumped in. The elevator operator kept a record of how many bushels of wheat we had brought to his elevator. He stored it there until we instructed him, at some point in the next year, to sell our grain on the wheat market. He took a small percentage for storage, and we got paid the remainder. Typically, the market was lowest during harvest because of the abundance of grain available to the market at that time. We would typically hold our wheat until early winter and sell it when the price was higher. Grain is a commodity. It has an intrinsic value that makes it wise to hold onto the grain over time. Grapes are a very different kind of produce.

John sees another angel (reinforcing our assertion that the first being is an angelic being). This angel does not have a cloud on which he sits. His mission is more specialized. While the Greek word here for "sickle" is the same as it was with the angel on the cloud, the word means, literally, "harvesting tool." Because of its specialized function, I have rendered the word as "pruning knife," the tool that a vintage uses to harvest grapes is a hand-held knife with a curved blade. Notice the connection with Jesus' words in John 15, as well as Joel 3. Right behind him comes the angel from the altar of fire – the one who filled the censer with hot coals and flung it to the Earth. This angel oversees the altar of sacrifice, and he calls the angel with the sickle to swing it and gather "the clusters of grapes." The angel swings his knife across the Earth, and the clusters are gathered, but they are not stored.

The grape clusters are thrown into the winepress of God. For the past sixteen years, my brother has been planting, cultivating, nurturing, and managing a vineyard. I see why Jesus used the vineyard and the grapes as the subject of several parables. I have watched my very patient brother learn some frustrating lessons from trying to manage a grape crop! You see, grapes ripen through the spring and summer. When the time to harvest them comes, the sugar content in the fruit is just right for fermentation. If one harvests grapes too early, there will not be enough sugar in the juice to properly ferment and preserve it. Wait too long, and the sugar content will be so high that the fermentation process will start prematurely while the fruit still hangs on the vine. When it is time to harvest grapes, they must be collected and processed immediately. It can be a bit of a frantic process.

The grapes are thrown into the winepress, outside the city walls, and then trodden underfoot to extract the juice. There are a good number of metaphors and mental images at work here. Winepresses throughout history have been manual or mechanical. The mechanical version is some manner of press by which a large plank, or "press," is forced by mechanical pressure against a solid base. The grapes in the machine are squeezed or "juiced." So tremendous is the pressure that all the juice is drained off, and all that remains in the press is grape skins and cluster sticks. The more ancient method of juicing is to load the grapes into a vat with a draining mechanism that will strain out skins and sticks, and have the friends and family stomp them. It stains skin and clothing. There are references in the Old Testament to judgment being like stomping grapes, and the stained garments being evidence of judgment having been carried out (Isaiah 63, for example).

What is meant by "outside the walls of the city?" If you think about it, most vineyards are in the country. Of course, their winepress would not be in the city. Bear in mind that we are not really talking about a grape harvest, are we? We are observing a metaphorical judgment taking place. Sin is being judged, and a sentence being carried out. In the Old Testament, there were clear laws about punishing or executing violators "outside the camp" or "outside the city." In Numbers 5, the unclean are to be taken outside the camp. In Numbers 15, those who are to be executed for capital crimes are to be executed "outside the camp." This practice continued into Jesus' time, as related in Luke 4:29. Visitors to Jerusalem remark in awe at looking across to the Mount of Olives, and seeing the hillside covered with graves, many of which date to Biblical times. Jews were buried outside the city. The significance was two-fold. The unrighteous had no place among God's people; and, the corpses of sacrificed animals or people punished by death would present a health hazard inside the city. Remember, the Bible says that Jesus was crucified "outside the city." (See Mat 27:33, Mark 15:22, Luke 23:33, John 19:17, and Heb 13:12)

Just in case we were totally clueless and missed the point here when the grapes are juiced, we are told that "the blood flowed." That truth snaps us back to the reality of what is being portrayed here. This is the final judgment of all sin, of all unrighteousness, in all people of all time. How do we know that this is the final judgment on sin? By the amount of blood that flows. It is a physical impossibility to accrue flowing blood to a height of five-to-six feet for a distance of 180 miles in every direction. Still, this passage is not about the physical world. The metaphor simply means that, when God's wrath comes against the rule of sin throughout history, it will come fiercely and completely. The fact that the measuring device is the bridles of the assembled horses points to war. God will, one day, lead His forces in a war against sin. His victory will be decisive and complete.

HOW MIGHT WE SHARE THIS?

I.   There will be judgment for the righteous

II. There will be judgment for the unrighteous

III. When the judgment happens, who will be ready?

QUESTIONS FOR FURTHER STUDY OR REFLECTION

1.   What symbolism does "sitting on a cloud" serve in the Bible?

2.   In the Bible, does a "sickle" commonly have a positive or negative implication?

3.   What other biblical accounts of the final judgment in the Bible correlate it with "harvest?"

CHAPTER TWENTY-NINE

THE SEVEN BOWLS OF GOD'S WRATH

WATCH, I AM COMING LIKE A THIEF

Revelation 15:1-16:21

THE TEXT:

"¹⁵:¹Then I saw another great and wonderful sign in Heaven, seven angels holding the seven last plagues, for with them the wrath of God was spent. ²Then I saw something like a sea of glass mixed with fire, and those who were victorious over the beast, that is, over its image and over the number of its name, stood near the sea of glass with harps from God. ³They sang the song of Moses the servant of God and the song of the Lamb:

> *Great and wonderful are your deeds,*
> *Lord God Almighty; Righteous and*
> *true are your ways, King of the nations.*
> *⁴Lord, who does not fear and glorify*
> *your name? Because you alone are holy,*
> *because all the nations will come to fall*

down in worship before you, because
your righteous judgments are clear.'

⁵*After this, I saw the Temple, precisely, the tab-
ernacle of testimony in Heaven, open ⁶and the
seven angels with the seven plagues emerged from
the Temple clothed in pure, shining linen and
with golden sashes encircling their waists. ⁷Then
one of the four cherubim gave to the seven angels
seven golden offering bowls full of the wrath of
the God who lives forever and ever. ⁸At that moment, the Temple was filled with smoke from the
glory of God and from His power, and no one was
able to enter the Temple until the seven plagues of
the seven angels had been accomplished.*

^{16:1}*Then I heard a loud voice from the Temple
telling the seven angels, 'Be on your way to begin
pouring out on the earth the seven offering bowls
containing the wrath of God.'*

²*The first one departed and poured out his bowl
on the Earth, and harmful and festering sores
afflicted those people who had the brand of the
beast and worshiped his image.*

³*Then the second one poured out his bowl on the
sea, and it became blood as from a corpse, and
every living creature in the sea died.*

⁴Then the third one poured out his bowl on the rivers and springs of water, and they, too, became blood. ⁵Then I heard the angel in charge of the waters saying: 'Righteous are you, who is and who was, the Holy One, for you have decided to inflict these punishments, ⁶because they poured out the blood of God's people and the prophets, and you have given them blood to drink; they are worthy.'

⁷I then heard someone from the altar say: 'Yes, Lord God Almighty, True and just are your judgments.'

⁸The fourth one poured out his bowl upon the sun, and it was permitted to burn people with fire. ⁹People were burned by the intense heat. They reviled the name of God who had the authority over these plagues, but they did not repent nor give glory to Him.

¹⁰Then the fifth one poured out his offering bowl upon the throne of the beast, so that his kingdom was plunged into darkness. Consequently, people bit their tongues because of the pain, ¹¹and they reviled the God of Heaven because of their sufferings and their sores, yet they did not repent of their behavior.

¹²*Then the sixth one poured out his bowl on the great river Euphrates, and its waters dried up, so that a road was made ready for the kings from the east.* ¹³*Then I saw three unclean spirits like frogs emerge from the mouth of the dragon and from the mouth of the beast and from the mouth of the false prophet.* ¹⁴*For they are spirits, that is, demons producing signs, who travel to the kings of the whole world to gather them for the battle on the great day of God the Almighty.*

*(*¹⁵*'Watch,' says Jesus, 'I am coming like a thief. How fortunate is the one who is alert and remains fully clothed, lest he go around naked and people see his shamefulness.')*

¹⁶*The demonic spirits gathered them together at the place called Armageddon in Hebrew.*

¹⁷*The seventh one threw the contents of his offering bowl into the air, and a loud voice came from the temple, that is, from the throne, saying, 'It is finished.'* ¹⁸*Then there was lightning and rumbling and thunder, and there was a great earthquake such as had never been since people have been on the Earth, the greatest quake ever.* ¹⁹*The great city split into three parts, and the cities of the nations fell. God remembered to give Babylon the Great the cup of wine, that is, His*

furious wrath, ²⁰and every island fled, and the mountains disappeared. ²¹Then large hailstones weighing nearly a hundred pounds fell on people from the sky, so that people reviled God as the result of the plague of hail, because that plague was so terrible." Rev 15:1-16:21

WHAT IS THE TEXT SAYING TO US?

I cannot back this theory up with any scholarship from any other scholar. But I see the three groups formed by the seals, the trumpets, and the bowls of wrath as connected to the Holy Trinity. The Lamb opened the seven seals. To me, they constitute the judgments of the Lamb. The seven trumpets were not motivated by any spoken word from the throne, or from Heaven. They come as a result of the opening of the seventh seal by the Lamb. It was Christ who released to us the Holy Spirit. It is Christ who opens the seal that releases the angels with trumpets. I see the trumpets as the judgments of the Holy Spirit. Then, I see the seven bowls as the judgments of the Father. You will notice how closely they resemble the plagues on Egypt. There is little wasted time in this chapter. The wrath of God is all that remains to be poured out on the Earth. The diamond floor appears to be glass on fire. There stand the victorious saints, who followed Christ rather than compromise their faith and suffer deception into doing the work of the beast or representing him in their world. See how they resemble the 144,000? The witness of God in our lives is in how we lived each day for Him. Holiness is expressed in our lives by our priorities and the rightness of our hearts. These redeemed now sing the "song of Moses and the song of the Lamb." The Old Testament and the New Testament meet at the throne of God. Those who found God through Moses are now one with those who found God through the grace of Christ. They sing both songs – the song of the Law and the song of the Lamb. What a beautiful sight!

The song sounds very Old Testament. It exalts God's greatness, His righteousness, His worthiness to be feared and glorified, His holiness, and right judgments. It is fitting, then, that the next thing we see is the Tabernacle of the Old Covenant – the Heavenly dwelling place of God. From it proceed the angels with the bowls of plagues. This is another reason I see these are God's judgments, as they come directly from His dwelling place. They come in royal dress, indicating that they have, indeed, come straight from the presence of the King. Then there is a Heavenly theophany – an expression of God's immediate presence. This is a nearly exact depiction of one of my favorite passages of scripture:

> *"Then the Temple of the Lord was filled with a dense cloud of His presence, and the priests could not perform their duties because the cloud of the glory of His presence so filled the Temple of God." 2 Chronicles 5:13-14*

There are those moments in the worship of God when His presence is so real and intense that no one wants to move or make a sound. I remember a worship service from my early days in ministry. I was a music and worship minister. The pastor had delivered a tremendously penetrating and convicting sermon. Finishing his message, he gave an invitation to any who wanted to come forward and pray at the altar or the first row of chairs in the sanctuary. Many came and knelt. Some were in tears; some prayed out loud, while others simply knelt quietly to themselves. The musicians began to play quietly. I led a song, very softly. I was accustomed to these types of moments in a service. We would give the folks who had come forward time to pray and do business with God, and then I would speak a word of dismissal. The group at the altar began to get up, so I prepared to wrap things up. Then, another wave began to fill the space vacated by the first wave. We continued to sing, but then I began to sense the heaviness – the density – of the presence of the Holy Spirit. I quit singing and sat down to pray.

One by one, the musicians stopped playing...silence prevailed. The only sounds were the muffled sounds of people weeping or praying to themselves or with others. Another wave of people approached the altars to kneel. I looked up and saw people kneeling at their place, just turning their chairs into prayer benches. Finally, those who had been on the platform returned to chairs or took a seat near the front. There was no sound, yet no one moved. I could not physically leave my chair. The pastor, through his wireless microphone, invited anyone who needed to leave to feel free, and those who wanted to stay could stay as long as they wanted. No one moved – not one. We sat there for easily 15-20 more minutes, no one moving, in the undeniable presence of God's Holy Spirit. Finally, we all felt the release. As we left, everyone stayed silent until we were outside the sanctuary. Many people remarked how they had never seen anything like that in their lifetimes. Most said that the presence of God was so clear that they did not dare to make a sound, for fear of disturbing the moment in His presence. It remains one of the mileposts of my life. If I never again experience the clear and present power of God, I remember that I once knew it without a doubt. In Heaven, the host will remain in this kind of subdued and worshipful silence until the bowls of wrath are all emptied.

In quick succession, the bowls of God's wrath are emptied on the Earth. The first plague is sores on those who took the brand of the beast and worshiped his cult statue. This is the same as the sixth plague on Egypt. The second bowl turns the sea to blood, congealed it like the blood of a corpse. Such was the first plague against Egypt. The third bowl extends the plague of water-to-blood to the rivers and streams – the freshwater of the world. There is a short interlude as the angels affirm that the followers of the beast deserved these plagues. The fourth bowl is poured out and empowers the sun to scorch only people with fire. The people curse God, recognizing the plague has come from Him. Still, they refuse to repent or give God glory. The next bowl brings a total reversal, and the kingdom of the beast is thrown into darkness, an exact repeat of the ninth plague against Egypt. But this is a spiritual darkness, for it only affects those who worship the beast. It also brings pain, and the followers of the beast bite their tongues in response. Still, they refuse to repent and continue to revile God. This is the same response that the plagues against Egypt elicited from Pharaoh. The sixth bowl is poured out, and the Euphrates river dries up so that the kings of the kingdom of the beast (it was the border of the Babylonian Empire) can come and do battle.

As you would expect, there is a pause before the seventh bowl is poured out. The true colors of the Dragon and the two beasts are now seen in their true form. In a vision reminiscent of the second plague on Egypt, there come frogs, but not from the lakes and rivers. The frogs are representative of the unclean filth that lives within the Dragon, the beast from the Abyss, and the beast of the Earth (here called the "false prophet"). John tells us that they are deceiving spirits – demons who will gather the power-hungry kings of the world for a final horrific battle. There is a brief parenthetical quote in which Jesus promises He is coming like a thief in the night with an admonition to stay ready – dressed through the night, as it were.

Before the seventh bowl is poured out, the armies of the world are gathered. They represent all of the world's concepts of power. They are the power of human strength, the power of human defenses, the power of human weapons, and the power of human strategy. They are everything in which the power-hungry who follow the beast trust and believe. All the might of the entire deluded world is gathered into one place. Har Maggido is an ancient Canaanite and Israelite city that sits in the Wadi Ara defile – a pass through the Carmel mountain range. It was through this pass that any attacking nation from the north or east had to come to attack Israel. Megiddo overlooked the Valley of Jezreel from the western end. Because it controlled the pass and overlooked the valley, Megiddo was tactically valuable ground. Deserted nearly 600 years before the birth of Christ, it had remained only in legends. Its location in the heart of the ancient Kingdom of Israel, and its legendary tactical position, makes it the perfect symbol for war against God. The armies are in place, but the battle will not happen. You will only hear it briefly mentioned once more in

Revelation 20! Here, it serves as the interlude before the seventh bowl pours out the last of God's wrath.

Now, the seventh bowl is not simply poured out, but thrown into the air. When it is cast into the air, the voice from the throne (the Bible's way of saying, "the voice of You-Know-Who!") announces that "It is finished." This is a direct quote from Jesus on the cross, recorded only in the Gospel of John 19:30 (hint), and now heard from the throne:

> *"30 Then when Jesus had drunk the soured wine,*
> *He said, "It is finished!" and bowing His head,*
> *He surrendered His spirit."*

There is a theophany such as creation has never experienced as it reacts to the final Word of God. The Great City, representing the seat of earthly power, splits into three pieces to reflect the Triune God, who has brought it to ruin. The other leading power centers of the world collapse. The power centers get the full measure of God's wrath until even the geography reacts by fleeing from the anger of God! Then one final plague, truly the seventh plague. It is the magnification of the seventh plague on Egypt. Seven, a holy and complete number. It is the number of perfection and finality. It is the number of the spirits of God Himself. Gigantic one-hundred-pound hailstones fall from Heaven! You can imagine the destruction such a thing would cause. They fall upon the people, bringing death and massive carnage, a near-extinction event. Still, the followers of the beast will not turn to God. In the face of all the destruction they witness, they blame God and curse His Name.

HOW MIGHT WE SHARE THIS?

I. God WILL Pour Out His Wrath

II. God is Worthy to Sit as Judge on the World

III. The Choice is Yours – Revere or Revile

QUESTIONS FOR FURTHER STUDY OR REFLECTION

1. How do we recognize wrong in the world without being judgmental?

2. Poetic justice is the Jewish idea that the punishment fits the crime perfectly. The Old Testament states this in terms of "an eye for an eye and a tooth for a tooth." How do you reconcile God's statements of poetic justice in Revelation with the loving God of the New Testament?

3. How do you believe it could be true that people could see the kind of plagues described in Revelation 14, and only revile God rather than turning to worship Him?

4. What do you think God means by, "It is finished," when we know the story still has several chapters remaining?

CHAPTER THIRTY

THE END OF THE GREAT PROSTITUTE
MYSTERY

Revelation 17:1-18

THE TEXT:

"17:1Then one of the seven angels with one of the seven bowls came and spoke to me saying, 'Come, I will show you the judgment of the great prostitute, who sits by the many waters, ²with whom the kings of the earth have fornicated, and with whom the people of the earth have become drunk with the wine of her immoralities.'

³ He then carried me in the Spirit into a wilderness. I saw a woman sitting on a huge scarlet beast that was covered with blasphemous names. It had seven heads and ten horns. ⁴ Now, the woman was dressed in purple and scarlet and adorned with gold, precious stones and pearls. In her hand, she held a golden cup filled with abominations and the impurities of her fornication. ⁵ On her forehead was written a mysterious name:

Babylon the Great
mother of prostitutes
and earthly abominations.

⁶ *And I saw that she was drunk with the blood of God's prophets, and the blood of those who witnessed for Jesus. I was deeply perplexed when I saw her.* ⁷ *Then the angel said to me: 'Why are you perplexed? I will explain to you the secret meaning of the woman and of the beast with the seven heads and ten horns. that carries her.* ⁸ *The beast, which you saw was, yet now is not, and is about to ascend from the Abyss and go to its destruction. The inhabitants of the Earth whose names have not been recorded in the Book of Life since the creation of the world will be amazed when they see the beast, because it was, is not, and will come once more.*

⁹ *This requires deep insight: The seven heads are seven hills on which the woman is seated.* ¹⁰ *They are also seven kings. Five have fallen, one is living, the other has yet come; but when he does come, he can remain for only a little while.* ¹¹ *The beast which was, and is not, is an eighth king. He is one of the seven and is headed for destruction.*

¹² *The ten horns you saw are ten kings who are not yet kings, but they will receive authority as*

kings for a single hour, along with the beast. ¹³ *They are of one accord and will relinquish their power and authority to the beast.* ¹⁴ *They will fight against the Lamb, but the Lamb will conquer them because he is Lord of Lords and King of Kings—and with him will be his called, chosen, and faithful followers.*

¹⁵ *Then the angel explained to me; 'The waters you saw, where the prostitute sits, are all peoples, crowds, races and languages.* ¹⁶ *The ten horns you saw, and the beast, will hate the prostitute and will strip her naked, defile her, eat her flesh, and burn her remains in a fire.* ¹⁷ *For God prompted them to do His will by agreeing to hand over to the beast their royal authority, until the words of God are fulfilled.* ¹⁸ *And the woman you saw is the great city that rules over the kings of the Earth.'" Rev 17:1-18*

WHAT IS THE TEXT SAYING TO US?

Now, in a way, we step out of time. As the judgment is taking place, with the armies of the Earth gathered for the final conflict, an angel approaches John. The angel invites him to come and see what the judgment has brought upon "the great prostitute, who sits by many waters." She is said to be the one with whom the kings of the Earth committed lewd acts, and the people of the Earth drank and partied in the immoralities she encouraged. This is not the first time the Bible has shown an evil empire as a prostitute. Compare what you read here with Isaiah 23:17, where nearly the exact description appears concerning the Kingdom of Tyre.

There is a line from Shakespeare's *Tempest*, which was adapted cleverly by an American politician's wife by the name of Billie Wilkie in 1940 that says, "Politics makes strange bedfellows." That is precisely the attitude behind this portrayal of the woman on the beast. Please remember, these are all symbolic figures of speech. John portrays them in language that would have shocked the people of his time, more than they do the people of ours. Still, the symbolisms are so very clear as not to be confused for anything else as we read them. The fall of Babylon has been proclaimed and hinted at for several chapters. Now, it is time to see what happens to her - in super-slow motion.

The angel carries John, "in the spirit," so you know that what he is seeing is not historical fact, but spiritual truth. He sees, in the wasteland, a woman sitting on a giant blood-red beast. Why is she in the wasteland? Because it is where the beast carries everyone who dares to follow it or ride on it in this case. When a horrible beast carries you off into a wasteland, desert, or wilderness - the ending will not be good for you. This beast is the same scarlet color as the Dragon. Again, this beast, not equated with the first or second beast, is a copy of the Dragon, the source of evil in the world. It has seven heads and ten horns, yet it is neither the beast from the Abyss nor the beast from the Earth. It is most similar to the beast from the Earth. You should understand it as another Earthly Kingdom, one John will identify for us. But first, he describes the woman.

We already know that she is a whore – the Greek word is *pornes* – the word from which we derive the English word "pornography." The point is not that she makes her living in the sex trade. She commoditizes immorality. Thereby, she is the pattern for every society after her, which will do the same. She trades in sin. She dresses in colors that only royalty can afford – purple and scarlet. She is affluence and wealth. She has gold and jewels and pearls. In her hand is a golden chalice. You might expect it to be full of expensive wine. But this cup overflows with abominations: blasphemous pagan religious practices, fornication, and secular sexual commodities. She is the worst of all worlds. She perverts spiritual worship with sex and sells sex in the secular world for money. She profanes both the sacred and the non-sacred.

Interestingly, she does not bear the name of the beast, nor his mark. Instead, so tremendous is her vanity that, on her forehead, is her own name – Babylon the Great! She is so blasphemous that she is trying to out-blaspheme the beast! She is proud to be the mother of all secular fornicators and sex marketers. Even more proud to be the mother of all earthly pagan worship prostitutes. She revels in her absolute nastiness. She is drunk on the blood of martyrs and would rather take the lives of witnesses than to have them tell her that her sexual marketing is immoral. She is not only vile and profane, but she is murderous as well. The three worst crimes in most jurisdictions are murder, rape, and child sexual exploitation. Throughout history, people have recognized that these three are the worst of the worst. In Revelation 17, the great prostitute is collectively all of those things in one being. When John realizes this, he says so great was the entirety of evil in her that he was astonished!

The angel asks John why he is astonished. After all, this is the nature of all political power systems. They murder, victimize, and exploit. To show John this truth, the angel explains, for all of us, the symbols here. The beast "once was, now is not, and will come up out of the Abyss and go to its destruction." It is a blatant parody of the description of God as the one "who was, and who is, and who is to come." Evil always parodies holiness. This particular reference is likely to the Roman Empire. It was founded as a Republic and reached its zenith as such under Julius Caesar. But the Senate and politicians of the day wrestled for power and murdered Julius Caesar. His nephew, Caesar Augustus, took the throne and cleverly took power away from the politicians and accrued it for himself. Rome became an Empire. Her days as a Republic were over. Augustus' successors, Caligula and Nero, commoditized sexual immorality and spent themselves in excess until Rome burned to the ground while Nero partied.

With Nero's suicide, the dynasty of Augustus and his family rule ended. The glory days of the Empire died. Civil war broke out until Vespasian reestablished control and took the office of Emperor. But the glory days of Caesar Augustus would never return. John uses this cycle of the Roman Empire to indicate the life cycle of the beast's master – the Devil. He ruled the world from the Garden of Eden until the Cross of Christ. At the cross, the Devil was defeated and can be continually defeated by the Church and the Word. Yet, today, those who do not know Christ are astonished at the Devil's power and believe that he is powerful. In our culture, there are many who think of the Devil as some mighty and counter-cultural party animal. Of course, he is not; and they are fulfilling this very word of Revelation prophecy.

The angel tells John that wisdom is required. Wisdom lies not in recognizing what the beast represents, but in understanding that the symbolism is not simply for a single empire, but for all Empires of the Earth. The beast has seven heads. They are seven hills – Rome is the city built on seven hills. The woman sits there or is enthroned there. She is the political and economic power of the Empire. To help us understand that the implication is that the beast represents all Empires, John is told that "five have fallen, one now is, and one is yet to come." The Empires that had affected God's people were: the Egyptian Empire, the Assyrian Empire, the Babylonian Empire, the Persian Empire, and the Greek Empire. The one under which the Revelation is written is the Roman Empire. The one to come will be the last of the world Empires. The beast himself becomes an eighth king who will belong to the final Empire before he is ultimately destroyed.

John is told that the ten horns – the power markers – represent ten kings who do not yet have kingdoms. Because they obviously belong to the future, many guesses have been made about whom they might represent. Please remember – they are symbolic. The number ten, as we have already discussed, is an in-between number. It is not the perfect number that seven is, or that twelve is. It is – a large number, but not holy. Their names do not matter. There will be many, but they will not be the ultimate power in your life. Empires will rise and fall – the Mongol Empire, the British Empire, the Russian Empire, the Qing Dynasty, the Ottoman Empire, the French Empire, the Caliphate, the Japanese Empire, the Third Reich – the list goes on and on. They have one thing in common: they each lasted for only a season. They had an hour of life, then fell. In the ultimate tally, Empire after

Empire will make war on the Lamb, but He will win the ultimate battle for He is the King of Kings and Lord of Lords. Who will be with Him in victory? He will bring all of His called, chosen, and faithful followers to victory with Him. It used to get on my nerves when people would refer simply to The Revelation by saying things like, "I read to the end, and we win!" Yet, as I have gotten older, and less willing to argue, I have to admit they are mostly right in that assessment. Still, what I hope you might take from this book – from The Book of Revelation – is that there are two forces at work in your life every day: Empire and Kingdom. One threatens and manipulates and rules by the appearance of power. The other loves and enfolds and gives you authentic power.

Then the angel explains that the waters are many nations, races, and languages, further affirming the representative nature of the beast and the woman. Immorality and power-hunger affect almost every nation known to humanity. But then a very curious statement: the beast, and his ten horns, hate the prostitute! They will tear her to shreds, eat her, and burn her remains. Why? Because she tried to out-blaspheme the blasphemers. She tried to ride their power and make it her own. She refused to take the mark of the beast or to worship his image or be beholden to the Dragon. She thinks she's better at being evil than the very source of evil. She has, in a way, blasphemed the Devil! Evil always eats its followers because evil systems refuse to worship God – or any other power. The truly evil believe they are the ultimate power and, in the end, are destroyed by their own evil and filthy hearts. She is the great city – at the moment, Rome. Yet she stands for every Empire that will ever rise or fall.

HOW DO WE SHARE THIS?

I.   The Woman

II. The Beast

III. The Lamb

QUESTIONS FOR FURTHER STUDY OR REFLECTION
---

1. How prevalent is sexual immorality in the world today? Where is it worst?

2. How does that sexual content affect the values of your culture, government, or **church?**

3. Do you see the immorality of the world being adopted by the church? In what ways?

4. Where do you believe you might see evil behind a governmental system in your world?

5. How does a Christian worldview affect how you live in this world?

CHAPTER THIRTY-ONE

THE LAMENT AND THE CURSE OVER BABYLON

"THE LIGHT OF A LAMP WILL NEVER SHINE IN YOU AGAIN"

Revelation 18:1-19

THE TEXT:

"¹⁸:¹ After this, I saw another angel with extraordinary authority descending from Heaven, and the Earth was illuminated by his splendor. ²Then he cried out with a mighty voice, saying:

'Fallen! Fallen is Babylon the Great! It has become the habitation demons, a haunt for every type of unclean spirit, and a hideout for every unclean and hateful bird.

³ For all nations have collapsed because of the maddening wine of her immoral passion. The kings of the Earth fornicated with her, and the merchants of the Earth grew rich from her excessive thirst for luxury.'

⁴ Then I heard another voice from heaven saying: 'My people, come out of her, lest you participate in her sins, or share in suffering her judgment. ⁵ For her sins are have reached to Heaven, and God remembers her crimes. ⁶ Do to her as she has done; pay her back double for what she has done. Pour her a double serving from her own cup. ⁷ As she glorified herself and lived in sensuality, give her an equal measure of torment and grief.

In her heart she brags, 'I sit on the throne as queen. I am not a widow. I will never know sorrow.' ⁸ Therefore her plagues will overtake her in one day: pestilence, mourning and famine; and she will be consumed by fire because mighty is the Lord God who has judged her.

⁹ The kings of the Earth who committed immorality with her and lived in her luxury will weep and mourn for her when they see the smoke rising up from where she once was.¹⁰ Terrified at her torment, they will stand at a great distance and cry: 'Alas! Alas, you great city, you mighty city of Babylon! Because your reckoning came in only an hour!'

¹¹And the merchants of the Earth will weep and mourn over her because no one buys their goods anymore— [12] *their gold or silver, their valuable gemstones and pearls; soft linen, rich purple, silk and red cloth; their citron wood, and all manner of articles of ivory, rare wood, bronze, iron and marble;* [13] *shiploads of cinnamon and spices, of myrrh and frankincense, of fine wine and olive oil, of finely ground flour and wheat; cattle and sheep; horses and chariots; as well as human cargo to be sold as slaves.*

[14] *And the ripe fruit you longed for is gone from you. All your expensive and beautiful trinkets have vanished, never to be recovered.'* [15] *The merchants who sold these things and got rich from her will stand at a far distance, terrified by her torture. They will weep and grieve* [16] *and cry out:*

'Alas! Alas to you, great city, who were dressed in fine linen, purple and scarlet, and adorned with gold, precious stones, and pearls! [17] *In a moment such great wealth has been totally destroyed!'*

And every sea captain, and all who travel by ship, the sailors, and all who earn their living on the sea, will stand far off. [18] *When they see the smoke from her incineration, they will exclaim, 'Was there ever a city like this great city?'*

¹⁹ And they threw dust on their heads, and cried, weeping and mourning: 'Alas! Alas! You great city, where all who had ships on the sea became rich from her wealth! For in a moment, she has been destroyed! ²⁰ Rejoice over her, you Heavens, And, you people of God, apostles, and prophets, For God has condemned her for condemning you."

²¹ A particular mighty angel picked up a boulder resembling a huge millstone and threw it into the sea and said: "With just this same violence will the great city of Babylon will be overthrown, never to exist again. ²² And the sound of harpists and singers, flutists and trumpeters, will never be heard in you again. No craftsman of any trade will ever be found in you again. The sound of the mill will never be heard in you again. ²³ The light of a lamp will never be seen in you again. The happy voices of the bridegroom and the bride will never be heard in you again. For your merchants were the world's famous people, and all the nations were deluded by your magic spells.

²⁴ And in her was found the blood of prophets and of the people of God, and of all who had been slaughtered on the Earth." Rev 18:1-19

WHAT IS THE TEXT SAYING TO US?

This chapter brings earthly closure to the story of Babylon The Great. The next chapter will show us the Heavenly response to Babylon the Great's fall. This is the earthly lament, or funeral service for the Great City, which represents economic and moral evil on the Earth. The first part of the chapter takes the form of a lament. The lament is an Old Testament form of expressing great pain. It accentuates the limitations of man by giving expression to the words a man utters when he comes to the end of himself. They typically begin with words such as we find at the beginning of Psalm 22, which Jesus quoted from the cross:

> *"My God! My God! Why have You abandoned me?" Ps 22:1*

In this lament, the formulation begins with "Alas! Alas!" They are words of total helplessness.

First, however, the tremendous angel flies through Heaven and declares that Babylon has fallen. There is nothing left of Babylon. She will now be a shattered ruin where unclean spirits and feral animals will take over. Not only will the capital of evil collapse, but it will take all of the major cities of the world, all based on the same selfish economy, with it. The symbolism is the collapse of all human government and economy. As a younger man, I thought this kind of collapse was impossible in the modern world. But while I was in college, I learned differently.

I was in college at Oklahoma State University from 1979 to 1983. In my early college years, an oil boom hit the state of Oklahoma. I remember driving home from college on Friday evenings and counting oil drilling derricks. It was just over an hour's drive, and at just about any point during the journey, one could stop and count fifteen-to-eighteen drilling rigs. The state was in an incredible economic boom. Money flowed smoothly, and no one did without anything they wanted. Banks were making huge money in speculative loans in the oil field. As a result, they were loaning money freely, and to people whose lives were also tied up in oil field speculation. The entire system was built on guessing where oil and gas might be found because the prices for the commodities were higher than anyone had ever seen them! One of the primary banks at the center of the boom was Penn Square Bank in Oklahoma City, Oklahoma. The bank had been around for decades. Everyone trusted the decisions of its wise and experienced bankers. Penn Square Bank built a new high-rise building with a collection of high-end boutique shops inside its facility. No one had ever seen such extravagance.

Many of my dorm mates were getting new clothes and new cars and living very extravagantly. Then, in 1981, oil prices began to drop. The Iranian crisis was behind us. A relatively peaceful Middle East was, once again, flowing with oil. Pressure on supplies eased, and prices relaxed significantly. With the reduction in possible profits, companies began to pull back on oilfield investment, and the big bank got nervous that it was over-extended. Penn Square Bank had dragged banks, savings and loans, and credit unions from all around the country into its speculative investment strategies. Looking to make a fast buck, they had jumped in with great enthusiasm. As prices retreated, investment income dried up. The banks began to lose money in their investments. They could not meet obligations to the return rates they had promised customers. In July of 1982, I was out touring the country with a musical performance group. I needed some cash and went to cash a check. When I presented the check for cashing at the local bank, the bank manager came over and informed me that my financial institution had closed the day before. Penn Square Bank had collapsed and had taken financial institutions across the country with it. My savings were federally insured, but it would be weeks before I could again access my money. In the meantime, friends made sure I was fed and cared for. Still, I will never forget that summer; and learning that financial institutions are not always as invincible as they seem. Money is, truly, only an illusion. It can all vanish in a moment.

That is precisely the point of the fall of Babylon the Great in The Revelation. The economies of the world function on an intricate system of supply and demand. If one part of the system collapses, the entire system suffers. If the central consumer in the system fails, everything falls apart around it. The lament in Revelation 17 comes from the lips of the merchants and sailors whose lives will fall into poverty because of the failure of the economic system in which they made their living. Their lament is evidence that all the people have not disappeared from the Earth. God's people are, in fact, still on Earth.

In verse 4, another giant angel calls to God's people: "Get away from her! Get out, lest you participate in her transgressions and, likewise, her punishment!" Even in the wickedest of times, God calls His people to a life of holiness. What is holiness? The Bible defines it with different words – but always the same idea: unique, separate, peculiar, sanctified, or set apart. When I was growing up, I remember a boy in my third-grade class who dressed differently than most of the kids. His haircut was very short. His clothes were always very plain. At some point during the year, he and I ended up working on a project together in class.

I remember asking him if he liked his haircut and clothes that way, or if his family was just poor. He looked at me with a funny look, offered a kind of choked-off laugh, and said, "No, Kevin. We are not poor. We dress this way to honor God. God does not care about fancy clothes and shoes and haircuts. God wants our hearts to be nice instead." I thought, "What a strange kid!" Throughout our school days, his church was known as the "holy rollers," and the "Jesus freaks." The girls wore dresses most of the time. We rarely saw them in pants, let alone jeans. They wore no makeup, no jewelry, and their hair was often long and straight. They did not take part in school activities on Sundays. They never really got into fund-raising sales efforts. They were different…unique… peculiar. Little did I know that one day, I would join them and be one of them!

God has always called His people to be separate from the political and economic systems of the world in which we live. While those systems will inevitably affect us throughout our lives, God calls us to invest our lives in His Kingdom and economy. We could spend ten more chapters exploring God's politic and economy. Those have been the subject of many great books, and I will leave you to research that further on your own. It is sufficient here to say that the Kingdom of God is based on true substance rather than appearance. The economy of God is based on generosity and service to others rather than acquiring things and money for oneself. I have a good friend who constantly calls the Kingdom of God, "the upside-down Kingdom." That is a very apt point-of-view, given that God's Kingdom is based on opposite values than those that rule earthly Empires.

The penalties called-for against Babylon are all based on what we call "poetic justice." She is to receive now all of the same things she gave, and twice as much. Did she live in splendor and extravagance? She will receive twice as much poverty and shame in return. Did she live in excess and gratification? She is to know twice as much misery and loss. Her collapse will come in a day – and it will take out all who partied and committed immoralities with her. The entire system will come crashing down because it was all built around the central idea of *"self."*

You see, nice clothes are not a sin. A new car is not a sin. A beautiful home is not a sin. Having nice things and enjoying good food and drink are not sins. Sin is not really any simple action. Sin is the attitude behind any action that seeks to exalt *self.* The drive to be better than someone else, to the extent that we will step on them to climb over them, is sin. The need to look better than, drive better than, wear better than, perform better than, or own better than someone else to exalt self over others, is the very engine behind sin in our lives. Such motives lead us to base our lives on appearances rather than substance. If we stay in that system of priorities, we become shallow and petty; we mistreat others in an attempt to make ourselves look better than them. If we live like this, we are living in the true muck of a sinful heart. Ugly actions cannot help but follow a heart lost in the ugliness of selfish motives. God calls us out of the deception of life in the systems and priorities of Babylon the Great.

The last section of the chapter is, in actuality, a curse. The world laments and grieves, throwing dust into the air to settle down on their heads. The curse is uttered by an angel who heaves a boulder the size of a millstone into the sea. There is a connection here with a quotation of Jesus that we quoted back in chapter 15:

> *"If anyone causes one of these little ones who believe in me to stumble, one day, he will believe that it would have been better for him to have had a large millstone tied around his neck and to have been hurled into the depths of the sea to drown." Matthew 18:6*

The world's political and economic systems have done exactly that – caused the children of God to stumble. As a symbol of judgment, the angel hurls the millstone-sized boulder into the sea and begins to proclaim the curse. Look at what it entails

There will never again be harpists, singers, flute players, or trumpets. No music again – ever. There will never be a craftsman at work there again. Nothing new will be built again – ever.

There will be no more grinding of grain there. No bread will be eaten there again – ever. The next one is tough: The light of a lamp will never be seen again in you. No light – ever. Never again will the city hear the voice of a bride or bridegroom. No weddings again – ever. What do all of those things have in common? They are expressions of celebration and joy. They are what the Jews call *"l'chaim!"*

Jesus said, in John 10:10, that He came to give His disciples abundant life. Life is meant to be abundant in blessing – not excessive in immoralities. Joy comes from enjoying the blessings that life naturally brings. The world twists the things that bring joy when it insists that they become instruments of excess in people's lives. In the curse, all of the joys of life are finished. This is a creative way of speaking total death as a curse. If anyone was left standing, they would find a way to express joy again. That is the way of the human spirit. We will sing. We will make music. We will create light. We will marry and celebrate! The total absence of joy is an indicator that no one is left. The judgment on the sinful structures of this world will take, with them, every single person who pursues them.

HOW MIGHT WE SHARE THIS?

I.   Sinful and Selfish Structures Are Doomed to Fail

II. When They Fail, They Take People with Them

III. Sin Has the Power to Cause the Collapse of All the Good Things in Life

QUESTIONS FOR FURTHER STUDY OR REFLECTION

1.   What is the function of a lament in the Old Testament?

2.   What is the significance of the fall of Babylon in Revelation?

3.   What values that you see in your world today are reflections of the values of Babylon?

4.   How should Christians differentiate our values from the values of the world?

CHAPTER THIRTY-TWO

THE DEFEAT OF SATAN AND JUDGMENT OF THE DEAD

THE WEDDING SUPPER OF THE LAMB

Revelation 19:1-20:3

THE TEXT:

"¹⁹:¹After this I heard what sounded like the roar of an immense crowd in Heaven shouting: 'Hallelujah! Victory and glory and power belong to our God, ²because true and just are His judgments. He has sentenced the great prostitute who corrupted the Earth with her immorality, and He has avenged the deaths of His servants she slaughtered.'

³ Then they shouted again: "Hallelujah! The smoke of her destruction rises forever and ever."

⁴ Then the twenty-four elders and the four living creatures fell on their faces and worshiped God, who is seated on the throne, crying out: "Amen, Hallelujah!"

⁵ *A voice came from the throne, saying: "Praise our God, all you His servants, you who fear Him, both common and great!"*

⁶ *Then I heard what sounded like a great crowd or like the roar of rushing waters or like loud peals of thunder, shouting: "Hallelujah! For our Lord God Almighty has begun to reign! ⁷ Let us rejoice and be glad and give glory to Him! For the wedding day of the Lamb has arrived, and His bride has prepared herself. ⁸ She was allowed fine linen, shining and pure." (Fine linen stands for the righteous deeds of God's people.)*

⁹ *Then the angel said to me, "Write: Blessed are the ones who have been invited to the wedding feast of the Lamb!" Then he said, "This is the true message from God."*

¹⁰ *Then I fell at his feet to worship him. But he said to me, 'Don't do that! I am a fellow servant with you and your brothers and sisters who believe the testimony of Jesus. Worship God! For the testimony about Jesus is the very Spirit of prophecy.*

¹¹ *I then saw Heaven standing open and there before me was a white horse, with a rider called Faithful and True. With justice, He judges and*

wages war. [12] *Now His eyes were like blazing fire, and on His head were many crowns. He has a name written on Him that no one knows but He Himself.* [13] *He was dressed in a robe dipped in blood, and his name is the "Word of God."* [14] *The armies of Heaven followed Him riding white horses, wearing fine linen, white and clean.* [15] *From His mouth projected a sharp sword with which to smite the nations, and He Himself will rule them with an iron crook, and He Himself treads the winepress of the fury of the wrath of God Almighty.*

[16] *And He has inscribed upon His robe and on His thigh this name: King of Kings and Lord of Lords.*

[17] *Then I saw an angel, standing on the sun, who cried in a loud voice to all the birds flying in midheaven, "Come, gather together at the great supper of God,* [18] *so that you may eat the flesh of kings, generals, and the mighty, of horses and their riders, and the flesh of all people, free and slave, great and common."*

[19] *Then I saw the beast and the kings of the Earth and their armies assembled to wage war against the one mounted on the white horse, and with his armies.* [20] *But the beast was captured and with*

it the false prophet who had performed miracles on his behalf. With these signs, he had deceived those who had received the mark of the beast and worshiped its image. The two of them were hurled alive into the fiery lake of burning sulfur. ²¹ *The rest were slain with the sword coming out of the mouth of the rider on the horse, and all the birds gorged themselves on their flesh."*

"^{20:1}*And I saw an angel descending from Heaven, holding the key to the Abyss on a great chain in his hand.* ² *He seized the Dragon, that ancient serpent, who is the Devil and Satan, and bound him for a thousand years.* ³ *He threw him into the Abyss, and slammed and locked it over him, to keep him from leading the nations astray any more until the thousand years were completed. After that, he must be released for a short period. Rev 19:1-20:3*

WHAT IS THE TEXT SAYING TO US?

Chapter 18 showed us the earthly view of the demise of the economies and political power structures of the Empires of the Earth. We can certainly see that all Earthly systems come to the same kind of ruin. Yet, there is an element in Chapter 18 that tells us that this portrayal is of the ultimate demise of Empire, and the ultimate victory of Kingdom. Fittingly, then, Chapter 19 opens with the perspective of the Heavenly celebration at the final collapse of Earthly Empires that set themselves to enslaving and misleading humankind and attempting to replace the need for God in the human heart.

Now, work backward with me a moment. We established that the woman was representative of human systems that position themselves to benefit financially and sensually from government and political structures represented by the beasts. The beasts of political power always come to resent those who profit from them and turn on them and devour them. The earthly beasts represent political and governmental systems committed to evil principles and not to the welfare of the people they rule. They rule only by power and by accruing more power. They serve the beast from the sea – the systems of evil on this Earth. The beast from the sea represents everything that seeks to replace the holiness and righteousness of Christ on Earth with sheer wickedness. The beast from the sea is the earthly embodiment of the Dragon – the Devil – the total spiritual embodiment of all that is evil. What we have, thus far, witnessed in the demise of Babylon the Great, is the collapse of the Earthly, human, pursuit of gratification. The power structure behind those sinful pursuits still exists and will next be dealt with by God.

There are some important things to note about the celebration in Heaven over the downfall of Babylon the Great. If you are reading along in the NIV, there is a chapter heading that says, "The Threefold Hallelujah. Yet, if you count them, there are four. The word "hallelujah" is a Hebrew word that means "praise to God!" The first hallelujah is like a roar from every voice in Heaven. It extols the righteousness of God and the fitting nature of His judgments. They shout the second hallelujah, because the smoke from Babylon's incineration rises up to Heaven, as prayer rose earlier in the vision. The third hallelujah comes from the 24 elders and the four cherubim. Predictably, they fall on their faces and shout their praise with their faces to the floor. The fourth hallelujah comes from a voice like mighty rushing waters, as though all of creation shouts it at once! The waters announce the wedding of the Lamb and His bride – the church. Of course, this is not a literal wedding, but the celebration of the fact that they are now together forever. The church has been dressed in white – the robes we saw the multitude in Heaven wearing in Chapter 7 of The Revelation. John is told that the white represents purity. Their sin has been forgiven. They have been redeemed. Their failures are remembered no more, and their standing with God is absolutely secured in purity, washed under the blood of the Lamb.

The angel gives John a particular blessing concerning those invited to the "wedding supper of the Lamb," that is, the Bride of Christ, the church. Because he belongs to this group, John is overwhelmed and falls down to worship the angel, but the angel tells him to stop. The angel corrects John, saying that he is just another brother with the brothers and sisters who have been forgiven and redeemed by the Lamb.

Then, once more, Heaven is opened to John's eyes, and he sees one more rider. But this is not one of the previous riders. He rides a white horse, like the first rider of the apocalypse, Conquest. But He is not named Conquest. He is named "Faithful and True." There is no faithfulness, nor truth, in the Dragon, the beasts, nor Babylon the Great. They turn on and devour each other. The one who is faithful and true does not wage war with weapons, but with justice. So great is His power that His Word – His faithful, true, and just Word – will vanquish any foe who stands against Him.

There is no weapon against Him. There is no law against Him. His eyes are like what? That is right…blazing fire. We first saw those eyes in Revelation 1:14. On His head are the crowns of every jurisdiction in creation, for He is the true King. On Him is written a name; that name that no one knows, that I believe John was prohibited from writing down in Revelation 10:4. He is dressed in a robe dipped in blood, and His name is the Word of God. (John 1 refers to Jesus as "the Word.") All the armies of Heaven, all of the righteous dressed in white robes, join Him in battle. Do not read past that small detail too quickly!

Take a minute to think about that. Who are those in the white robes? They are the saints who died believing in Christ, whether martyred, or beheaded, or died through time, or taken up in the final harvest. They are the army of the power of God, and they will do battle with Evil. Here is the entire point of the Book of Revelation! Yet, it is so easy to just read right past in our hurry to get on to the New Jerusalem. But here is the power. If you live in a tiny church in an obscure mountain village in the vast Asian province of the Great Roman Empire, it might be easy to feel like you have no power. The Roman Empire is immense and could crush you in a second. But that is the power of the Dragon and the beasts!

The real power lies in the host in white robes in Heaven. Those brothers and sisters of the Lamb and all who believe in Him – *your* brothers and sisters! *Your* powerful family! They ride on white horses and are ready to do battle with Evil on your behalf anytime. What are you afraid of? Why should you feel powerless?

All the might of all the armies of Heaven will fight on your behalf. My friend, Keith Maule, has always said, "One day, you are going to walk into Heaven, and you are going to say, "Oh, wow. I should have believed for more! What was I ever afraid of?" I believe he is spot-on. Please do not leave The Revelation and miss this point. Is life overwhelming right now? That Empire does not rule you. Have you gotten a bad diagnosis? That Empire does not rule you. Have you had to walk through divorce, or the loss of friends or the loss of a loved one? That Empire does not rule you. If that loved one you lost walked with Jesus, they have just joined the force that fights on your behalf. Here is the reason that the Bible says,

"No weapon formed against you will reach you, and any voice raised against you will be silenced." Is 54:17

"What shall we say in response to all that God has done for us? If God is on our side, who can stand against us?" Rom 8:31

"For I am sure that neither death nor life, neither angels nor demons, not the present, the future, or any power anywhere; not height nor depth, nor anything in all of creation can separate us from the love of God that is in Jesus Christ, our Lord!" Rom 8:38-39

Are you catching on now? Do you hear me? You have more power at your back than you have any idea, or any ability to comprehend. The angels who come to people with messages from Heaven always say, "Do not be afraid." They say that because they *know* the power that works in your benefit. They *know* you cannot lose in whatever battle you are facing!

A missionary once told me the story of the people with whom he was working in what my church calls a "creative access" area of the world. Those people live under constant threat of execution should they preach the Gospel of Christ. A church leader in that area was entrapped by a man who approached him seeking to hear the Gospel. That seeker was a mole for the government and turned the pastor in. The pastor was arrested, taken in for interrogation, and beaten nearly unconscious. The interrogator held a gun to his head and said, "Disown your Jesus this moment, or I shall pull the trigger and send you off to your God."

The pastor said, "Go ahead, pull the trigger. The worst you can do is exactly as you say – send me home to my God. But know this, the moment you pull that trigger, you spill my blood on every word I have ever spoken, on every pamphlet I have ever handed out, and on every Bible I have ever given to a new believer in this country. The moment you pull that trigger, you transform me from an impoverished preacher to a martyr for the cause of Christ. You will elevate me to legendary stature among our people. They will tell of the penniless preacher who gave his life for Jesus, who was unafraid as the officer shot him in the head. You will make me thousands of times more effective and thousands of times stronger for Christ than I could ever possibly be by myself. Pull the trigger!"

The missionary said that the pastor told him the man stood frozen for what seemed a very long time. His hand began to shake in anger as he realized the truth of the words the pastor had spoken. The pastor said he did not know what hit him, only that he woke up alongside the road at the entrance to his village. A note had been stuffed into his pocket that said, "This is what we will do to anyone we find talking about Jesus." The church grew in that man's region by incredible leaps as word of how God had delivered him, and his bravery in the face of certain death spread like fire through the villages.

How would you live if you could see the armies of the host of Heaven right behind you every day? You would fight like David in the face of Goliath:

> *"You come against me with a spear and a shield and a sword. But I come against you in the name of the Lord Almighty, the God of the armies of Israel, whom you have defied.* [46] *Today the Lord will hand you over to me, and I will strike you down and cut off your head. Today I will give the carcasses of your army to the birds and the wild animals for a feast, and the whole world will know that there is a God in Israel." 1 Samuel 17:45-46*

I do not really hear any fear there, do you? This is the point for which I have written this entire book! I have been waiting through the entire story to get here. If you could only focus for a moment on who it is you serve, who it is that fights for you, whose power lives within you, and the amazing things of which that power is capable, you would live with far less fear and far more faith. You would step into today and tomorrow and every day that lies ahead forever, knowing that this world cannot harm you. The worst it can do is send you home. It can only send you to join the armies of God, fighting on behalf of your brothers and sisters who have yet to graduate. You have nothing to fear. Nothing.

Christ is mounted up and comes to fight in your place. Out of His mouth comes the double-edged sword. In His hand is the iron scepter. His robe is stained with blood because it is He who treads out the winepress of God's wrath on those who come against you. On His robe and on His thigh His name is branded:

"King of Kings and Lord of Lords"

You really have more power on your side than you know. You truly have nothing to fear.

At the moment before the final spiritual battle starts, an angel calls all of the birds to come and prepare to feast on the carcasses of God's enemies. David does not fight alone; neither do you.

The beast from the sea and the beast from the Earth are captured before the battle can begin. They are thrown, alive, into the lake of burning sulfur and fire. The rest are no contest; they are killed by the double-edged sword coming from the Lord's mouth – His Word! He defeats them, as it were, with one hand tied behind His back. He does not even have to use the power of His church on these puny foes. Then, an angel does the clean-up work! The angel flies down from Heaven and grabs the Dragon (I envision him grabbing the Dragon by the throat!) and drags him over to the shaft of the Abyss and flings him in! The angel slams the door to the shaft of the Abyss and locks it with the heavy chain he carries. The thousand years? Remember it just means a very, very long time – 500 generations – 200 lifetimes. That Devil is not coming back anytime soon.

That is the real power that always has your back if you are a part of the Body of Christ.

"Stop being afraid." Revelation 1:17

HOW MIGHT WE SHARE THIS?

You may see this from any number of perspectives: literary structure, eschatological victory, or expository proclamation. I preach only one point from this section:

I. Stop Being Afraid! (That's a pretty good single-point sermon)

QUESTIONS FOR FURTHER STUDY OR REFLECTION

1. How would you really live if you were not afraid of anything?

2. Why are you not living that way now? Of what are you afraid? Why?

3. What is the first step you would take if you understood that the entire force of the armies of God was behind you, right now?

4. Can you get started? What is in your way? What is stopping you?

5. Who could pray with you or help you put down your fear today?

CHAPTER THIRTY-THREE

THE GREAT WHITE THRONE
HEAVEN CAME DOWN

Revelation 20:4-15

THE TEXT:

"20:4 I saw thrones, and people sitting on them who had been given authority to judge the souls of those who had been beheaded because of their witness to Jesus and because of the Word of God and who had not worshiped the beast nor its image and who had not received its brand on their foreheads or their hands. They were raised to life and ruled with the Messiah for a thousand years. 5 The rest of the dead did not come to life until the thousand years were over.

(This is the first resurrection. 6 How fortunate and holy is the one who has a share in the first resurrection. The second death has no authority over them, but they will be priests of God and His Messiah, and they will reign with Him for a thousand years.)

⁷ When the thousand years are completed, Satan will be released from his prison ⁸ and will go out to deceive the nations at the four corners of the Earth, Gog and Magog, and to gather them for battle. Their number is like the sand on the seashore.

⁹ They marched across the entire Earth and surrounded the camp of God's people and the city He loves. Then fire came down from Heaven and consumed them.¹⁰ And the Devil, who misled them, was thrown into the lake of burning fire and sulfur, the same place the beast and the false prophet had been cast, and they will all suffer torment day and night forever.

¹¹ Then I saw a great white throne and the One who was seated on it. The Earth and the Heavens fled from his presence, but there was no place for them. ¹² And I saw the dead, famous and commoners, standing before the throne, and books were opened. A particular book was opened, which is the Book of Life and the dead were judged on the basis of what they had done as recorded in the books. ¹³ The sea gave up the dead in it, and death and Hades gave up the dead in them, and each person was judged according to their works. ¹⁴ Then even death and Hades themselves were cast into the lake of fire. This is

the second death, the lake of fire. ¹⁵ And if any-
one's name was not found recorded in the Book
of Life, that person was thrown into the lake of
fire. Rev 20:4-15

WHAT IS THE TEXT SAYING TO US?

In Revelation 3:21, at the end of the message to the church at
Laodicea, we heard the promise that the one who prevailed would
earn the right to sit with Christ on His throne. Here, that promise
is portrayed as fulfilled. This is a judgment scene, but those on the
thrones are not going to judge anyone, but the Devil. Remember
how he was overcome - by the Church and the Word? Now it is
the Church and Christ (the Living Word) who will pass judgment
on the Devil.

Those who have died for their testimony are shown to have a
sort of priority in God's eyes. They are the first resurrected. Going
back to the Christian end-times movies of my youth, this was a
scene with which they terrified us. In those last days, we may all
have to endure being beheaded for daring to remain faithful to
Jesus. That is not really what John is saying here, thank the Dear
Lord Above. Beheading was the ultimate form of capital punishment in the Roman Empire. It remains so in the cultures of many
Middle Eastern countries yet today. History reports that some
martyrs were, indeed, beheaded though most were boiled in oil or
burned at the stake. Still, the Greek word here for "beheaded," is a
very specific word. The Romans had two forms of beheading that
they instituted for capital punishment. The honorable and merciful

method was beheading by sword. The more cruel and vindictive method was beheading by the ax. The word used here is for beheading by an ax. These who have been murdered for sharing the Gospel were murdered with animosity and vengeance. For those who give their lives because people hated them for sharing the Good News of Christ, there is a special place and a priority in Heaven.

Now we come to the famous "thousand-year reign," the millennium. You are likely aware that different traditions have ascribed differing interpretations to this concept. There is a group known as *"amillennialists"* who believe that the thousand-year time frame is a generic reference to the Christian age from Augustine to the present. The *"premillennialists"* believe that Christ will return to Earth before the thousand-year reign. This group is also sometimes called *literalists*. They belong to the group of people who adhere to the *Dispensationalist* theory of God's activity in history. Then there are *"postmillennialists"* (like me) who believe that the reign of Christ is the fulfillment of Jesus' own words in Luke 17. Listen to the words of Jesus as He describes the coming of the Kingdom of God:

> *"20Once, when asked by the Pharisees when the kingdom of God would come, Jesus replied, 'The coming of the kingdom of God is not something that can be observed, 21nor will people say, "It is here," or "It is there," because the kingdom of God is in your hearts.'" Luke 17:20*

Be aware that I have taken a bit of liberty with that final phrase. The Greek literally says, "on the inside, it exists." The Greek word for "on the inside" is only used twice in the entire New Testament: in Luke 17:20, and in Matthew 23:26 where Jesus instructs the Pharisees to "first clean the *inside* of the cup." In that verse, Jesus is specifically speaking of the tendency for legalistic people to worry about how they appear on the outside when His priority would be that they have clean hearts. I would submit that Christ's use of the word is prescriptive and that we should understand the Kingdom of Christ in terms of His own words. Remember that, to John's readers, the term "a thousand years" is a way to say, "an unimaginably long time." Christ promised that His Kingdom would be in the hearts of people.

Further, you have likely noticed that I almost always insist on interpreting The Revelation from the symbolic point of view. It simply seems, at least to me, to be academic dishonesty when scholars repeatedly switch between the literal and figurative when attempting to interpret The Revelation. I believe that it is just that kind of inconsistency that has led to confusion and to the general hesitancy to engage with this text where most people are concerned. I think it is most honest and consistent to see the Book of Revelation as a book of spiritual figures and to consistently see it that way. For that reason, I have chosen to see the reference as a spiritually figurative statement, rather than a literal time frame. Of course, that makes me different from the preachers and authors you will read in the non-academic world of Revelation expositors. Please remember that my overarching purpose in writing this book was to help people engage in a sensible way with The Revelation of John. If you prefer a more literal and historical perspective, that is just fine. I pray you will find insight and blessing. I hope you might use my guidance as a starting point from which to venture out into the questions about what it all means and come to hear for yourself the message of this book. Then, I will be gratified to have accomplished my purpose and have helped you interact with The Revelation!

I believe that the discussion about the "first resurrection" versus the "second resurrection" should be understood to simply mean that those who die for their testimony will be exalted in Heaven. They are a type of "first fruits," a promise that all who lived in Christ will also join them. You see the same kind of device in the popular resurrection account in 1 Thessalonians 4:

> *"¹⁵According to Christ's own word, we tell you that we who are still alive, at the moment of the coming of the Lord, will certainly not get precedence over those who have died in Christ before us. ¹⁶For the Lord Himself will descend from Heaven, with a loud command, with the voice of the archangel and with the trumpet blast of God, and the dead in Christ will rise first. ¹⁷Then, we who are still alive on Earth will be caught up together with them in the clouds to meet the Lord in the air, and then we will be with the Lord forever. ¹⁸Encourage one another with these words." 1 Th 4:15-18*

The issue of two resurrections is, I believe, as simple as showing respect for those who have paid the highest price. Notice also; there is no "first death" as opposed to a "second death" in The Revelation. Clearly, we are to understand that physical death is the first death and final, negative judgment is the second death.

The text includes something of a retelling of the final battle and the judgment of the Devil. What does it mean that, after the millennium, the Devil will be released from his prison and go out to gather the nations for battle? Stick with me here: first, in James 4:7, the Bible clearly teaches that Christians, by the power of God at work in them, can "Resist the Devil and he will flee from you." That is because, since Christ's victory on the Cross, the Devil is a defeated foe in the lives of Christians. He is, in effect, restrained. Ultimately, if the Devil is to cause trouble, he will have to go do that among those who are not...get ready for this...those who are not the child born to the woman in Revelation 12! Remember her? She is Israel. The child is the church. The child is swept away to be protected by God.

When the Devil could not reach the child, he went after the woman. When he could not reach her, he raised up the beasts to take out his wrath on the people of Earth. Ultimately, in his unrestrained state, he can only use the armies of the unsaved in his attempt to bring about the fall of the saved, and of God. Gog and Magog are an intentional reference to Ezekiel 38-39. In that reference, he is "Gog from Magog." He is listed as allied with Meshech and Tubal, two other entities that scholars cannot positively identify with known people groups. Further allies are Libya, Ethiopia, and Persia, all of whom we can identify easily, but who would constitute a near-worldwide alliance in Ezekiel's time.

In Revelation, they represent all the armies from the four corners of the Earth, not literal countries or armies. When I was a child, teachers abounded who taught that Gog and Magog were Russia and China. Thankfully, since the fall of the U.S.S.R., that kind of interpretation has mostly stopped. Whomever they are, they fall into the fate of those who challenged the two Witnesses in Revelation 11, namely that fire comes from their mouths and consumes the enemies of God! In Revelation 21, that fire falls from Heaven and consumes them. Note that there never is any battle. Then the Devil is thrown into the lake of burning fire and sulfur. Here, we see that we may equate the lake of fire with the Abyss. The Devil (the Dragon) and both beasts have been cast into the place of eternal punishment and will not come back.

Then John sees the "great white throne," and the One who sits on it, from whom all of creation retreats. All the citizens of Earth from the sweep of all time stand before the throne. They have come for judgment, yet they are not arbitrarily judged. There are books. The books record everything ever done. This is a direct reference to Christ's own account of the final judgment in Matthew 25:35-40, where humankind is judged based on whether or not they fed, clothed, or cared for the "least of these." There is an implication that, while everyone is to be judged on their works, one book takes precedence over all others: The Book of Life. All the dead of all time are given up by wherever their soul and body had gone. Even death and Hades, the inescapable place the Greeks believed that souls went in the afterlife, cough up their dead. God breaks their intimidation by emptying them of those whom they held and then crushes their power by throwing them into the lake of fire. The chapter ends with the revelation that only one book really mattered. Anyone whose name was not in the Book of Life was cast into the lake of fire, suffering the same punishment as the Devil and his beasts.

In John 8, the Pharisees try to set a trap for Jesus. They bring Him a woman whom they claim to have caught in the "very act of adultery." Interestingly, she was apparently caught in this act alone. No man is flung into the dirt at Jesus' feet. John says in his Gospel that Jesus crouches down and writes in the dirt. The Pharisees press Him for an answer. Should they be allowed to stone this woman, as the Law of Moses dictates, or not? They think they have Jesus trapped. If He says they should stone her by the Law of Moses, He will lose all credibility, having taught His followers about the love and grace of God. If Jesus says they cannot stone her, He will have blasphemed the Law of Moses, and they may stone Him! It is a pretty clever trap. Jesus rises and gives His answer. "Stone her." There had to have been gasps of surprise on all sides. Wait, Jesus continues, "As you prepare to stone her, be sure that it is the one who has no sin who throws the first stone." Once again, He crouches down to write in the dust. What is He writing? Anytime the Bible repeats something, you should take that as a cue to do a bit of research and find out what is going on there. In John 7, you see the account of Jesus interrupting their service the night before. In that interruption, he shouted out. "Is anyone thirsty? Let him come to me, and I will give him living water to drink, just like this scripture says!" (John 7:38)

Where does the Bible talk about "living water?" Only in two places. The one they were most likely reading during that service appears in Jeremiah 17:13:

> *"Lord, you are the hope of Israel; all who deny you will be put to shame. Those who turn away from you will have their names written in the dust because they have forsaken the Lord, the spring of living water."*

Then, in John 8, Jesus is writing in the dust. He is writing their names! He does not know them. They do not know Him well enough to even arrest Him without having one of His followers kiss Him on the cheeks to identify Him for them. Yet, He knows their names. I envision Him, crouched down, writing their names upside down and backward – so that they can read them perfectly. As each person steps up to throw their rock, they see their name written in the dust, drop their stone, and walk away. John tells us in John 8:9 that even His disciples left until only Jesus and the accused woman were left. He proclaims that He will not judge her. The one person in that entire courtyard who could have judged her by His own standard that day...would not. That judgment, it is implied, will wait until the end of time. Here in Revelation 21, we see that names are written in the Book of Life. The question, then, is simple. Is your name written in the dust, or in the Book of Life?

HOW MIGHT WE SHARE THIS?

I.   There Will be a Judgment

II. Your Works Matter

III. Your Life in Christ Matters More

IV. Where is Your Name?

QUESTIONS FOR FURTHER STUDY OR REFLECTION

1. For whom do you believe the array of thrones exist? Does Revelation give us any clues?

2. Why do you think the Devil's judgment is retold here?

3. How do you feel about a loving God who ultimately will throw people into the lake of fire?

4. What does the word "impenitent" mean?

5. Does God set any kind of deadline past which a person cannot repent? What if a soul comes to the great white throne and falls down on the glass-on-fire floor, and repents? Would God still send that soul to the lake of fire?

6. What do you believe God will do with people like Adolf Hitler or Osama bin Laden?

CHAPTER THIRTY-FOUR

THE NEW HEAVEN AND THE NEW EARTH

"IT IS DONE."

Revelation 21:1-27

THE TEXT:

"21:1Then I saw a new Heaven and a new Earth, for the first Heaven and the first Earth passed away, and the sea no longer existed. 2I saw the Holy City, the new Jerusalem, descending from Heaven from God, prepared as a bride adorned for her husband. 3Then I heard a loud voice from the throne: 'Look! The home of God is now with His people, and He will dwell with them and they will be His people, and God himself will be with them as their God. 4And He will wipe every tear from their eyes. And death will no longer exist, neither will grief or crying or pain, for the previous order of things has passed away.

5Then the One seated on the throne said, "Look! I am making everything new!" Then He said, "Write this down, for this message is trustworthy and true."

⁶ *Then He said to me: "It is finished. I am the Alpha and the Omega, the Beginning and the End. To the thirsty I will give water freely from the spring of living water.* ⁷ *Those who prevail will inherit all things, and I will be their God and they will be my children.* ⁸ *But the cowardly, the unbelieving, the vile, murderers, the sexually immoral, sorcerers and idolaters and who lie, they will be sentenced to the lake of burning fire and sulfur. This is the second death."*

⁹ *Then one of the seven angels with one of the bowls of the seven last plagues said to me, 'Come, I will show you the bride, the wife of the Lamb.'* ¹⁰ *And he carried me away in a prophetic trance to a great and high mountain, and showed me the Holy City, Jerusalem, coming down out of Heaven from God.* ¹¹ *It beamed with the glory of God, and its brilliance was like that of a very precious jewel, like jasper clear as crystal.* ¹² *The city had a thick, high wall with twelve gates. Twelve angels were at the gates and the gates were inscribed with the names of the twelve tribes of Israel.* ¹³ *There were three gates on the east, three on the north, three on the south and three on the west.* ¹⁴ *The wall of the city had twelve foundation stones, and on each was the name of one of the twelve apostles of the Lamb.*

¹⁵ *The angel speaking with me had a golden measuring rod with which to measure the city, its gates, and walls.* ¹⁶ *The city was laid out with four equal sides, as long as it was wide. He measured the city with the rod and found it to be 1,400 miles in length and width.* ¹⁷ *The angel measured the wall using human measures, and it was 200 feet thick.* ¹⁸ *The wall was made of jasper, and the city of pure gold, clear like glass.* ¹⁹ *The foundations of the city walls were decorated with every kind of precious stone. The first foundation was jasper, the second sapphire, the third agate, the fourth emerald,* ²⁰ *the fifth onyx, the sixth carnelian, the seventh yellow topaz, the eighth beryl, the ninth blue topaz, the tenth chrysoprase, the eleventh jacinth, and the twelfth amethyst.* ²¹ *The twelve gates were twelve pearls. Each individual gate was made from a single pearl. The main square of the city was pure gold, like transparent crystal.*

²² *I did not see a temple in the city, because the Lord God Almighty and the Lamb are its Temple.* ²³ *The city has no need of sun or moon to illuminate it, for the glory of God illuminates it, and its lamp is the Lamb.* ²⁴ *The nations will walk in its light, and the kings of the Earth will bring their glory into it.* ²⁵ *The gates of the city will never close by day, and there will be no night there.*

> ²⁶*People will bring the glory and honor of all nations to it.* ²⁷*But nothing unclean will ever enter it, that is anyone who does what is shameful or false, but only those whose names are written in the Lamb's Book of Life." Rev 21:1-27*

WHAT IS THE TEXT SAYING TO US?

The judgments all concluded; John's vision moves on to the glory of God's Kingdom come to Earth. The emphasis of the first paragraph is that the old "order" of things is gone, and a new order has come. There are a "new heaven and a new earth." Remember, these are spiritual representations! There is no longer any sea. The sea was equated with the Abyss, and that has been locked away. Spiritually, after the cross, there is no need to separate Heaven from Earth, because Heaven has come to live in the hearts of the redeemed. There is no need for a sea – a place where monsters like the leviathan could hide – because all has been made known and laid open. The loud voice from the throne affirms the path on which we have already started to think. After the cross, the Bible tells us:

> *"For you are the temple of the living God. As He has said:*
>
> *"I will live with them and walk with them; I will be their God, and they shall be My people." 2 Corinthians 6:16*

And in Acts 7:47-48,

> *"It was Solomon who built a house for Him.*
> *⁴⁸But now, the Most High God does not live in*
> *temples made by human hands."*

Do you see it? Since Jesus' victory on the cross, God's home is in the hearts of those who acknowledge Christ as savior. You might say, "But, Kevin, what about this bit about wiping away every tear from their eyes?"

The next statement, indeed, says no more tears, death, mourning, or grieving. It seems like, surely, this must be talking about the future. But perhaps it is not. There is an account in John 11, in which Jesus raises his friend, Lazarus, from the dead! In the account, messengers come to Jesus to let Him know that His dear friend, Lazarus, is deathly ill. Still, John's Gospel tells us that Jesus chose to wait two more days before going to be with His friend Lazarus and his sisters Mary and Martha. In the end, we find out that it would not have mattered. By the time Jesus gets to Bethany where his friends live, Lazarus has been in the tomb for four days. When Jesus arrives, Martha affirms that if He had been there, Lazarus could have been saved. Jesus tells her to stop weeping (see that?) because her brother is going to be raised from the dead. She affirms that she has faith that Lazarus will rise at the resurrection. Jesus tells her, "I am the resurrection and the life." In typical Johannine fashion, she does not understand what He is saying, even after He asks her to affirm that she believes.

Martha sends Mary to Jesus. Mary takes Him to the place where they have placed Lazarus in a rock-hewn tomb. Standing all around are friends and family, as well as professional mourners who came to get paid for raising a big fuss. Mary falls at Jesus' feet, weeping. Then John tells us this:

> *"³³When Jesus saw her weeping, and the Jews who had come with her weeping in the same way, He was deeply moved and troubled in His Spirit. ³⁴ 'Where have you buried him?' he asked. 'Come, we'll show you, Lord,' they replied. ³⁵ Jesus wept." John 11:33-35*

The logical question is, "Why is Jesus weeping?" Did He not just say that HE is the Resurrection and the Life? He did. Does He not intend to raise Lazarus from the dead? He does. Does Jesus not know how this is going to turn out, with Lazarus coming out of that tomb? Oh, He does. So why is He weeping? Look at verse 33: Knowing all He knows, Jesus looks around. His dear friend is lying in the dirt weeping. All around Him are friends and family, genuinely weeping with her. There is also this troupe of professional weepers who make money off of the grief of others. These people have no clue. Even the couple that knows Him and has seen Him do many miracles have no clue. Even after He tells them what He's about to do, they have no clue. Jesus weeps, not for Lazarus, not for Mary or Martha, certainly not for the professional mourners. He weeps for humanity, who cannot see that death is not the end. He weeps because, until He goes to the cross, there will be no redemption, no hope. Until His resurrection, people will continue to believe that death is a dead end.

After the cross and His resurrection, we understand that He was only the first of the coming resurrections. Whether we are all resurrected at once at some point in the future – as the Jews believed, or inherit new life the moment we pass from this Earth – passing from "glory to glory" as the Apostle Paul believed (2 Corinthians 3:18) – the bottom-line is the same: the old order of death and the grave were defeated on the cross of Christ. If we lose loved ones on this Earth, we need not grieve like those who have no faith (1 Thessalonians 4:13). We know that what we see as death in this world is only the birth of eternal life in the believer! Time after time, in my career, I have sat with families who have lost a loved one whose faith was clear and strong. They cry, they shed tears, but they do not weep in dark grief. They experience the inevitable sadness of parting. Yet, they also laugh through their tears as they recount the great things, the great causes, the beautiful acts of ministry that their loved one accomplished because of their faith. There is now *hope* in the time of parting since Jesus opened up the way from the cross!

The One on the throne exclaims, "Look! I am making everything new!"

The true and solid words are spoken. It is done, finished, over, accomplished. God proclaims Himself the beginning and the ending, and everything in between. He is every letter, every number, every combination, every puzzle, every riddle, every truth, the answer to every question, and even the one who made the questions possible. Knowledge is often illustrated in the Bible as thirst, and God promises to give free water to the thirsty in abundance. Those who are victorious, those who prevail, are the heirs, they will be treated as God's own children. Those who finally refused to believe and lived in wickedness – judged by their own deeds, will be thrown into the lake of fire.

This is the second death, about which John was told in Revelation 20:6, that would have no power over God's children whose names are written in the Book of Life. Then, John sees the Holy City of God coming down to Earth from Heaven.

Jesus had taught His disciples the outline of the prayer He wanted them to use when they asked Him to teach them to pray. In one line of that prayer, He taught them to petition God: "Your Kingdom come, Your will be done, on Earth just as it is in Heaven." How does that Kingdom come? It comes when God dwells with His people. Where does God dwell with people? He dwells with people in their hearts! Since the cross, God's tabernacle is no longer off in Heaven, but in the hearts of those who love Him! John sees the Holy City descending. It is resplendent! It is a cube of 1,400 miles in any direction. Would you care to just venture a wild guess of the distance from Jerusalem, Israel to Rome, Italy? How did you know it was 1,400 miles? It is! That may be a simple coincidence, but I do not think so. God's Holy City takes in the fallen Kingdom of Israel and the world power of Rome. It unites the twelve tribes of Israel with the twelve apostles of Christianity. The walls are 200 feet (144 cubits) thick. Here, again, the square of the number of tribes or apostles…a multiple of perfection. The entire thing is made of the most precious and impressive materials known to humanity. Its worth is beyond estimation.

Then John realizes that there is no temple in this Holy City. How can a Holy City be holy without a temple to its Holy God? It does not need a temple because God the Father and Son live by the Holy Spirit in the hearts of His people! The city does not need the light of day or night, because the glory of the Lord will be all the light – the revealing and the guidance – that it needs. It never closes, because city gates were closed at night or during a siege. In God's Kingdom, there is no night and no siege. Who may enter? Those whose names appear in (notice the subtle name change here) The Lamb's Book of Life are welcome.

In the Psalms, there is sometimes a one-word interlude. It is *"selah."* It indicates a pause, a time to simply reflect on what you have heard, and worship along in joyous reflection of the Glory of God and His love for you.

Selah.

HOW MIGHT WE SHARE THIS?

I. The Old has Gone, The New Has Come

II. Living in a World with So Much Hope There Are No Tears

III. Heaven on Earth – In Our Hearts and Lives

QUESTIONS FOR FURTHER STUDY OR REFLECTION

1. What do you think is meant by "a new Heaven and a new Earth?"

2. What kinds of things would you look forward to in a world without pain or tears?

3. Do you feel like you have the light of God in your heart right now?

4. What does it mean that there will be no more night in the Holy City?

5. Do you agree that we no longer need a "temple" because God lives in people's hearts?

CHAPTER THIRTY-FIVE

THE FINAL VISION
"I AM COMING SOON"

Revelation 22:1-21

THE TEXT:

"²²:¹Then, the angel showed me the river of liv-ing water, sparkling like crystal, flowing from the throne of God and of the Lamb ² down the main street of the city. On each side of the river, there were Trees of Life, producing twelve kinds of fruit, each yielding its fruit every month. The leaves of the trees are for the healing of the na-tions. ³And the curse of war will no longer exist. The throne of God and of the Lamb will be in the city, and His servants will worship Him. ⁴They will see His face, and His name will be on their foreheads. ⁵ There will be no more night, and people will have no need for the light of a lamp or sunlight, for the Lord God will illuminate them. And they will rule with Him forever and ever.

⁶ *The angel said to me, 'These words are faithful and true and the Lord, the God of the spirits of the prophets, sent His angel to reveal to His servants the things that must soon happen.'*

⁷ *'Watch! I am coming soon. Blessed is the one who obeys the words of this prophetic book.'*

⁸ *It was I, John, who heard and saw these visions. And when I heard and saw them, I fell down to worship at the feet of the angel who revealed them to me.* ⁹ *But he said to me, 'Don't do that! I am a fellow servant with you and with your brothers and sisters, the prophets, and with all those who keep the words of this scroll. Worship God!'*

¹⁰ *Then he told me, 'Do not seal up the words of this prophetic book, for the time is near.* ¹¹ *Let the one who is unjust continue to be unjust; and let the morally depraved person continue to be morally depraved; let the righteous one continue to do be righteous; and let the person who is holy continue to be holy.'*

¹² *I promise, I am coming soon! And I am bringing with me the reward to pay each person according to their behavior.* ¹³ *I am the Alpha and the Omega, the First and the Last, Beginning and End.*

¹⁴ 'Blessed are those who wash their robes so that they may have access to the tree of life and may enter the city by its gates. ¹⁵ Outside are the dogs and the magicians and the fornicators and murderers and idolaters and everyone who loves lying.

¹⁶ I, Jesus, have sent my angel to give this word to you for the benefit of the churches. I am David's descendant, the bright Morning Star.'

¹⁷ The Spirit and the bride say, 'Come!' Let the one who hears say, 'Come!' Let the one who is thirsty come; and let the one who desires, receive the free gift of the water of life. ¹⁸ I testify to everyone who hears the words of the prophecy of this scroll: If anyone adds to them, God will add to that person the plagues described in this book. ¹⁹ And if anyone takes away and words from this book of prophecy, God will take away that person's inheritance in the tree of life and in the Holy City, which is described in this book

²⁰ He who testifies to these things says, 'Truly, I am coming soon.' Amen. Come, Lord Jesus.

²¹ The grace of the Lord Jesus be with all the saints. Amen. The Revelation by John." Rev 22:1-21

WHAT IS THE TEXT SAYING TO US?

Now, we reach the final chapter. The last chapter of the Bible reassures us of the restoration of the Garden created in the first chapter of the Bible, The Garden of Eden. Through the middle of the new Kingdom flows the river of God's mercy and forgiveness. On either bank of that river grow trees of Life – life abundant! They bear the fruit that gives life to the dying, hope to the hopeless, healing to the sick, sight to the blind, hearing to deaf, words to the dumb, and dancing to the lame in every season. And the leaves of the tree are for the healing of all hurt in every nation. As it was in the first Garden, there is no more curse, for the sin that separated humanity from the first Garden, and God's presence is gone. God lives among His people. They are marked as His. They live by His Light, for God is Light (1 John 1:5). They live under His rule and reign with Him in true power forever and ever.

Then John relates the final words he gets from the angel who has been his guide through this process. There is first, an affirmation that these are, indeed, the trustworthy and true words of Christ – the Word. There is further affirmation that these are things that must come to pass soon. Then you hear Christ Himself speaking through John:

> *"'Watch! I am coming soon. Blessed is the one who obeys the words of this prophetic book."*

John recounts the moment when he fell at the feet of the angel to worship him, but the angel forbade it and told him to worship God. This time, the exhortation includes all who will keep the words of "this book," this Revelation.

The angel tells John not to seal this scroll. A sealed scroll could not be read by any except the one to whom it was addressed. In effect, the angel is telling John to send the scroll around unsealed so that anyone who touches it can read it. He is encouraging John to trust that the contents of the scroll because they are the Word of God, will accomplish their purpose in the hands of whoever comes in contact with them. I have faith that the same is true of this effort at making the old truth more accessible to the people into whose hands this book falls.

Then there is this very interesting admonition to let people be themselves. It is a reminder that God is the judge; I am not. Christ is the savior; I am not. The admonition should not be lost on any of us. The writer, the preacher, the teacher, the friend, we are all vessels, tools in the hands of God. He will speak His Word through us, but it is His Word, not ours. We are allowed, even empowered to work by His Spirit, but it is not ours. We get to experience His power, but it is not ours. It is often so hard to simply be a conduit for God's Word, His grace, His love, and not want to force people to respond! The angel says to John, "Let them be who they will be. God will work His plan. Let it be."

Why should I let people simply be who they are? Because Christ says, He is coming soon. Each will be treated as his works deserve. God will judge righteously, and I cannot. I am not the Alpha and Omega; God is. He will sort the children from the dogs, those who belong in His family from those who will not. It is not mine to sort people. God will allow the children to walk straight into his Kingdom.

Wait, late in the book, there is a very interesting point. "...that they may have the right to the Tree of Life and may walk straight through the gates into the city." Now, I may be a mile off here, but that says something very profound to me. The righteous are not made to wait in some "paradise" or "purgatory." (Though, I was a counselor many times at Jr. High Camp, so I am pretty sure I have paid any purgatory dues I had accrued!) They walk straight in! There is no grave any longer, right? There is no Hades. There is no waiting for the resurrection because Jesus IS the resurrection and the life! I am convinced that this is testimony that, in the moment we pass from this life, we walk straight into the gate of the eternal Kingdom of God's Glory!

In my ministry, I remember sitting with two saints as they passed from this life to the next. Each testified to being able to see Heaven, while still perfectly cognizant in this world and this moment of reality. In both cases, they were not looking at the ceiling, but at the door to the room. They each described what they saw as they crossed over what they described to be a loud, rushing river. Their descriptions were precisely the same. They would describe their vision, then turn and address me by name, asking if I could not see what they saw. They both described hearing singing – the singing of millions of souls singing the same song all together. They both said that they could not see a person, but that they knew there were millions there; that they could feel them and knew them all.

One even began to sing the song. Then stopped and said, "Oh, Pastor! I've never sung this song, yet I know it perfectly!" Each of those gentlemen came to a moment when they looked over at me and said, "Pastor, do you see Him? Jesus is here to take me home now." Neither was afraid. They both paused to say farewell to the loved ones gathered around their bedside, then closed their eyes and breathed their last. Both were excited to go home. As I have read through The Revelation in the past 35 years, their stories ring true at so many points in John's vision. Their joy at seeing Jesus, at knowing their spouse, or their brother, or their sister, or their parents, or the baby they lost at birth in 1946…inspires my faith and keeps me from any fear of what comes next. I am deeply convinced that we get to step straight in and eat from the Tree of Eternal Life.

Jesus affirms that it is He who has given this message to John to share with the churches. Now we are all invited. The word from the Spirit and the Church is, "Come on!" Our proper response when our ears hear the truth is, "Come on!" Are you thirsty for truth and knowledge and wisdom? Come on! Would you like to drink of the free gift of the refreshing and renewing Water of Life? Come on!

Then, there is a pause, a final warning: Do not add to the words of this prophecy, nor take away from it. Let it stand as it is and do not make your preaching or your writing about it a distraction to its central meaning. I pray that I have been able, here, to make the truth of this ancient book more accessible – and I pray I have not been any kind of distraction or discredit to its truth.

Jesus affirms, "It is true! I am coming soon!"

Our response is, "AMEN! Come on, Lord!"

May the grace of the Lord Jesus, truly, be with you as you journey toward home. Come on!

HOW MIGHT WE SHARE THIS?

I.   There is a garden restored in Heaven for You

II. There is a place in Heaven set aside for You

III. Come on!

QUESTIONS FOR FURTHER STUDY OR REFLECTION

1. What do you think of as you read this last chapter of Revelation?

2. What responses do you feel within your own spirit or mind?

3. Do you find this invitation exciting or troubling? Why?

4. How do you feel when people invite you to "Come on!?"

"LET THE ONE WHO HAS AN EAR, HEAR WHAT THE SPIRIT SAYS"

As I finish this book, it is a gray and rainy day in February. Six weeks have passed since I wrote the first words of the Prologue. I have written or listened to the words of The Revelation every day. It has been a tremendously healing and restoring process in my soul. I should have done this a long time ago. Thank you, Ted, for believing I could genuinely do this. You were right.

This process of living with The Revelation has given me one new insight, and it may be the most important one I have ever had where this book is concerned. I now see its purpose in the life of the Apostle John. Exiled to Patmos and in the final days of his advanced years, he has seen things of which you and I could only dream. He walked with Jesus. He saw the blind given sight. He saw the lame walk. He saw the dead raised! He had likely walked through the ruins of the Colossus of Rhodes. He watched Jerusalem fall and be destroyed by the Romans. He saw the beloved Temple of Solomon torn down and ruined. He lived alongside the Apostle Paul. He grew up with Peter and James. Legend tells us that he had honored the request of Jesus, and cared for Mother Mary until her death, likely in Ephesus. This letter was the last thing that we know he wrote.

He had one final chance to tell the story of our salvation history from that little room on Patmos. He could get one last communique out to the brothers and sisters. What would he say? He wrote this: The Revelation of John. He wrote it in symbols; yet, it is the entire story of God at work in the world. Do you see it? In this book is the story of the Garden of Eden, the advent of sin, the source of sin, the nature of sin, the power of sin, and the final result of sin. In these pages are Abraham and his treaty with God and God's promise to him. Here is Moses, and the Promised Land, and Elijah and Jezebel. Here are the prophets of old, especially Daniel and Ezekiel, and the symbols with which they spoke of the end of all time. Here are Jesus and the disciples; all gone but himself when John writes, his brothers in the faith and the calling of Christ. In these pages, you see the influence of Paul and Barnabus, and of many unnamed churchmen, whom John knew would read his letter in their church. Here are God and Satan, the original battle for the souls of a couple in the Garden, and the final battle for the souls of all humanity. It is all here! This is John's gift to the church and to the world. If he could only tell the story once more, this is how he chose to wrap it all into one telling. With only this book (remember, there was no Bible when John wrote this), with only this scroll, a person could start a church and give them the essentials they would need to live the Christian life.

He wrote it in the power of the Holy Spirit, and it carries that power with it into this day. He reminds us that, on those days when the world in which we live seems so totally overwhelming, power-hungry, savage, or brutal, authentic power – the power to push back all of those things and know peace – comes from God through Jesus Christ.

As I put down my pen or, more accurately, close up my keyboard for the last time on this endeavor, I pray that I have magnified a bit of the power of this ancient book in your life. I pray that, at any moment that you feel powerless, you might find assurance and strength in The Revelation. I pray that in knowing that God could use an exiled old 90-year-old man, nearly spent, to send His Word of power and affirmation out into the world like a hot laser beam – you will know that God can use you for things you have never yet dreamed possible.

"So it is with me, brothers and sisters. I came to you, not with great eloquence or human wisdom as I shared with you this testimony about God. In fact, I determined to know nothing in the time we spent together, except that I knew Jesus Christ – even if only the crucified Christ. I came to you in weakness and with great fear and insecurity. My message is not with wise and persuasive words, but with a demonstration of the Spirit's power, so that your faith might be bolstered, not by my feeble words, but by the power of God." 1 Corinthians 2:1-5

Selah.

BIBLIOGRAPHY

Aune, David. (1997) *Revelation 1-5, Volume 52A Word Biblical Commentary.* Zondervan. Grand Rapids, MI.

Aune, David. (1998) *Revelation 6-16, Volume 52B Word Biblical Commentary.* Zondervan. Grand Rapids, MI.

Aune, David. (1998) *Revelation 17-22, Volume 52C Word Biblical Commentary.* Zonderan. Grand Rapids, MI.

Barton, Bruce B. (2000) *Revelation Life Application Commentary.* Tyndale House. Carol Stream, IL.

Boring, M. Eugene (2011) *Revelation (Interpretation: A Bible Commentary for Teaching and Preaching).* Westminster John Knox Press. Louisville, KY.

Beale, G.K. & Campbell, David H. (2015) *Revelation: A Shorter Commentary.* Wm.B. Eerdmans. Grand Rapids, MI.

Fee, Gordon. (2011) *Revelation A New Covenant Commentary.* Cascade Books. Eugene, OR.

Gordon, Michael J. (2011) *Reading Revelation Responsibly: Uncivil Worship and Witness: Following the Lamb Into the New Creation.* Cascade Books. Eugene, OR.

Hoskins, Paul (2017) *The Book of Revelation: A Theological and Exegetical Commentary.* CreatSpace Independent Publishing Platform. North Charleston, SC.

Mounce, Robert H. (1977) *The Book of Revelation.* W. B. Eerdmans. Grand Rapids.

Paul, Ian. (2018) *Revelation. Volume 20 Tyndale New Testament Commentaries.* InterVarsity Press. Downers Grove, IL.